I0528669

THE LIFE AND TIMES
of
HENRY J, AND ELSIE FLUSCHE FUHRMAN
Their Biographies, Family Records,
and
Other Related Information

by

Alvin M. Furhman

ISBN 978-1-961358-18-8 (paperback)
ISBN 978-1-961358-19-5 (digital)

Copyright © 2023 by Alvin M. Furhman

All rights reserved. No part of this publication may be reproduced, distributed, or transmitted in any form or by any means, including photocopying, recording, or other electronic or mechanical methods without the prior written permission of the publisher.

Printed in the United States of America

CONTENTS

PART I

My Remembrances
By
Elsie Flusche Fuhrman

PART II

Maternal and Paternal Family Records
of
Elsie Flusche Fuhrman

PART III

Introduction to Biography of Henry J. Fuhrman

PART IV

Flusche Brothers: Historical Data and Personal Journal
Translations and Information

Introduction to the Flusche Brother's Activities
in America

The Poems of the Steinmetz, Flusche Family

Wilhelm Flusche's Tribute to the Sesquicentennial

ILLUSTRATIONS

PART I

PART II

PART III

PART I

"My Remembrances"
Written by
Elsie Flusche Fuhrman

PART I

"My Remembrances"
Written by
Elsie Flusche Fuhrman
Begun, 1978; Completed, 1985

1985: Ninety-one-Years-old

Henry and I

Our Engagement Picture: 1921

Our Last Picture Together: January, 1975

Our Wedding Picture, March 29, 1921

My First Meeting of Henry's Family in Iowa, April, 1921

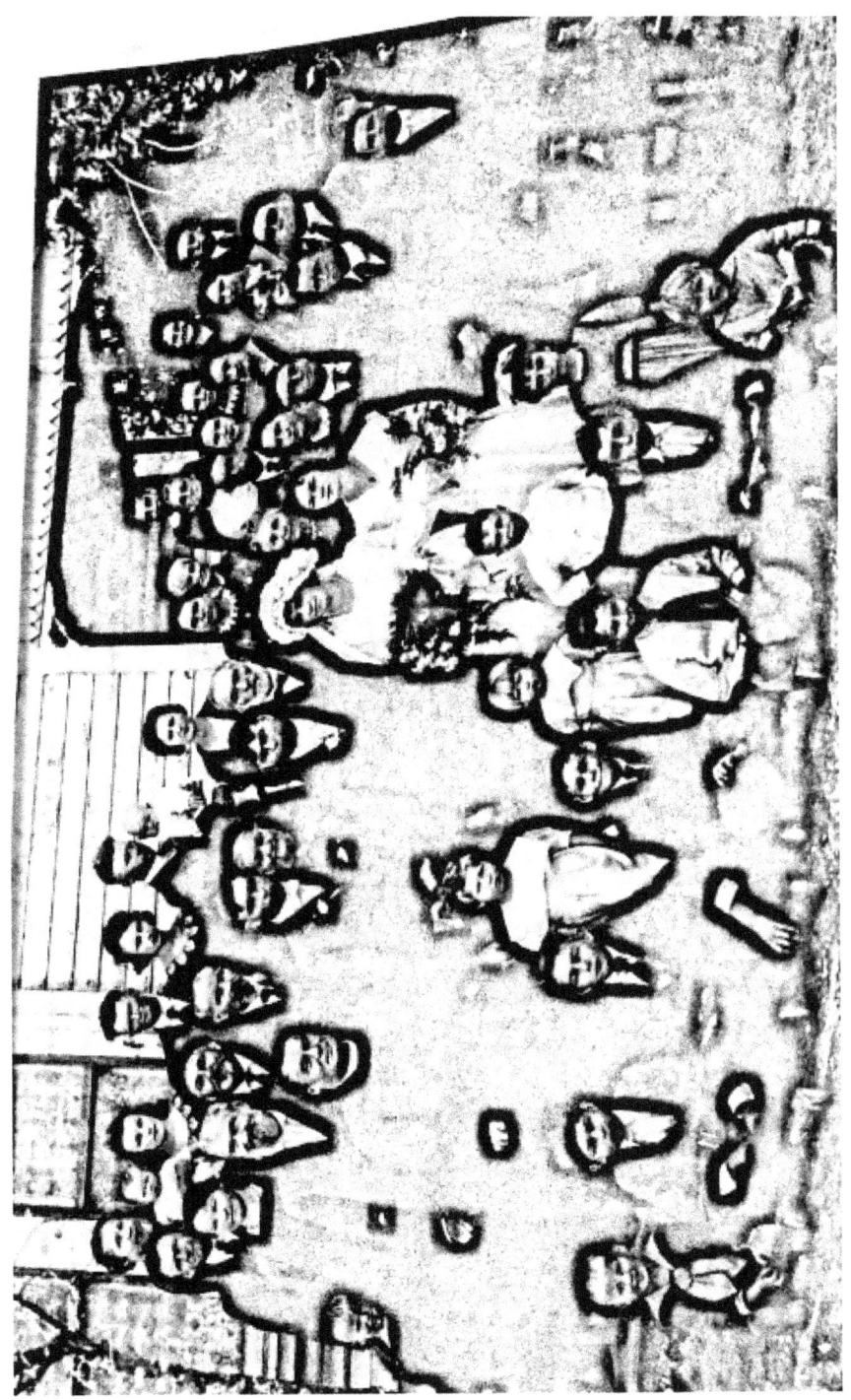

Our Wedding Reception in Lindsay: March 29, 1921

PREFACE

(Excerpts from a feature article about Mrs. Henry
(Elsie) Fuhrman
by Betty Stephenson in the magazine,
"All Around Gainesville,"
March/April, 1984)

In Lindsay and Muenster's formative years, there was a great rivalry between the two growing communities.

Young people were always having dances and picnics as their main form of recreation, and oftentimes, they were "infiltrated" by boys and girls from their neighboring townsites.

Mrs. Henry (Elsie) Fuhrman remembers the disputes well. "Lindsay and Muenster used to fight like cats and dogs," she grinned. Now nearly 90 years of age, she has seen a lot of progress as well as some of the steps taken backward in her time. She grew up in Lindsay, one of the towns established by her uncles and her father, Wilhelm Flusche. The three younger Flusche brothers got all of the credit for establishing the towns, she said, but it was her father who financed their transactions.

Her father and his brother, Tony, came to Lindsay in 1892. She was born two years later . . .

She and a date often rode the train to Muenster for 35 cents to attend a dance. A train came back the other way in a few hours, just right for catching it back to Lindsay.

It cost 15 cents to ride the train to Gainesville and she did that often, too. Her date would come to the town of Lindsay from the farm on horseback and tie up the horse at one of the stores. Then they would walk to the train depot, ride to Gainesville to see a movie, then go to the drug store for a soda. All for a little over a dollar for both of them.

Keeps Busy

There were nine children in Elsie's family, and she is the only one left. but Mrs. Fuhrman still lives by herself in Muenster. She keeps active by crocheting bedspreads and afghans for her six children, 22 grandchildren and seven great-grandchildren. She also pieces quilts by hand and gives those to her heirs as well. "It gives you something to do and to look forward to," she said, somewhat explaining her longevity.

She married Henry Fuhrman, who visited quite often in Texas from his native Iowa. She was very young when they met, "but he waited for me," she said. They moved to Iowa after their marriage where they lived for three years before his asthma got too bad and they moved back to Lindsay in 1924.

. . . Henry dies in 1976 at the age of 90. "We had been married 55 years when he died," she said, displaying their 50th anniversary picture.

"I have seen nearly five generations in my day," she added. "I now sit here alone with all my memories, but I'm glad I have them."

REMEMBRANCES

Henry and I

At the request of my children, I will try and recall some of the ups and downs that finally led up to our marriage after what our pastor called it in our Golden Wedding homily, "Eight years of playing hard to get."

I was eighteen and Henry was twenty-seven when we met for the first time in 1913. He and his sister, Teresa, had come to Lindsay, Texas, to visit his uncle and Godfather, Henry Fuhrmann. We were together at several parties: once at our home where we played blindman's bluff, drop the handkerchief, hide and seek, etc. and at one wedding dance at which I asked him for lady's choice. At that time, I thought I was going with someone else. I learned later, the affair was all in my head; it was a sad episode in my life. At that time, I discovered I was losing my hearing and no one can imagine the grief and the terrible depression I suffered. My only wish was to find a specialist who could help me to regain my hearing.

Four years had gone by when Henry's uncle died in Towa and Uncle Henry from Lindsay went there for the funeral. While in Iowa, if that girl, Elsie Flusche, ever got married. Uncle Henry said no and he didn't think she was going with anyone. So Henry wrote to me and we corresponded together. I had an aunt living in Milwaukee, Wisconsin. I decided to see a specialist about my hearing and to stay with her while I was there. I wrote Henry that I was going to Wisconsin and I sent him my address. The State Fair was going on and Henry came to attend the fair. He and I had a good time together and he proposed to me, but I was so determined to keep on trying to get my hearing back that I could not think of anything else. Henry went back to Iowa; he wrote me a letter saying if I ever wanted him back, I had to make the first move. When he left Milwaukee, I knew then and there I had made a big mistake. The doctors could not help me, so I went back to Texas more disappointed and depressed that ever. Four years went by again.

In the meantime, Henry was running his father's thrasher machine and had had a sunstroke; he was very sick for a long time. It was decided that he should have a change of climate. He went to Saskatchewan, Canada, to visit his brother, Val, who had taken up a homestead there and had married. But it got so cold there, Henry did not stay there long. He went further west and landed in British, Columbia, where he worked at a lumber camp close to Chilliwack; he stayed there two years. As for me, I worked for my sister Augusta and at other different places. All of my classmates were married and my sister, Clara, and my brother, Alex, were so much younger than I. I had written several letters to Henry, I never mailed then. Papa Theisen mailed it in Gainesville for me. My uncle and aunt were in the Lindsay Post Office, and I was afraid they would tell somebody that I had mailed a letter to Henry. The letter reached his parents' home in St. Joe, Iowa. They stuck the letter behind their mirrow and forgot about it. After about two months, it fell down on the floor and Uncle Nick, (God bless him), picked it up and mailed it to Henry. I had mailed it in October. and Christmas had come and gone and I did not hear anything, so I was sure Henry was married, etc. All at once after New Years, I received a package with a string of pearls and soon I had letter from Henry. He wrote that he was pulling up stakes and was coming to Texas as soon as he could wind up his business there; he said he would be in Lindsay in time for his birthday which was January 28th. Again, his birthday had come and gone with no sign of Henry. I went to the Post Office every time a train came in, hoping for a word from him. His Uncle Henry was also there every time I was. Finally, I asked if he was looking for Henry Fuhrman and he said yes. Then he asked if I was also looking for him. About that time, I had a card from the Dallas Health Department. It said: Henry Fuhrman detained with small pox--that's all. Uncle Henry and I were going to Dallas to see him but his son-in-law told us we wouldn't be able to see him because he was quarantined. So on Valentine's Day, February, 14th, Henry finally arrived, No one will ever know how happy I was when I saw him. In my imagination, I thought he would have pock-marks all over his face from the smallpox, but there he was, with a fair complexion and with pink cheeks like a girl. He weighed 208 and pounds was a handsome-looking man. He had been away from his home in Iowa for two years. We would have gotten married right away, but Lent had started and no one married during that time. He wanted to go home to Iowa, but we decided he should stay and married we after would Easter. So we had a six-week courtship. Uncle John Bezner had a new Studebaker car and we could drive it whenever wanted it. I was making preparations for our wedding. Mama had old-fashioned ideas from Germany: a bride had to have so many bedsheets, so many pillow cases, so many towels, etc. I also had a nice wardrobe; Mama was a real generous. I bought a navy blue suit for $50.00 and a beautiful hat with geathers on it for $13.00. Since I had my own sewing machine, I had sewed myself a real nice, black taffet dress according to the latest style. I also sewed a peacock-blue taffeta dress. I had a purple overcoat which I had bought the year before.

Our Wedding Day

Our wedding day finally arrived on March 29, 1921. Henry looked handsome in his new navy blue suit. Since crepe de chine shirts were in style. He bought two for $14.00; one white for the wedding and one with tiny red stripes. I think we were a real handsome-looking couple even if I have to say so myself. I had a white, crepe georgette wedding dress. The wedding reception was at our home and about sixty quests attended. Lizzie Kubis and Mrs. Hoelker cooked the wedding meal; Mama recited a poem she had made-up.

Iowa

So we were married and I wish I could say we lived happily ever after. We went to Iowa right after the wedding to make our home. Since Henry had been away from home for two years, I thought surely his folks would kill the fatted calf to rejoice the long lost son's return. Well, it wasn't at all like I had imagine it would be.

My Three Years in Iowa
(This part was written 1-27-85)

We arrived in Bode, Iowa on Thursday, April 5, 1929, at about three o'clock. Henry called his home and they said they were papering and that we should wait until they had finished the job. Henry went out on the street and met a lot of people he knew for he had been gone for two years. I sat in a drug store, wondering what I had gotten myself into. About six o'clock, Uncle Nick came to get us. When we got to Henry's parents' home, they all stood outside. Anna Faber was holding Raphael, a baby of three months. Grandmother Engert, Mama Fuhrmann's mother, was there. She was about ninety-years-old and looked it. Her dress looked like something out of the eighteenth-century. And Papa Fuhrmann! He had so many wrinkles in his face. I never saw a person with so many wrinkles as he had. Mama Fuhrmann was a tall, heavy-set woman. She was nearly as good a talker as my Mama. We sat down in the parlor and Mama Fuhrmann asked all about the relations in Texas. She had been to see them in 1904 at the double wedding of Mike and Katie Fuhrmann: Mike to Mary Mosser, Katie to Fritz Mosman. Henry and I had not eaten since we had breakfast on the train. There was Adolph, the chief cook and bottle washer. He was sixteen years old, six foot six inches tall, and weighed ninety-eight pounds. He was standing no sign of in the doorway and had to hear everything. There was no sign of supper yet at eight o'clock. Finally, Mama Fuhrmann told Adolph to start a fire and to put potatoes with the jacket on to cook. He left and shortly after, I noticed smoke was coming from the direction of the kitchen and Adolph was leaning against the door again. The smoke got thicker and thicker. Mama Fuhrmann got up to see what was going on. To make a long story short, he got supper on about nine o'clock. Everybody up there would fry down a whole hog and eat it three times a day. We had potatoes with the jackets and this meat to eat. That was it. By that time, the shivaree bunch arrived--about twelve in all--making much noise. Henry reached in his pocket and gave them his last five dollar bill.

We got there on Thursday and I did not get to see the rest of the family until Sunday. Mama Fuhrmann called Anna (Faber) and Clara (Plathe) and told them that they didn't have to come to bake cakes or pies; Elsie could do that. I had sent Henry to Algona to have my wedding dress cleaned and pressed. I thought Sunday would be a second wedding with his family. I baked about four lemon pies and they turned out too soupy. I also baked about two cakes. Sunday morning, Mama Fuhrmann and I went to early Mass because we had to cook the dinner. The others did not show up until it was time to eat. The table was set for about ten people. Clara Plathe and her three boys and Adolph sat at the first table; Adolph could eat for three. Not a one had a wedding present. No one asked if I wanted to put on my wedding dress, etc. I was about ready to go upstairs and lie down, but for Henry's sake, I kept a grin on my face. I had my big trunk in their pantry; it was a large room. Later on, I opened my trunk and showed some of my wedding presents. Clara Plathe said I had more than she had, that I didn't need anymore presents. So, we didn't get any. Pete Erpelding did give us a colt. Joe gave us a young calf and that was it. Henry had told me on the way to Iowa that they gave different presents in Iowa than they did in Texas. My brothers were all so hard up. I had five dresser scarves that my sister-in-laws had made. I did get a nice mantel clock from John and Gusta, and a silver knife and fork from Robert. Tanta Tonchen and Uncle Tony gave me a real nice bedspread. Willy and Anna gave me a good linen tablecloth.

I couldn't wait until we were in Joe's house to live. We moved in on Monday. It was a nice, two-story house. Joe had all Grandma Engert's furniture; it looked a hundred years old. The bed had a top on it that nearly reached the ceiling. The foot-end was wide enough for Henry to stand on in his sleep and dive down, head first. When Henry was real tired, he would get nightmares. Usually, he was trying to hold back a team of run-away horses. He would yell whoa, whoa. If I tried to wake him, he would get even more excited because he thought I was with him and in danger. So I learned to be quiet until his nightmares were over. But in time, he didn't have them anymore.

Henry had 165 acres of good land. We had planned to build it up and fence it off. In the meantime, Joe and Henry did the farming together. Joe had the farm buildings and machinery. Joe was so glad to get a house-keeper that he promised us the blue of the sky. He was to pay half of the grocery bill; but in time, he paid less and less. We got to Iowa in time to put in a corn crop. Joe had a bunch of young heifers that he and Henry broke for milking. I would go to the pasture to get them in the evening for milking. They were so wild, Henry would be wringing wet with sweat, then he would sit in a draft to milk. I often think that was partly the reason he got asthma. All went well though until October when Henry and Joe were picking corn together. Henry caught a bad cold which he could not get rid of. He would sit up in bed half of the night, coughing. We went from one doctor to another but none of them could help him. It was after Christmas before we knew that he had asthma. Henry did not go outdoors from October until March.

During that first year in Iowa, my sister, Clara, came to visit me. She worked for Mama Fuhrmann. Nick, Louis, and Adolph were there. All three of them would have liked to have dated her. When she first got there, Nick would introduce her like this: "Meet the hired girl." No name, no nothing. It sure made Clara mad but that's the way it was.

All in all, I got used to everything and also the people. There sure was a big difference between their ways and ours. In Iowa, a couple wouldn't get married without a firm foundation. All winter, they would hibernate. On March 1st, they woke up to get the land ready for a crop. In Texas, we were used to working all the year-round. In Iowa, the hired hand got his room and board in the winter by feeding the hogs and milking the cows. When the farmers did begin field work, you couldn't get to go to a dance, party, or movie until they had the oats and corn planted. It was as though they had a one-track mind. People in the South were more carefree and light-hearted.

My sister, Clara, was in Iowa from August to November before she came home from a dance all excited because she finally met boy like a Texan. That was Hubert Becker. He was home for the Thanksgiving holidays from Conception College in Missouri. He was different from most Iowa boys. In Iowa, a boy wouldn't ask a girl for a dance unless he was introduced first. Whenever we had a big snow storm, Joe wouldn't go to church on Sunday but Hubert would come, honking his horn a mile off. It sure made Joe mad. Henry and Joe knew what kind of boy Hubert was. When Hubert graduated from high school, he got a one-seated Ford car for his birthday. Then, the Beckers were the aristocrats of St Joseph. One time, Hubert and two boys vandalized a Public School and his father had to pay stiff fine for him. His dad said he didn't mind paying the fine, but he didn't like the gossip and the bad name it gave Hubert. Whenever Mr. Becker was thrashing at different places, he would make it a point to get in the house to see if they were clean enough for him to eat there. Anyway, it was because Henry and I were living in Iowa that Clara met Hubert Becker.

Birth of First Child Elsie

Clara worked for me when our first child, Elsie, was born January 19, 1922. Henry had been real sick with asthma since early fall. When Elsie was born, he had not been out of his clothes for two weeks; he had to sit up to breathe. One year after we married, get he weighed 135 pounds. Because Henry was sick, we had to get a hired man to help Joe with the farming. Our hired man was Joseph Klemm. He and Lizzie Ruf came over from Germany together. Papa Fuhrmann had sent Lizzie $300 dollars for her trip over to America and she worked for Mama and Papa Fuhrmann for three years at five dollars a week to pay it back. When she had it paid for, she and Joe decided to get married. That meant Henry and I had to get out. I would ask Henry, "What will we do?" He would only shrug his shoulders. No answer. Many years later, he told me he didn't care if he lived or died because he felt so bad. I had to make all the decisions. On February 12, 1924, we moved back to Texas. I was expecting our second child; we couldn't wait until Joe and Lizzie got married. We left most of the possessions we had acquired: pots and pans, dishes, and my sewing machine. I had bought the sewing machine before I married and we had had it shipped to Iowa. We had a baby bed, and about three-hundred canned fruit jars in the cellar. I don't know why we didn't have a sale. We left it all. We only took a trunk with our clothes. Henry had helped to build a nice hog shed for Joe; he built the outside and finished the inside during the winter months. We had about sixty hogs that were not ready for the market; we left enough corn to fatten them. Henry even gave Joe one hundred dollars to feed the hogs. The day we left, there was a real Iowa blizzard. It snowed so hard, you coudn't see ten feet ahead. They would take the wheels off from a wagon and make a sled out of it. That's how we drove to Bode, Iowa, to catch the train for Texas. Elsie was two years old then and was very lively; she would run all over that train. We arrived in Gainesville, Texas. It was still cold, but nothing like Iowa.

Lindsay Texas: 1924

Birth of Second Child William

We had planned to rent a farm from my brother, Robert, on the highway halfway between Lindsay and Gainesville, but it was rented out until November, 1924. We rented a small house right south of the Hoelker house and grocery store. Our oldest son, William, was born there March, 10, 1924. My mother lived about three blocks north of us and Henry would go there each morning to milk Mama's cow. That way, we had milk and Mama did too. Henry worked anywhere he could find work during that summer. In the fall, he drove a cotton seed truck for Nick Dieter. Nick had the cotton gin in Lindsay. In November, we moved on my brother's farm. We rented the farm on halves and we were furnished all the farm equipment, etc.

Birth of Third Child Alvin

We lived there five years and our second son, Alvin, was born on February 3, 1927. My sister, Augusta, and Mike Fuhrmann were Alvin's Godparents. It so happened that Mike Fuhrmann had a son the same time and the two boys were baptized the same day by Father John Nigg. Mike's son was named Arnold and our's Alvin. Arnold got leukemia later and died at the age of 25.

Henry got tired of renting and started to look around for a farm of his own. We still owned the 160 acres in Iowa. We had about six different renters for that land and one was a bigger crook than the other. The last renter was our brother-in-law. He was a sorry farmer: he never fixed any fences and allowed the cattle to roam at will. Other farmers would harvest 100 bushels per acre; our renter would have 35. We never received a statement showing how much rent we should get. Henry finally decided to sell the farm. We had hung on all during the depression: corn sold for 25 cents a bushel, oats at 10 cents. At one time, we were $500 behind with the interest. We turned the farm over to a loan company. At one time, they had built a ditch through our farm and cut it in two pieces. It cost us $2400 and we couldn't do anything about it. In 1938, we were caught up with our interest and Henry decided to sell the farm. We got $87 an acre. Land prices were at their lowest. Oh, Henry never aimed to get rich! He worked hard to keep a roof over our heads.

When Henry finally decided to buy the farm we called the French place in 1930, we borrowed $8000 on our farm in Iowa. We paid $60 per acre for 100 acres. We had to do a lot of improvements on it.

Birth of Twins Rosalie and Coralie

On January 20, 1930, our twin girls, Rosalee and Coralee, were born. It was the first time I went to the hospital to give birth to any of our children. Henry had worked so hard on our house to have it ship-shape for our new baby. The weather was so cold. When Henry went to town to see the doctor about coming out to our farm to deliver the baby, the doctor advised him to bring me in to the hospital because he was afraid that he may not be able to come out. We lived about five miles from town and the roads were slick with ice, so I went to the hospital. At that time, in order to induce the mothers to go to the hospital to have their babies, they offered cheap rates at $2 per day. The doctor charged us $25 and I was in the hospital ten days. Our twins cost us less than $50. It was a surprise for both of us that we had twins. I never went to the doctor so I did not know I would have twins. Coralee was born three minutes before Rosalee and weighed 6 lbs. and 8 ounces; Rosalee weighed 5 lbs. and 4 ounces. When I saw them the first time, I knew they were not identical twins. Coralee had a long, narrow face and Rosalee had a round face that was no bigger than an apple. The second day when I was nursing Rosalee, she hemorrhaged all over me. She turned blue around her mouth and I thought surely she would die. They took her back to the nursery and I did not see her for two or three days. Was I glad that she was alright. Fuhrmann was a nurse at the hospital and she baptized Rosalee. Uncle Louis, Henry's brother, was staying with us on a visit. After I got home with the twins, we did not baptize the twins for two or three weeks because the weather was so bad. Everyone who came to visit us had a set of names for the twins. I should have kept a list of them; I think there were more than fifty names. Mama's choice of names was Augusta and Henrietta. She was determined one should be named for her, and the other should be named for Henry.

We loved eight years on this place. We called it the French place because our neighbor was Eugene French.

Birth of Third Son Gerald Max

On December 11, 1934, our third son, Gerald Max, was born at home on this French place. My brother, Max, and Katie Mosman, Henry's cousin, were sponsors for Jerry--as we called him. After eight years on the French place, we decided that we needed more room for our growing family. We only had four rooms. How we managed it that long is a mystery to me. Our neighbor, Phillip Berend's farm was for sale. It had a nice, six-room house on it, and it had lots of shade trees and about thirty fruit trees. It became a four-way deal: Leo Mosser bought our farm, Leo Neusch bought Leo Mosser's farm, and we bought Phillip Berend's farm. We all agreed on the same price of $90 per acre. It was then that we had gone to Iowa in 1938 to sell our farm there. We had the Berend farm of 125 acres all paid for. Henry, William, and Alvin worked hard to get it all in good shape because we thought it would be our home from here on out. But it was not to be.

World War II

World War II was raging in Europe. Camp Howze was built north of our home. 250 families with land in that area had to give up their farms. We thought we were safe but only three months later, we found out that the government was going to build an air base and that it would use a strip of our land. Twelve other families had to give up their homes for this project—a project that was never finished. No one can fully realize how it felt for us to give up our home and get out in two weeks. It was heart breaking. We signed the papers on July 1, 1942. I told the two men who came to our house to sign away our home that all they needed was a gun in their hands and we'd have it here just like the Germans had it under Hitler. These men jumped up in disgust and said we didn't sign, etc.

As I said, we had exactly two weeks time to get off of our farm. We had to pay $300 to buy our buildings back or they would pile them up and burn them. Henry put an ad in the Gainesville paper saying that on July 15th, he would auction off his home to the highest bidder. Then the people from town came in droves to look the house over. Our family would be sitting at the table eating and they would walk all over the house. A six-room house like ours would sell for about $250. The army camp was built about three months before us, so people had been buying up farm houses and farm buildings from the farmers who had to leave that area. That cheapened the market for the air base buildings. When the 15th came, Henry stood on a chair and auctioned his home off to the highest bidder. We did get $600 which was higher than most of houses sold for then. When we first found out that the government was going to take our farm, I would walk around the house at night and think it couldn't be; that it was all a dream. Our son, Alvin, was fifteen at the time. I went into his room and he was sitting on his bed, crying.

I had a third of a share in our home in Lindsay. My mother had willed the ancestral home to me and to my two sisters, Augusta and Clara. Since my sisters agreed we could live in this house, we were luckier than most of the others who had to find a farm in two weeks. So we moved to Lindsay. We took our chicken coop with one hundred chickens and four cows along. John Bezner took some of our hogs to his place. Charlie Strauss, a good friend of ours, took our sheep. We lived in Lindsay from July until November. Since Mama's water well went dry, we did not have water. John Bezner, my brother-in-law, would take the water wagon from the thrasher machine and go to Gainesville five miles away and fill it with water and would dump the water in a shallow well-hole on the place. There were frogs and snakes in this well. We had to pull the water up with a bucket and a pulley for the cows and chickens. We had to get drinking water from our neighbors in milk cans, and I had to do our washing at John and Gusta's place.

In the meantime for months Henry would leave with different real estate men to look for a new farm. The irony of it all was that the very first place we had looked at was the farm we finally bought. After five months of looking all over Cooke County, parts of Oklahoma, and neighboring counties, we bought the John Yosten farm east of Muenster. Our first impression of the Yosten farm was that the house was too small for a family of eight; the barn was leaning to the south.

1942 was the year that was! It was the year Uncle Sam promoted us from the town of Lindsay to Muenster. In that year, the green bugs destroyed our grain--all the oats and wheat except for one load. We had twenty acres of cotton ready to harvest when we left in July and corn also was ready; it was in the roasting-ear stage. The people from town would go to the farm and help themselves to the corn. Our peach trees were loaded with peaches but we didn't get any. Some people even dug up our shrubs around the house. We had a large barn that we sold for $250. Our cotton was snow-white and we couldn't pick it; we had to put a bid on it at the courthouse. It looked like it would yield many bales so we put a big bid on it. When we finally were allowed to pick it--they gave us two days to pick it--it had hung so long, it was as light as feather and it only made two bales.

When it was certain that the government would take our farm, Father Conrad, our pastor, told the people on Sunday from the pulpit that the neighbors should help all who had to give up their farms. Now one Monday morning our neighbors, Henry Zimmerer and Albert Kubis, came to see us. I quickly ran in to tell Henry who was sick in bed that our neighbors were coming to help us. That spring, the green bugs had eaten up all our wheat and oats except for one load which Alvin and Bill had taken to the Zimmerer place to thrash. It had not been enough grain to haul the machine to our place. And do you know what our neighbors came to us for? They came for the six dollars that it cost to thrash our one load of wheat. Now wasn't that nice and neighborly?

John Bezner had about twelve trucks that were used for hauling gravel to the army camp. Since he needed truck drivers, he got Bill to drive a truck for him. But when we found out we had to move too, we kept Bill home to help us since Henry was sick and couldn't do anything. Bill and Alvin rolled up the fence wire, etc. At that time, we couldn't buy fence posts or fence wire. My sister, Gusta, said we should leave that old junk alone and let Bill drive the truck, that we'd make more money that way. Labor was in demand with the building of Camp Howze. Anyone who could hold a hammer was considered a full-fledged carpenter and could receive about six to eight dollars an hour. You couldn't hire anyone to help for love or money.

Muenster

We moved to Muenster in November, 1942. The children were all happy to move here. Elsie was in Dallas, going to beauty school; she was twenty. Bill was eighteen and dreaming of becoming a pilot. The war was still raging in Europe. When his draft call came, he was rejected as 4-F; it was a severe blow for him. When Bill six years old, he had to have his foot operated on because of a bone infection. The doctor removed a bone from his second toe the middle of this foot. It did not impair his walk at all. The left foot was just a little more narrow. He really was disappointed because of the 4-F classification. He then joined the Merchant Marines.

Alvin was fifteen. We had a tool shed on the farm and he was tinkering in this shop until all hours of the night. For instance, he would figure out ways to make his burden on the farm a little easier. Henry would tell him to harrow the east forty and Alvin would go up and down the rows like a streak of lightning in order to get through so he could tinker on his pet inventions. We had a hammer mill in the hallway of the barn and an oats bin on the north side. In order not to carry the oats bucket ten feet to the hammer mill, he built an elevator that carried the oats and drop it in the hopper at a precise time. You know in time, all his tinkering paid off. It helped him to develop his future vocation.

Henry had to build everything over on the Yosten farm except the house. We lived on this farm twenty-two years and it was while we were on this farm that our children did most of their growing up and their learning. They all married while we lived on this place. All at once, Henry and I were left all alone there.

(Children: Updated in 1985) Elsie was the first one to marry. She married Gilbert Endres on June 29, 1949. Gilbert and Elsie have one daughter, Lou Ann; she is married to David Spaeth and their children are George, Brenda, and John. William married Kay Eigel on August 11, 1956, in St. Louis, and they have four children: Bob, Tina, Kathy and Amy. Alvin married Gracie Friske on October 20,1953; they have two sons, Kent and Gene. Kent married Sammye Wibble. Coralee married Robert Pulte on October 18, 1951, and they have five children: Michael, Christopher, Don, Steve, and Diana. Don married Belinda Donald in Arlington on September 15, 1984. Rosalee married Robert Bayer on May 7, 1953; they have seven children: Carl, Carolyn, Dolly,

Betty, Allen, Henry, and Susan. Carl is married to Norma Richardson, and they have two sons, Travis and Mark. Carolyn married Charlie Lawrence; Dolly married Harold Owen and they have one son, Jeremy. Betty is married to Tim Cole and they have a daughter, Wendy. Jerry married Carolyn Brinker on September 13, 1958, in San Antonio; their children are Glen, Elizabeth, and Mark.

In 1964, we had a good offer for our farm and we sold it to Paul Fetch at $300 an acre. We then built our home in Muenster. Henry was seventy-nine years by then and he kept saying that it was my house because he wouldn't be in it as long as I. So, I had to plan how to build it. Alvin had drawn up a plan but I deemed it too elaborate and big. Now with the energy crisis, I'm glad my utility bills are not higher.

Henry died April 6, 1976. Today as I am writing this, he has been gone two years already. The children are all happily married and have their own homes and families, and I thank God everyday for the blessings I've had during my lifetime; especially for having had such a good husband and father to our children. We've had our ups and downs but we always had all we needed and we were really happy. Henry told me so many times that he was glad he found me. I have no financial worries and I am happy and contented. The children are all so nice and considerate to me. With four of them living close by, I go to a different one every Sunday; I look forward to this. This summer, God willing, I shall go again to visit Jerry in Houston, and Bill in Fort Worth. I'm hoping and praying that I won't be a burden to the children.

Reflections

I pondered for a long time to tell you children about episodes of our woes. When Henry came to Milwakee to propose to me, was a fairly well-to-do man. His father had sold out all the farm machinery and livestock to Henry, Joe and Nick; each one gave in a homestead in Papa $10,000. Uncle Val was disillusioned over a love affair with an Iowa girl. Papa Fuhrmann had a stake in a homestead in Saskatchewan, Canada, so Val decided to make his fame and fortune there. Papa Fuhrmann gave him a freight car full of farm implements and cattle when he moved to Canada. Not a word was said about the $10,000 that Henry and Joe had paid into the equipment Val took with him. Henry had worked hard and saved his money but when he returned from Milwaukee, disillusioned and disappointed, he loaned Val $1,700 in 1917 and another $700 in 1918, $2,400 in all in two different notes. Interest in Canada was 12% at that time. At the same time, I also had a big disappointment in my romance didn't really know nor care what to do. I was afraid if I grabbed the first chance to marry, I wouldn't be good to him since I pretty headstrong and hot tempered; that's why I did not accept Henry at that time. If I think back now, I know it was for the best. I learned to control my emotions and I also learned to accept the fact that I couldn't hear good. I only wanted to find someone who could restore my hearing. Henry was too nice to ever hold it up to me that if I would have accepted his proposal in 1917, everything would have been so different. We would have had an easier start than we had in 1921. Val sent us one hundred dollars for interest over thirty years. In 1951, he sent Henry $1,500. He still owes $700, but Henry never pressed him for that and who was I to say something about it since I begin with. I learned to abide by his wishes. We never had hard words or arguments; that was the result of four years of waiting. I learned to hold my tongue and temper. May God rest his soul. Amen.

MY BIOGRAPHY

Mama and Papa

Now since I have plenty of time to think, I will try to recall events of my childhood days and of the past. (Written in 1978)

I was the sixth of nine children, born on October 22, 1894, in Lindsay, Texas, to Augusta Steinmetz and Wilhelm Flusche. My Papa was the oldest son of Stephen and Eva Katherina Flucht Flusche: he was born, August 9, 1839. My Mama was born April 1, 1860. In other words, Papa was twenty-one years older than Mama. My grandfather, Stephen Flusche, was a school teacher in Liesterscheid in Germany. When Grandfather Flusche died in 1867, my Papa took his teaching position. By 1872, four of Papa's brothers had immigrated to America: Joseph, Carl, Anton, and Emil. Papa Flusche wanted to marry Christina Flucht, his first cousin, but neither the church nor the government would allow the marriage. Then Papa, Grandmother and Papa's youngest Flusche, Grandmother's sister, Aunt Anna, brother, August, immigrated to America in 1873. The family pine farm of eight acres was sold to a man named Teipel, their hired hand. Papa acquired 700 acres of farm land in Westphalia, Iowa. Beside acting as over-seer of this land, he worked in a post office. Papa married his first wife, Christina Flucht, in 1875. Christina died in 1881 leaving two children, Willie and Clara, who were six and five years old. Papa put them in an orphan home in Dubuque, Iowa, at a considerable expense. One time, he visited them and he asked Clara if Willie was going to school. Clara answered, "No, he sits in the basement and peels potatoes all day." So Papa decided he had to make a home for them. He wrote a letter to the priest in Attendorn, Germany, asking if he knew of a girl that would be willing to come to America, marry him, and take care of his children. This priest in Attendorn gave the letter to my mother who just happened to be home on a visit. My mother answered the letter. My Mama was twenty-five years old at that time, and had worked out from the time she was sixteen years old. Her parents were poor. My grandmother, Elizabeth Walter Steinmetz, had been from a prosperous family. She married my grandfather, Wilhem Steinmetz, against her parents' wishes. They told her that this Wilhem Steinmetz would never amount to nothing.

Grandfather Steinmetz

My grandfather was a tailor and a good one. He'd squat on middle of a table with all his material and tools all around him and sew on a man's suit all week. His customers were Buergemeister, doctors, etc. By Saturday night, he had the suit ready and he would deliver it himself. Then he would go to the Wirtshaus or saloon and celebrate with his friends all night. Sunday morning when people were going to church, Grandpa Steinmetz would be going home. He had a nice voice and he'd sing! You could hear him all over Attendorn. People would shake their head and say, "There goes Wilhelm Steinmetz home." He would then sleep off his roush or his katzenjammer. Monday morning, he would sit

The first birthday of each of our children

ELSIE

BILL

ALVIN

JERRY

THE TWINS: ROSALEE AND CORALEE

The succession of homes I've lived in since I married

The French place

Our retirement home in Muenster

On Uncle Robert's place in Lindsay

The Yosten place in Muenster

In Joe Fuhrmann's house in Iowa

The Berend place in the air base

"We lived on this farm (in Muenster) twenty-two years, and it was while we were on this farm that our children did most of their growing up and their learning."

Family picture: 1951
Back Row: Jerry, Alvin, Bill and Elsie
Front Row: Rosalee, Henry, me (Elsie) and Coralee

Our Golden Wedding Anniversary, March 29, 1971

Back Row: Robert (Bayer) and Rosalee, Robert (Pulte) and Coralee,
Alvin and Gracie, Bill and Kay.
Front Row: Jerry and Carolyn, me (Elsie), Henry, Elsie and Gilbert (Endres)

"The school pictures of our twenty-two grandchildren"

LOU ANN ENDRES, 1951

MIKE PULTE, 1952

CHRIS PULTE, 1953

CARL BAYER, 1954

CAROLYN BAYER, 1955

DON PULTE, 1956

DOLLY BAYER, 1956

BOB FUHRMAN, 1957

BETTY BAYER, 1958

GLEN FUHRMAN, 1959

STEVEN PULTE, 1960   ALLEN BAYER, 1960   KENT FUHRMAN, 1960

TINA FUHRMAN, 1961   ELIZABETH FUHRMAN, 1962   HENRY BAYER, 1962

KATHY FUHRMAN, 1963   GENE FUHRMAN, 1964   SUSAN BAYER, 1965

MARK FUHRMAN, 1965   DIANE PULTE, 1966   AMY FUHRMAN, 1971

MY SEVEN GREAT-GRANDCHILDREN

BRENDA SPAETH   JOHN DAVID SPAETH   GEORGE SPAETH
Children of David and Lou Ann Spaeth

JEREMY OWEN
Son of Harold and Dolly Bayer Owen

WENDY COLE
Daughter of Tim and Betty Bayer Cole

TRAVIS BAYER

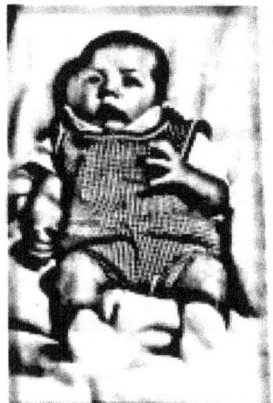

MARK BAYER

Sons of Carl and Norma Richardson Bayer

The Fuhrman family members present at Tim and Betty Bayer Cole's wedding: 1978

on the table and sew again. The money from his last week's suit was all gone and poor Grandmother Steinmetz had to take in washing and boarders to make ends meet.

Mama's Life Before Her Marriage to Papa

There were eight girls and one boy in the Steinmetz family. Mama was one of the younger ones. When she entered school, the teacher asked for her name. Mama said, "Augusta Steinmetz." teacher said, "Ain't that nest about empty?" As a child, Mama would herd the cow in a hay meadow just outside of Attendorn. Grandma Steinmetz had inherited this land. In the center of this meadow was a mountain which was called Mike's head, or in German, Michael's Koypf. Mama was first employed in Cologne; and later on in Berlin. She was a cook for Major and Mrs. Herman vonStahow and their two girls. The vonStahows lived at a Kaserne or as call it, a military camp. When Mama was twenty-one, she came home to announce to her parents that she was getting married to Ernest vonFragstein, a Lutheran. Her parents forbid her to marry him. At that time, children obeyed their parents even when they were twenty-one years old. On Christmas, 1881, her fiancee committed suicide by shooting himself. I think this tragedy remained with Mama all over her life. Mama was vain about her looks. She always told us three girls that none of us were as pretty as she. She had seven points of beauty: a heart shaped mouth, a swan neck, a Roman nose, a widow's peak hair line-- I forget the other three.

The Courtship of Mama and Papa

When Papa wrote the letter to the priest in Attendorn, Mana answered it. Since Papa was a retired school teacher, and Mama could write nice and could write poetry, they corresponded for a while. Mama was persuaded to accept Papa's proposal of marriage through their exchange of letters. Papa sent her the money come to America. They were published while she was still on the ocean. Up until then, the only thing she remembered of Papa was when she saw him at her first communion when she was about 12 years there were maybe old. Papa had brought his class from a neighboring town to Attendown for their first communion. That way, there were maybe several hundred

from the neighboring towns and villages making their
first communion in Attendorn. Each class was represented
with their teacher. Mama remembered that this teacher,
Herr Wilhelm Plusche, was counting them off four abreast
for the procession into church and that Papa had held his
hand on her shoulder.

Mama and Franz Hesse

Mama had a first class ticket on the ship to America,
and there was a man on this ship who was also from
Attendorn; his was Franz Hesse. Papa had written Mama
about him. Franz traveled on what they called the zwishen
deck; in other words, it was way down in the basement.
Mama had to dress up to go to the table, etc. She would
take apples and oranges down to Franz Hesse and he would
give her herring which was plentyful down there. There
would be black kettle full of cooked potatoes with the
jackets and a big barrel of herring: the passengers would
help themselves. This Franz Hesse had gone to Germany to
find a wife; he was forty-two-years old. In those days
in Iowa, girls were scarce. Most men would go to America
first to make their fame and fortune; then, they would
go back to Europe and bring their wives or brides back.
When Franz Hesse and Mama came to Iowa, my Uncle Carl
in Westphalia had just hired young girl by the name of
Elizabeth Muller. Mama and Franz stopped off at Uncle
Carl's place and this girl came out to open the gate for
them; they were with a team of horses and wagon. When
Franz sav this Elizabeth Muller, he said, "That's going
to be my wife or no one." Sure enought, a year later they
married. They were the parents of all the Hesses here in
Muenster.

Mama Meets Papa: They Marry

Now when Mama saw Papa for the first time, she turned
around and cried. He had written her that he had lost one
eye when he had typhoird fever so she knew he only had
one eye, she thought he would be wearing a glass eye. Papa
was nice about her disappointment and did not press her
further. He was staying at his house and Mama was staying
with his brother, Carl. In those days, a girl would not
live under the same roof with her intended husband. After
a few days, Papa told my mother it was alright; she could

go back to Germany. He would pay her way back. But Mama had talked so much about going to America and about getting married to a rich man, etc. A doctor in Germany had told her she couldn't have children because she had anemia; she thought there wouldn't be any children if she married him. She decided to go through with it. They got married on October 29, 1885, in Westphalia, Iowa. In 1886, Grandpa and Grandma Steinmetz and their youngest daughter, Anna, lived with Mama and Papa arrived in Westphalia, Iowa. They all lived with Mama and Papa until Mama and Papa went to Texas in 1890; then, Grandpa and Iowa with Grandma Steinmetz lived on a farm in Iowa with Anna until Anna married Uncle Paul in 1892.

The Flusche Brothers and Papa

About that time my uncles, Anton and Emil Plusche, were establishing German Catholic Colonies. Uncle Emil and Anton started Westphalia, Iowa in 1872; then Westphalia, Kansas and Olpe, Kansas. They named them after Westphalia, Germany and after Olpe, its county seat. My father was well situated in Westphalia, Iowa. He had 700 acres of good land all paid for. He was the oldest of six brothers when his father Stephen Flusche died in 1867. My father Wilhelm, being the oldest, had to promise he would always help his brothers when in need. So when he got the telegram from Anton and Emil from Westphalia, Kansas, that they were bankrupt, Papa put $300 in his pocket and went there; Anton had a drugstore and Emil had a grocery store.

At about that time, August Pulte from Texas had a letter in the Ratfoliphn Rundshan, a German Catholic paper. He wrote that he was getting lonesome for some of his countrymen from Westphalia, Germany. He wrote that where he was living, there was good farm land and that it would make a good place to start a German colony. So one of the Flusche brothers wrote to him and Uncle Anton and Uncle Emil went to Texas. That was how Muenster was started in 1889. My father really was not the organizer but was what you might call the power behind the throne. He was the first one to buy land in Muenster and also in Lindsay. In order to keep his brothers going, he had to sell one farm after another in Iowa to help out. He paid for their life insurance and when Papa died he didn't even have insurance for himself. When Mama went back to

Iowa in 1912, the people all told her if Wilhelm Flusche had stayed in Iowa, lain on his back, and stuck his feet in the air, he would be a rich man.

Mama and Papa Move to Texas

My father brought his family from Iowa to Texas in 1890. The family consisted of my parents, Willie, Clara, Robert, Fritz, and Gusta. He had bought 100 acres of land south of Muenster where Arthur Bayer now lives. My mother was expecting Otto and the Texas water made her sick. When her time came, she went back to Iowa to have her baby; Otto was born August 18, 1891. My Uncle Carl Flusche, who was a doctor, had delivered her first three children in Westphalia, Iowa. When Mama came back to Muenster with Otto, there was trouble brewing in Muenster. It seemed that two of the Flusche brothers' best friends were stirring up the people against them; even the Muenster priest was against them. There were about sixty families in Muenster by then. The Flusches had sold all the land that they had leased from Gunter and Wellesly of Dallas and they went back to Dallas to lease some more land. But these two good friends had gone to Dallas and leased the land the Flusches needed, so the Flusches could not get more land. Mama had the baby and they couldn't buy milk. Someone stuffed rags and stuff in their chimney so they couldn't start a fire. So the Flusches shook the dust of Muenster from their feet and moved on. At that time, five Flusche families lived in Muenster. Papa and Anton moved to Lindsay where they organized that community in 1893. I don't know too much about the circumstances involved in the re-location of the other Flusches: Joseph Flusche moved to Tioga; Emil organized a colony in Pilot Point and a colony north of Wichita Falls called Mount Carmel; and August helped organize Windhorst. In all, the Flusches organized seven Catholic colonies.

Papa and Uncle Anton Organize Lindsay

At first, the Muenster people made fun about Lindsay. They said it was too close to Gainesville and that it would never amount to much. Uncle Tony was really the main organizer: Papa helped Uncle Tony. Anton leased a certain amount of land from Judge J. M. Lindsay who owned all the land around there, and named the colony after him. J. M. Lindsay donated eight acres for the church and donated ten acres of land for the Lindsay park east of Papa's house. Papa bought the first land in Linday: 100 acres of farm land (Lindenau) and twenty acres in Lindsay. Papa built the second house in Lindsay in 1892; it was a large two-story frame house that had stairs going up to the second floor and to the attic. To measure the land, Uncle Tony tied a white rag on a spoke of the wheel; then, young Tony had to sit on the back of the buggy and count how many times the wheel turned to make an acre. Tony was about twelve-years-old then. Uncle Tony had a buggy but he did not have a horse. When a settler came, he would send young Tony down to Papa for a horse so they could drive settlers around to look at land. We had a three room house on our north farm which we always called Lindenau; it was named after a health resort close by Berlin, Germany. When the first settlers came, they would live on Lindenau until they found living quarters on their farm. Mama said it was home for thirteen different families. This house on Lindenau where so many first settlers lived was so full of bed bugs everybody had bed bugs in those days; we had them too. Mama would paint the mattress with carbolenium. It did kill the bugs but it would sure did have a strong smell, especially when it rained. My father went to the merchants in Gainesville to ask them to allow the settlers credit; he said he would stand good for them. Very few settlers had any money when they first came. Some even said later that they had to stay because they didn't have the money to leave. Papa even paid for Uncle Tony's housekeeper: Tanta Tonchen was sickly. When Uncle Anton moved from Westphalia, Kansas, to Texas, he brought his maid, Katharine Eikof, along with his two children, Tony and Emilia. Every Saturday, Tony came to get $3.00 Katharina. Katharina later married Fred Herr; she was the mother of Mrs. Ben Luke of Muenster. The first years were trying days for all involved and today as I drive through Lindsay I can't help but wish that my parents and to all the first settlers could see what a nice town it turned out be after all the trials and hardships they went through.

Events Beginning With My Birth

My brother, Herman was born December 20, 1893, and I was born October 22, 1894, in Lindsay. In 1895, Grandpa and Grandma Steinmetz and Uncle Paul's family moved to Texas from Iowa. Grandma Steinmetz died from cancer shortly after they came to our place. Uncle Paul and Aunt Anna lived on Lindenau the first year. Uncle Paul was no farmer so the first thing he did was to open a saloon. Grandpa Steinmetz then made his home with Uncle Paul and Aunt Anna. Grandpa Steinmetz still owned a hay meadow that Grandma Steinmetz had inherited by Attendorn, Germany. Mama herded the family cows on the mountain side when she was a child. In 1906 they discovered a large cavern under this mountain that they called Mike's head, but they did not tell Grandpa Steinmetz about the cavern. All at once in 1910, they offered Grandpa 1000 marks for his property in Germany. Since he had been a poor man all his life, he accepted the offer. Grandpa Steinmetz died in 1910; he was 90 years old. Alvin was in this cavern in Attendorn. He said that it's not as big as Carlsbad but it sure was worth a lot more than what Grandpa got for it. The cavern is now a major tourist attraction in Attendorn.

My earliest remembrance is when I stayed with my Aunt Anna in Tioga. Mama was expecting Alex, Max was about a year-and-a-half old, and I was three: I guess we were a sorry looking bunch. My Aunt Anna, Uncle Joseph's wife, visited my mother and when she saw all of us little ones, she told Mama that she was going to take Elsie along with her. I don't know just how long I was with her. Uncle Joseph had died in 1896 in Tioga but he was buried in Muenster. Their oldest girl, Anna, had married Theodore Wiesman and was living in Muenster. Aunt Anna's oldest and only and four daughters were at home yet. I can remember when I stayed here that everyday I would wait for a certain hen to lay her egg behind a shed, and I would take the egg to Aunt Anna. Uncle Emil, my Godfather, went on a visit to Aunt Anna and afterwards, he told my father that he better take that Elsie away from Aunt Anna; they were spoiling her so that she would never fit in with the rest her brothers and sisters anymore. When I came home, I'd push Mama away and ask for my other Mama. One day, I stood at the edge of our porch and Max pushed me off and said that I didn't belong there.

Robert and Fritz struck by Lightning

When Robert and Fritz were about twelve and thirteen, they were struck by lightning. A sudden thunderstorm came up just as they were about ready to leave the field. Willie had left a little earlier and made it to the barn. When he returned to Robert and Fritz, they were still unconscious. A doctor told Mama that this could have caused the mental problems Robert and Fritz had when they were older.

Our house burned down in 1899; it was the second house built in Lindsay and the house I was born in. The night of the fire, my father carried all of us children outside to the park across the street. My brother, Max, was three years old and was so shy. There were so many people around that he had gone back upstairs to his room. Since he couldn't crawl into his high bed, he sat down behind the door. No one missed him. Mama was so full of grief and sorrow because the next day the doctor was going to amputate the finger of my youngest brother Alex. For thirty-five days Mrs. Eikof, a friend of ours, had taken six-month-old Alex to Gainesville to the doctor with the horse and buggy. My mother had had a visitor who had a child the same age as Alex; the child was cutting teeth and running a high fever. The two children were playing on the floor when this sick child bit my brother on the middle finger of his left hand and caused blood poisoning. Mama was determined to save the finger, but the doctor advised her that in order to save the hand, he had to amputate.

Therefore, unknown to everyone, Max was upstairs. The fire had started up by the chimney and the alarm had been given that no one should enter the house anymore because the roof was ready to cave in. One of the men who had been helping to save whatever was possible from the lower parts of the house and cellar was Peter Fuhrmann. He said later that it seemed to him that there something upstairs that he had to get; it seemed as though someone was pulling him upstairs. There were five rooms upstairs and he didn't know which was Max's room; yet, he went straight to his room, picked him up, and carried him out to the park where the rest of us were. This was just minutes before the roof caved in. Now my mother was so full of grief and sorrow, she never even missed Max. Days later, Max would hold up his little foot to Mama and say, "It was hot but it did not burn."

During the process of saving what could be saved, Mama called for a green box on her dresser; she had knitted twenty-four squares for a bedspread. They carried out all sorts of boxes, but not of them was her spread. My Uncle Paul Wiese was carrying a handmade dresser which was upstairs but he couldn't get it down the stairs so he threw it out of the window. When it hit the ground, it was pile of kindling wood and later it burned up. Uncle Paul weighed two-hundred-fifty pounds and got a rupture from carrying this heavy dresser and had to be taken to the doctor. There was twenty-gallon barrel of wine in the cellar with a sand sack on the opening. They rolled this barrel out and all the wine ran out. We also had twenty-five gallons of molasses in a barrel which they rolled out but was left too close by the house; it was one hard lump of molasses. Mama said we kids licked on this lump for days. Robert and Fritz had many agate marbles which melted into one lump.

At the time of the fire Mama was also expecting her ninth child, Clara, who was born February 28, 1900. My mother was in such shock and despair, she revolted against God because she felt he had sent her all this misery. When Papa told her to go to church, get on her knees, and thank God that Max was saved from the fire, Mama was consoled.

Unknown to anyone at the time, Mama was terribly upset during the fire for another reason; inadvertently, she caused the fire. I did not learn about this until in 1960, when Gusta was dying from cancer; she told me what happened that night of the fire. Gusta said Mama needed to sew some bands on our cotton sacks and she needed some cotton which was kept in a big bundle in our attic. Mama told her to get it for her, but Gusta told Mama that she was scared to go up there in the dark. Mama told her to go. That she needed it. Gusta said that she got some matches and went up into the attic. When she got up there, she lit a match and it fell on the cotton. In seconds, the whole bundle was on fire. She ran down as fast as she could and hollered fire. I can barely remember Papa and Mama carrying buckets of water up to the third floor but it was too late. At the time, you could not get insurance if you kept cotton in the house. Since the fire was first seen by the chimney on the house, Mama always said sparks from the chimney started the fire. Poor Gusta had to carry this secret with her the rest of her life. She was about twelve years old when the fire occurred.

Mama and Papa did get $500 from the fire insurance and another house just like the house that burned, only the new house didn't have a stairway going to the attic. We all stayed in the three-room house on Lindenau while the new house was being built. During this time, Papa became ill. The fire happened during the first part of September and started about midnight; it was cool then. My father became overheated, then chilled by running in and out of house; he caught a bad cold which he couldn't get rid of. It settled in his throat; a year and a half later, March 26, 1901, he died. At that time, they called his ailment T. B. of the throat. He was sixty-two-years old. He left Mama with nine children, the oldest was fourteen, and the baby, one year old.

After the fire, we all stayed at Uncle Anton's. Papa carried our most priceless possession, a large clock, on his back as we walked to Uncle Anton's that night. Mathilda, a daughter of Emil who was staying with Anton at that time, carried little Alex--I don't know who carried Clara. When the estate was settled in 1942, the only thing that Max asked for was the clock that Papa saved from the fire.

What I Can Remember of My Papa Before He Died
Written: May 1985

As I think back, I can't help but think what a nice childhood all of us had while Papa was alive. We had a vinyard of grapes. Papa made about 25 gallons of wine a year. We had a fruit orchard with peaches, pears, plums, and a lot of bee hives in the orchard. I remember we had a big hive of bees in a tree east of our house. Papa had a special net that he would put over his head. He would catch the bees and put them in a hive.

We also had ducks and geese. One big gander threw me down when I was about two or three-years-old, and he stood on me and kept packing on my neck. I yelled all I could and Mama came and chased him off. I swtill have a scar on my neck from that gander.

I also remember that Papa would purt mwe up on his shoulders and say that I was "the apple of his eyes," and I remember that we kids would have to look for his pipe. Papa always smoked a pipe; he would put it down when he worked and forget where he put it.

From Papa's Expense Account of New House

While looking through the yellowed pages of my father's diary, I got to thinking that his record of the new house's expenses would be interesting. These are some of his notations: [Our house burned down on September 5, 1899; it was insured for $500]. The new house was built about the same as the old one, only two feet longer. Expenses: Paid Eugene Vetter, 36 1/2 days, $45.00. Carl Lavatsch, 29 days @$1.50 per day, $43.00. Peter Jensen for the foundation, 5 1/2 days @$1.50, $8.25. Wall paper for 3 rooms, $6.50. Nails and hardware, $50.00.

Life With Mama
Fritz in Subiaco

My brother Fritz was very smart and could learn easily. Mama had in her mind that he should be a priest. So in the fall of 1902 when he was fourteen, he went to Subiaco, Arkansas, to begin his studies for priesthood. During that school term, Subiaco burned down. Fritz had a nice new trunk which he carried out on his back. He saved the trunk but he injured his back. This injury caused him a lot of trouble later in his life.

In 1902, Mama had to have an operation. The doctor had to remove the lowest joint of her spine. This bothered her the rest of her life. But the most serious threat to the family occured during a typhoid fever epidemic in Lindsay in 1903; five of our family were stricken with it. We were all on the farm except Mama, Clara and Alex- -Clara and Alex were too small to work in the field. Otto always had to go home to milk the cows and to bring us groceries; he was the first to get sick. Then Gusta had to help out and she got it. Robert was next in line to help the others, and he got it worse than anyone. His fever got so high, it scared Mama. Willie got it and then Max; that left Herman and me alone on Lindenau. Mrs. Niernhaus, a neighbor, went to Mama and bawled her out because she left us sitting alone there like some lost chickens. Mama told her to take us, which she did. I was eight-years-old and Herman was ten. We were there about two or three weeks when all at once, Mama got a big bill from Mrs. Niernhaus for our board. Mama thought she had taken us in out of charity. So then I went to stay with the sisters and Herman stayed with the Eikofs. Clara and Alex were at Tanta Mari Loerwald. All recovered without serious effects except for Robert. Mama always wondered if the fever was the possible cause of the mental problems he had later in his life.

Otto and the barbed-wire Accident

Three events of importance happened in 1905: Otto was sick, I got scarlet fever, and Mama decided to marry Mr. Theisen. When otto was about fourteen years old, he was sick all the time. He was running a fever and he had sacks under his eyes. Mama even took him to the hospital, but they couldn't find out what he had. That was about the time Mama got married to Papa Theisen and she would often spend the weekend with him in Gainesville. This one time she had given Otto strict orders to stay at home. He was just released from the hospital. All of us kids went to our neighbors that Sunday night and otto didn't want to be left alone at home so he went along. We played pump-pump pull away. Anyway, we all had to run and Otto ran right into a barbwire fence. He cut his face open from ear to ear. Herman and I took him home. He was bleeding something awful. Whole chunks of blood could be seen with every step he took until we made it home. I couldn't find enough rags to stop the bleeding so I took bed sheets. Herman called Mama over the phone and told her what had happened. She said to bring him to Gainesville the next morning. We kids sure had an anxious night but you know after that, otto was not sick anymore. He had the scars on his face the rest of his life. I don't know how many stitches the doctor put in him the next day.

My Illness of Scarlet Fever

About this same time, I was eleven-years-old and we were all on Lindenau chopping cotton, when we had one of those sudden downpours of rain. I was soaking wet before I got to the house. I got real sick and Gusta would set a cup of water by my bed and she'd go out in the field and chop cotton with the rest of them. I lay there the rest of the week. My fever went so high, I would see all sorts of things on the ceiling. They did not take me home to Mama until Saturday; I was already peeling off. Mama got scared and called the doctor. I had scarlet fever, the worst kind. I peeled off from head to toe and my hair all came out. I was put under quarantine for a month in our front room. At that time I could hear good yet. I knew when I was alone in the house. I would prowl all over and hunt me something to read. When I heard anyone coming, I'd stick my book under the pillow. It's a wonder I did not damage my eyesight because I was supposed to have been in a darkened room already on the farm. But it seems it may have affected my hearing more than my eyes.

The next important event that happened in 1905 was Mama's "love marriage" to mr. Theisen. Mama had told us that her first marriage to our father was a convenience marriage.

Mama and Papa Theisen

During 1905, we were all at a picnic. Mama had told us younger ones to be home by nine o'clock. When we came home, the parolor was all lit up and Mama had a date with Mr. Theisen. We kids all candy from him. He was to be our step-father later on. He was very handsome and sophisticated. Now Mama had always warned us girls never to go by the looks of a man. She had a German saying which meant: "A handsome man, a good-looking man, set him on a table and eat from him." In other words, he wouldn't be a good provider. How true this turned out to be for her. When Father Nolan from Gainesville heard that Mr. Theisen and Mama were going to get married, he sent Mama a note that he had to see her. So Mama went to him. He gave her good advice. Mama was pretty well-to-do at that time; she owned three farms. Father Nolan told her to make out papers stating black on white, that Mr. Theisen could not claim any of her property. Texas has a law that half of the wife's or the husband's property automatically goes over to the spouse. that advice. So Mama had the papers drawn up on that advice. Father Nolan's second advice was that since Mama had all nine of us at home yet and Papa Theisen had six children at home, that he couldn't boss us and Mama couldn't boss any of his. Boy, was that a God-sent advice in later years. His third admonition to Mama was that Papa Theisen was a crank. Now Mama didn't know what a crank was, but she soon found out.

Before their wedding, Mama had bought a new buggy called a Phaeton. It was low on the ground so older people could get in easier and it opened on each side. It had rubber tires and a lamp on each side. Mama had a new horse which had to be kept curried. Not one of our plow horses could harmonize with this fancy Phaeton. The horse also had to be gentle so Mama could drive it. The first few months, Mama would dress up in her best clothes and drive to town and pick up Papa Theisen at the court house where he was employed as the county tax assessor. They got married November 6, 1905; the wedding reception was held in our home in Lindsay. We had several hundred people invited. My cousin, Bill Loerwald, and his brother, Charlie, had loosened the screw on the wheel of this Phaeton. At about nine o'clock on the wedding night, Mama and Papa drove to Gainesville to spend the first night at Papa's house. They got as far as the poor farm, about three miles east of Lindsay. There was a deep dip in the road, and the wheel came off and rolled down this dip. It was dark and there they sat. A black man who peddled vegetables came by with a cart. Mama got on the cart with this colored man and Papa Theisen rode the horse to Gainesville in his wedding tuxedo. They left the Phaeton sit until the next day. Bill and Charlie Loerwald followed and watched what happened. They sure got a big kick out of it.

Papa Theisen was director of the choir in Gainesville and Mama was with the Lindsay choir for thirty years. Now Father John, who had been director for the Lindsay choir for many years, was transferred to Windthorst where he had started a new choir. When Mama and Papa Theisen got married, he invited them to come to Windthorst on their honeymoon. The first night, he invited his choir to be there with a keg of beer for a sing-a-long party. By the time they were all there, it was nearly nine o'clock. Just whenthey had started singing, Papa pulled out his watch and said, "Nine o'clock. Time to go to bed." Mama said to him: "Are you nuts?" Papa went to bed; Mama stayed on and sang with the choir until twelve o'clock. When she went to bed, he turned his back to her. Then she knew what a crank was. She was to find this out many times in later years.

As for Mama not bossing his children, or he not bossing us, the agreement was to our advantage. Since we always stayed on farm during the week, we would only be in town on weekends. Luckily for us, that was when Papa Theisen would be in Gainesville. You see, he had a nice home in Gainesville with eight acres of land right north of the Fairview Cemetery. Was that a setup for an ideal marriage, Papa in Gainesville and us in Lindsay?

Sometimes, though, Papa would come out on weekends on the Katy train that went west from Gainesville. He had a certain place to hang his hat in our living room. Now the first train would come to Lindsay about seven and the train going to Gainesville from the west would come about seven-thirty; it was timed just long enough for Papa to walk to our place and back to the station. If he found Mama in bed with one of her migraine headaches, he would grab his hat and beat it back to the station to go back to Gainesville. We and Mama would not see him again for six weeks. We were all happy when he did that because if he stayed, we had to have the meal on the table at a precise time, and we kids were supposed to be in bed at nine o'clock. Papa Theisen's life-style interfered with our life-style. There wasn't much for us young folks to do those days. First we'd all meet at the Post Office and if nothing else was cooking, we'd go to our house. Mama never cared how much noise we made or how late we stayed. Herman could hear a new song one time and then he would play it on the piano. We would all sing along or roll back the carpet and dance. Now Papa and Mama had their bedroom next to our living room. Papa would go to bed, yellow and green from anger, but he couldn't say nothing. Mama always sat up until twelve; she could knit and read at the same time with nothing but a coal oil lamp. But it wasn't always that Papa Theisen could catch the train to Lindsay on weekends.

My half-brother, Willie, was against Mama marrying Papa Theisen. He told her that smart city slicker's kids would teach her boys all sorts of tricks--which they did. There was Bennie Theisen; he was the same age as Herman. My Uncle Tony Flusche was depot agent in Lindsay and in those days, they would ship five-gallon, wooden buckets with candy. Now Bennie showed Herman how to unscrew the lid, take out a big sack of candy and put the lid on it again. All sorts of tricks like that.

Now Papa Theisen's son, Albert, had married Iva Culp whose father was a lawyer. This Albert was cashier in the Muenster bank and he embezzled a large sum of money and caused the bank to close. One night about midnight, lawyer Culp, Albert, and Papa came to Lindsay and got Mama out of bed. Albert knelt down in front of Mama and pleaded with her to sign a certain piece of paper to keep him out of the pen. Mama stood firm and did not sign. This really cooled off what little affection Mama still had for Papa. She told us much later that it would have cost her one of her farms if she would have signed that paper. Albert then moved to San Antonio where he was employed byJaska's store. In time, he did the same thing there. The time came when he could not find a job in Texas. Papa Theisen sold his nice home and his eight acres of land for $4,000 and paid Albert's fine. This made him dependent on Mama for thirty years.

Papa Theisen tried different ways of supporting himself but it all was a flop. I could write a book on all the different projects were he tried out. He owned a movie picture show at one time but he was too poor to take out insurance and within a year, the show burned down. It left him more poor and discontented than ever. He was so hot-tempered, everyone of his six boys ran off when they fourteen, fifteen-years-old, to make their own way in the world. So when Papa got old and helpless, the children told Mama they didn't owe him a thing. On Papa's seventy-fifth birthday, his children were scattered all over the U.S.A. and they wrote Mama that they were going to come and take Papa out to the Turner Hotel in Gainesville for dinner. This was the swankiest hotel in Gainesville and the Theisen children would get their names in the paper--which was the main idea of it. But Mama wrote back that it wasn't such a good idea. First of all, Papa didn't have a suit fit to wear to this gala dinner, and secondly, he needed the money that this dinner would cost to buy him some new clothes to wear. So when the time came for the big surprise, we cooked the dinner for the thirty people that came. Everyone had a good time. It so happened that Papa had been white-washing Mama's chicken coop and was wearing the oldest clothes he had and when they all came, he did not change to better clothes. Then Julia, his daughter, asked Mama if that was the best clothes he had. When it came time to leave, Mama grabbed a hat and went around for a collection and the whole amount of money came to $23. If they would have had the dinner at the Tuner Hotel, it would have cost hundreds. With $23 money, Papa couldn't buy much. Mama always said she would take care of him and feed him but she would not buy any clothes. He stayed in his room upstairs and Mama was in her room downstairs. He had no money, home, property, or old age pension. Mama couldn't get old age pension because she still had a farm, but she had no income. There they were; she begrudged every bite he ate. Before she died, she wanted us to promise that we wouldn't take care of him; she wanted his children to take care of him. Mama died after suffering a stroke in 1940. Papa Theisen lay with a broken hip for two years before he died in 1941. That was the end of Mama's "Love Marriage."

Mama married Papa Theisen in 1905 but for us children, it was still life as usual with Mama. Fritz had gone to the seminary in 1901, Robert had his first bout of mental illness in 1904, but the rest of us worked together and Mama prospered. We had the 177 acres on Lindenau. We helped work Willie's farm until he got married in 1906, and we farmed the 200 acres south of Lindsay. Each of us more or less had specific work to do on the farm; for instance, when we baled hay. We would bale as many as ten thousand bales. Herman would cut the hay with a horse hitched to a mower and he kept his mower blades sharpened. Alex would run the sulky rake that put the mowed hay into wind-rows. Gusta would run the buck rake; it was a wide rake that brought the hay to the tray beside the hay baler. When our hired hand, Arthur Galasky worked for us, he'd put a block into the baler to section off the bale. Sometimes, Herman would use his foot to stomp down the hay into the hopper between the packing of the plunger. As the bale moved out of the baler, Otto sat on the north side of the bale and I sat on the south side of the bale; we'd put the wire through the hay bale. If we had trouble getting the wire to go through the hay, we'd yell at the one who sat on the middle of the turn-stile to make the horses stop. Two horses walked in a circle and moved the gears that powered the baler. Usually the youngest one sat in the middle and drove the horses; that was my first job. Max was a general flunky; he'd work wherever he was needed: he'd help Herman stack hay bales and haul them into the barn. On Saturday night, we'd go home to Lindsay. The bales would be stacked six layers high on the wagon. The only thing holding the bales on the wagon was ropes attached to the front of the wagon, brought over the bales, and tied down on the back. When the loaded wagon made turns, the bales would lean way over; we thought they would fall off. We would drive the hay wagon in on Saturday and unload it on Monday. We kept some hay on the farm and some at home in Lindsay.

When we moved from Lindenau to the South farm, all the cooking utensils were put into a wooden box, put into the back of a buggy and taken along too--even the stove. There was a cook shack on the South farm. I slept on a cot in the cook shack; the boys slept in the barn. On the side of this summer kitchen was a table that would seat ten or twelve people. Everyone sat on hay bales while they ate. We had a rain barrel for drinking water on a sled; the barrel caused the water to have a pickle taste. I had to go about a half mile to Sandmans with the barrel on the sled to get water. The Sandmans sold butter in Gainesville. Since they had no ice, they kept the butter under the storage tank by the windmill. When I got the barrel of water, Mrs. Sandman would give me a slice of butterbread. [Rosalee and Ray Sandman live there now; that would have been Ray's grandmother.] When Gusta got married in 1908, I did part of the raking for awhile. The baling would take up to a month or six weeks until cotton picking time in August. When we all worked together like that, Mama made a profit from farming. When the boys were older and on their own, they just couldn't make a go of it.

My Year at St. Mary's School, 1906-1907

I made my solemn communion in the spring of 1906; that fall, I attended St. Mary's School in Gainesville. When you made your solemn communion in Lindsay, it was as if you had your Ph.D from the four grades taught there. Mama wanted me to have higher learning, so until Christmas, Otto and I drove to Gainesville with the horse and buggy to attend school at St. Mary's: Otto was fifteen and I was twelve. Herman, fourteen, was in Conception, Missouri two years; it was the same place where Fritz was in the seminary. Mama made a deal with Captain and Mrs. Wright for me to stay with them for the second semester at St. Mary's because it was oo cold for me to drive with the buggy: Otto then rode a horse to school. The Wrights lived right across from St. Mary's Church. For my room and board, I had to feed the horse. I also had to hitch it up to a buggy and bring it to the front of their house. Mr. and Mrs. Wright would take a ride in the afternoon. After school, I then had to take the buggy and horse to the back and unhitch it. Noboby but Mama could figger out a deal like that without asking it I'd do it. I also had to husk a load of corn that they had in grainery. I'd husk and read a book at the same time. I took music lessons twice a week. Mama told Mrs. Wright to be sure I practiced one hour after school every day. At that time I could hear good yet. I would prop the book up on the music stand and read it and at the same time, I'd play a piece of music that I knew by memory. I'd play that piece of music over and over until I heard Mrs. Wright coming. I'd quick sit down on my book and keep practicing. She said that she was tired of hearing that same tune all the time. Needless to say, the money spent on my music lessons was wasted. My brothers Fritz and Herman were good musician, but I was not.

While I stayed at the Wrights, I ate a lot of grits; it tasted real good with gravy. The neighbor lady asked me one time if I got enough to eat. I said yes. I remember when Mrs. Wright was practicing a speech that she had to give at the dedication of the Confederate Monument in the Gainesville City Park. While stirring the soup, she would make motions with the soup laddle. On Friday noon, I'd take the train to Lindsay at five o'clock; I always enjoyed that.

Rogation Day Processions

In the early days, we used to have rogation days. We would have processions three days in a row to pray for a bountiful harvest. The parade would go down main street in Lindsay until Hoelker's store; then, north pass our house, and then back to the main street.

Mama told us about the rogation day processions in Germany. They would go out into the country-side, pass the wheat fields, all the while singing the all-saints litany. The priest would lead and the people would answer, "Ora pro nobis"; which meant, pray for us. Now they would come to a wheat field that was real thin and short. The priest would pray, all in the same tune, "Prayer won't help here; needs manure." Then they'd come to a field where the wheat was real tall and thick. He would say, "Quit praying or it will lay down." The people answer, "Ora pro nobis."

John and Gusta

It seems that John Bezner and my sister Gusta were sweethearts from childhood on. Just what John saw in Gusta was a mystery to me. He had a roving eye for pretty girls and Gusta was so shy and timid. I remember once when Gusta was staying in Gainesville with the Eppingers where she did housework, that I needed to try on the first communion dress that Mrs. Eppinger was sewing for me.

John Bezner, Julia Theisen, and I drove to Gainesville in a buggy: Julia would stay with us during the summer vacation. I was sitting in the middle, John on the right side driving the horse, and Julia on the left side. He spent the whole time at Eppingers with Gusta. On the way home it was late, and the horse knew its way home alone. I pretended I was sleeping and John and Julia smooched all the way home to Lindsay. One time while John was courting Gusta downstairs in our parlor, Julia Theisen was upstairs with her ear to the floor; she could hear every word they said. She got pleasure from that.

I remember another flirtation of John's. At one of the Loerwald's weddings, John and Gusta were engaged already. I was about twelve-years-old and we kids played hide and seek. There was a big tent set up to eat under and I ran behind the tent. There was John and Lena Friedman, hugging and kissing. Of course, I never said nothing to Gusta. This Lena Friedman later married Joe Gieb.

The night John and Gusta celebrated their engagement, a lot of people were there and we kids were playing in what we called the cow and horse yard west of our house. There was a big trough in the middle of the yard where the horses ate and we kids were running around the horses. All at once Dick, a white horse, kicked me on the side of my knee. I flew against the fence and I kept yelling for some fresh water because I was fainting. None of us ever called on Mama to help us when we got hurt. Otto and Herman dragged me up the back steps upstairs, got water and a rag and washed out my wound, put salve on it, and put me to bed. I had a big hole there from the horse's hoof iron. I still have the scar there.

On August 20, 1908, was Gusta's wedding. Now the Loerwalds always had big weddings but Mama was determined that Gusta's would be bigger and better. So there were five-hundred people from Muenster, Lindsay, and Gainesville. We butchered a hog for sausage and a beef for roast and roll-mops as Mama called them. The roast was distributed far and wide. Our neighbors and friends, who would roast them for us the day before, brought them to our place the wedding morning since no one had ice in those days. Mama made five hundred roll-mops: she'd take a piece of steak about four inches square, put chopped onions, salt, pepper and sprinkle flour on it, roll it up and tie a string around it; then, she baked it in the oven the day before. We had a tent all along the north side of our house with tables under it for the wedding feast, and on the north side of that, we had a big wooden platform to dance on later. All in all, it was a gala affair. The bridegroom had to furnish the music for the dance and to pay for the beer and the cigars; it cost John $300.

At the time Gusta was not quite twenty. Mama made Gusta wash the white Sunday shirts for the boys. Robert was sick; Fritz was gone to the seminary, so that left Herman and Otto who weren't old enough to do the farming. We had two farms. We had two hired hands at the time of Gusta's wedding, Arthur Galasky, and Willie Muller, a greenhorn just in from Germany. There I was, fourteen years old and left with all the work. We had hard water and the homemade soap would swim on top like some grease. The men all wore their overalls all week without washing. Lots of times, the overalls were just as dirty after I washed them as they were before. Herman always had his traps set in the picnic park for skunks, and I never did get all the odor out of them. On Monday morning, I'd start the fire under the black kettle in the wash house and I'd maybe get the white clothes on the line. We had five beds to change sheets and pillow slips and the underwear for six to eight people; the laundry pile was higher than me. At about ten A.M., I'd go up to the dining room to get dinner started. Most of the time, Mama had the table full of papers and she was writing letters a mile long to Germany. Her mind was more in Attendorn than in Lindsay, Texas. Anyway, I then would quit washing and maybe go in the garden and dig up potatoes and start the cook stove and cook the dinner which I had to take up to the farm for six boys and men. I'd then run to the pasture and try to run the horse into the barn so I could hitch it up to a two wheel cart. We always had such wild horses. By the time I got to the horse by the barn and I got there, the horse would turn around like a streak of lightning and with his tail up, he would run back to the pasture. By that time, I had to go back to the kitchen and look after the dinner. Sometimes, the fire was out again. When I finally got the horse in the barn, I couldn't get the bridle on it; it was so wild. I'd stick my head through the little window on the south side and ask Joe Gieb, who was going by our place to go home for dinner, if he would come in the barn and put the bridle on the horse. Finally, I'd have the horse hitched up and the dinner bucket in the cart. As soon as I had one foot in the it cart, the horse would go like a streak of lightning. How I made up to the farm all in one piece I'll never know. When I got to the boys with the dinner it was 12:30 and I got a big bawling out too yet. When I got back to Lindsay, it was two o'clock. Then, I'd start the fire again under the black kettle and wash the colored clothes until dark; and all this was washed on a washboard.

Leaving Cheaply in the Goood ol' days
Written, May, 1985

We had a hired hand five years for $30.00 a month with room and board. Mama would charge at the grocery store (Fritz Mosman) and at Zackarias clothing store a whole year, and paid them when she sold her cotton about Thanksgiving. The grocery bill was about $125.00 for ten-twelve people. How about that?

A carpenter got $1.00 per hour and dinner; he got only $1.25 without dinner. When Robert build his bungalow in 1912, he paid one dollar an hour and we cooked the dinner (in Lindsay) and took it to his place. When they built up on Camp Howze, the carpenters got $5.-$6. per hour. Since then, everything went up. Before we had ice, one farmer would kill a cow and peddle the meat at 5 cents a pound. Every Saturday, it would be a different one. That way, we'd have enough meat for all of us for about 50 cents. We would take a load of wheat to the Gainsville flour mill and grind it into flour and got about 27, fifty-pound sacks. We did the same with sugar cane. We would take a load of sugar cane to Galasky's molasses mill and we'd get about 25 gallons of molasses. Mama would put about 25 gallons of pickles with dill in salt brine, and during the winter canned them as we needed them. The same was done for sauerkraut.

We had about 30 fruit trees in our orchard: peaches, plums, pears, etc. It seems like we were canning all summer in that hot summer kitchen away from the house. We always raised about three hogs--that was Mama's chore. She would chop off sugar cane and carry two-three arms full to the hogs. In the winter we'd butcher the hogs and a beef. We would grind up the beef half and half with pork for sausage. We would have about 20 gallons of lard. We always raised about 50 bushels of potatoes. She had a big garden and had her own eggs and milk. You can see why we didn't have a big grocery bill.

We used to raise a lot of cotton. My brother, Herman, would go to Gainesville, with a long hay wagon with bales

of hay for seats and bring 25 colored men to chop cotton
from sun up to sun down for $1.25 a day. When they made a
law of eight hours a day, if the men were in the middle
of the field when it was eight hours, they'd drop their
hoes and quit. It was the same with picking cotton-- $1.25
a day and 25 cents less if we cooked the dinner. Until
they made the law at so much per one hundred pounds, it
started with 50 cents per one hundred pounds. Toward the
end of the cotton boom, it was $1.00 per hundred pounds.
In this one hundred acre farm, the Sod, you could tell
where Senator Bailey had a race track. The cotton was
about a foot high where it had been, and the rest would
be five or six feet high.

Even courting was cheap in those days. For instance,
if a boy was too shy to ask for a date, he would send
you a postal card with a lot of sweet nothings on it. I
had 500 cards. Selbs gelobt stinkt. (Self praise stinks)
I sure wish I would have kept them. When the guy was
jilted, you'd get real ugly ones. For instance, I got one
that had a girl primping in front of mirrow that said,
"Beauty is only skin deep." You could get a card for 5
cents and postage was 1 cents.

We would go to the State Fair in Dallas for a dollar,
round trip ticket. We could ride on everything they had
for 10 cents a ride. We'd go to Gainesville on the train
for 15 cents, Muenster for 35 cents. A ticket to the
movies was 50 cents. We'd and to give a party and serve
lemonade (without ice) and homemade cookies. We knew
about a dozen different parlor games and everybody had
a good time.

The Buggy Accident

When I was fifteen or sixteen-years-old, Mama had
bought another 300 acre farm which was half way between
Lindsay and Gainesville on the north side of the highway.
It was called "the sod" because it was prairie and had
never been plowed. It had a three-room house on it and
we would batch there during the cotton chopping and the
cotton picking season. We had as much as a hundred acre
patch of cotton all in one piece. The north end was so
far away from the house that I had to cook the dinner and
take it out to the boys with a horse and buggy. Clara and
I were going to take the dinner out one day and there was
a sawed-off tree stump about two feet high on the north

side of the house. We had the dinner in the buggy and I crawled in first. Clara got in; she had a hold on the top of the buggy on the other side. I wasn't even sitting yet when the horse took off. I was thrown out when a wheel went over this stump. If Clara had not hung on to the side of the buggy, it would have tipped over. I fell between the wheel and the buggy. I had on a new calico dress and the spokes of the wheel rubbed the whole back out of my dress before I fell down and the wheel went over my head. All I remember was falling out of the buggy. When I came to much later, I was lying on the bed and Mama was leaning over me. Clara said that she finally got in the buggy, got a hold of the reins, drove out to the boys, and told them what had happened. They got scared and got Mama. A few years later when I noticed I was losing my hearing, Mama always claimed it was from the time the wheel went over my head. Who knows?

This wild horse we had was Robert's pride and joy. It had been a race horse at one time. Once I was going to take lunch to the farm. I had the sandwiches in a shiny, new one gallon molasses bucket. The horse shied when he saw the bucket. It started to run when I had only one foot in the stirrup. It ran up main street, the lid flew off the bucket, and the sandwiches were scattered all along the street. The horse stopped in front of the church.

Mama had fifty head of cattle on Lindenau. When feed got scarce there, the cattle had to be moved to the south farm. I remember herding the cattle through downtown Lindsay to the farm. [Ben Sandman bought this farm later; he married the oldest Hermes girl.]

When Mama had bought "the sod" farm from Joe Bailey, she had to buy 450 acres in order to get it for $50 an acre; the Bailey ancestral home was on it. [A. Voth bought that farm later.] Since Mama had promised each of the girls $2,000 and each of the boys a hundred acre farm, she used this farm to arrange for the settlement of her plans of endowment. In 1913, Gusta got her $2,000 when Mama gave her 150 acres of this Bailey farm land; she was twenty-five years old. Gusta and John had been living on his farm on Wolf-Ridge. [John got the Wolf-Ridge farm with the $4,000 inheritance he got from his father.] John then built a new house on the north side of the highway; later, he bought the bottom land across the highway because it was better land. He sold the 150 Bailey acre farm to Henry Fuhrmann and Henry Fuhrmann eventually sold the farm to a Rauschuber. Therefore, in 1913, Mama had 677 acres of land: 177 in Lindenau, 200 acres in the South Farm and 300 acres in the Bailey farm (or the sod farm). All we had heard was that she wanted a farm for each of her six boys. That was Papa Fuhrmann's dream too; he also had six sons and 700 acres of land in Iowa. Now there is not a one Fuhrmann in St. Joseph Iowa, anymore. The same goes for Mama's six sons; there is not a one Flusche in the town of Lindsay except a son of my half-brother, Willie.

Robert and Mary Endres

In 1913, when I was eighteen years old, Robert and I took a trip to Westphalia and Erling, Iowa. Robert then went to Wisconsin to visit Mary Endres whom he had met in Muenster while she had been visiting her cousins, the Werner Endres family. While visiting her, Robert told her that it would be best if he wouldn't get married because of his recurrent mental problems. She told him that she would not get married either. In the meantime, I was having a good time in Iowa. I met a young man by the name of Peter Heese. I liked him very much and we often went out together. One night, we went to a tent show where they had a live drama and humorous show. Everybody was laughing around me but I could not make out what the jokes were. So the next day, I told Robert that I could not understand what was going on at that tent show. He said to me, "You dumb cluck, don't you know you can't hear?" That is how I found out that I was losing my hearing. It was a blow that I will never forget. The rest of the family knew it but had kept it from me. I still had a good time with Peter Heese and when I went back to Texas, I got a birthday ring from him. He planned to come to Texas and spend Christmas with me. But under the persuasion of somebody that I thought was my boyfriend in Lindsay, I waited awhile before I thanked him for the ring and the delay ended that romance. Many years later when Henry and I got together by a miracle, I knew it all had to be that way.

Mama and Max's Trip to Germany

In April of 1914, Mama and Max left on the Nord Deutscher Lloyd steamship, "Breslau" out of Galveston to Europe. Mama took this route because it was cheaper even though it took longer to get there. She saved with cheaper travel arrangements so that when she got there, she could impress her friends and relatives on how prosperous she had become while she was in America. But it backfired on her on one occasion. She had written ahead of time just what day and hour she would arrive in Attendorn. On arriving at Bremen, Germany, May 1, 1914 she and Max took a railroad ticket, third class, as far as the town of Finnentrop, the last stop before Attendorn. Now the townspeople of Attendorn had made plans of meeting Mama and Max at Finnentrop on the date that Mama had directed, and not at Attendorn; they even had a band with them. So when Mama and Max arrived at Finnentrop, lo and behold, they crawled out of this third-rate car. Mama had planned to get a first-class ticket in Finnentrop to Attendorn. Max said he was embarrassed when all these people saw them get out of what they called a cattle car.

Mama and Max stayed with Mama's niece, Lischen Haverkamp, who was a full-fledged dressmaker. Since she did not have a large apartment, she put a bed for Max in her sewing room. Lischen had about eight to ten girls sewing for her. In Germany, if a girl wanted to become a dressmaker, she had to sew three years for nothing to learn the trade; that was also true for all the other trades.

My sister, Gusta, never forgave Mama for taking Max along to Germany with her. He was only eighteen years old then and was the most handsome of all my brothers. Mama and Max visited the VonStahow family in Berlin where Mama had worked as a girl. The father, Herman, was gone, but the mother and her two spinster daughters, Marga [Margaret] and Ellie [Elizabeth] were there. The two daughters both fell in love with Max. While in Germany, Max traveled all the way down the Rhine with only a knapsack on his back; he stayed at special hostels for travelers along the Rhine.

They visited around until in August of 1914. They were in Lucerne, Switzerland, when World War I broke out. They had to hurry and get back into Germany before the borders were closed or they would not have been able to get their trunk out; they had only taken some suitcases along to Switzerland. It turned out that they couldn't leave Germany until November. Before Mama and Max were able to leave Germany, Mama joined the Red Cross in Attendorn. She took care of some of the first wounded German soldiers of the war. Since Germany had to go through Luxembourg to invade France, preparing [France was to invade Germany by going through Luxembourg), the Luxembourg people were extremely hostile toward the German soldiers. Mama said some of the first wounded boys had their eyes punched out by the Luxembourg women. Also, the streets were very narrow in the Luxembourg towns and she said when the German soldiers marched through these streets, Luxembourg women poured boiling water from the upper stories of the buildings on the soldiers marching below. Later when Mama got back to America, she read in the American papers that the German women did this same thing to the French soldiers. Because Mama had witnessed the first few months of the war, she did not believe the propaganda that came out during the war; she remained sympathetic to her homeland.

On November 14, they left Rotterdam, Holland on the Dutch Steamer, Rotterdam, arriving in New York, November 24, 1914. (It was a Luxembourg steamer.) On the way back, they were harassed by the Belgians who hated the Germans. Mama said one woman had a long hat pin and she would point it at her like a spear.

While Mama was in Germany, she would write that nobody drank water there; they all drank wine. So I got a bushel of grapes and made some wine. I had asked somebody how to make it. It turned to be pretty good stuff. Clara and I bottled it and we put it up in the attic. We got a step ladder and Clara crawled up in there and I handed her the thirty-two bottles. After a few weeks, we went to see if they were still there and about half of the bottles were missing. So we got what was left and put them in the attic of the summer kitchen. We didn't look at them anymore and when Mama and Max came back around Thanksgiving, all the bottles were gone. It was Herman!

In November while Mama and Max were waiting to leave Germany, I was bridesmaid for Josephine Wagner and Lambert Hartman. I asked Herman if I could get a new dress. He was holding the purse strings while Mama was gone. He said no, that there was no money. So I wore one of Josephine's dresses since we were both the same size. I was unable to hear any of the wedding ceremony. I was twenty-years-old.

When Mama and Max came back from Germany, Mama decided that Max should become an architect. Grandpa Theisen's sister was married to a building contractor named Kemp in Dubuque, Iowa. Max went to Dubuque to work for Kemp. He had to start at the bottom which meant he dug ditches. Max was a good worker and received promotions.

He was dating the oldest of Kemp's three daughters—we in Lindsay didn't know anything about this. Max told Sister Christina that he would have married that girl if he had stayed in Dubuque. He could have had a good position in Kemp's business and maybe eventually have had the whole building contract business but after he had been there a year or so, Mama wrote him that she needed him. So Max went back to Lindsay. Mama was having financial problems because of Alex. I don't know how Max was expected to help Mama. Mama made plans for all her children but somehow, they didn't work out as she expected. There is German saying for this; in English it means: Man proposes, God disposes.

Mama's Property Distribution Plan

When Otto got married in 1916, Mama sold him 150 acres of the western part of the sod farm and sold Robert 150 acres of the eastern part of the 300 acre sod farm. Mama gave them 100 acres of land with a house, barn, windmill and well. Since Otto and Robert wanted more land, they had to pay her $60 per acre for the extra 50 acres. Mama had planned to give each of the boys 100 acres of land; she figured it at $30 per acre, or $3,000. Now Herman got married in May of 1916: Mama gave him 100 acres on the north side of the south farm and she gave Max the 100 acres on the south side of this farm. Herman's land had a house, barn and a well, but Max's did not. Max's land didn't have these improvements because Mama charged him $500 for his trip to Germany and Max didn't even want to go! Alex was promised 100 acres in Lindenau and was expected to farm the remaining 77 acres as income for Mama. We girls were promised $2,000. Gusta got her $2,000 when Mama bought the sod farm in 1912 when she was twenty-five-years old. Clara and I got our money later when Mama's empire was crumbling. Mama had good plans but they didn't work out. When we all pulled together and each of the boys would do what he did best on the farm, the farming went well; but when they had to farm by themselves and had to do everything alone, they just couldn't make a go of it. For example, Otto always did all the plowing. Since we always raised a lot of cotton, Herman would always take care of the cotton pickers and cotton choppers. He'd go to Gainesville in a long wagon and get about twenty-five black people to chop cotton. We'd cook dinner for them and they'd get $1.25 per day. One after another, my brothers lost their farms except Robert. Even though he had a relapse of his mental problems every four years, and had to be admitted to Terrell for about six months, he'd return and farm.

Mama watched her well-intentioned plans for us children fall apart and she experienced many bitter disappointments, but I was absorbed in my own problem of trying to get back my hearing. In the fall of 1917, Gusta and I went to Iowa; Walter was a year old. When Gusta discovered she was pregnant again, she went home, and I went to Milwaukee.(That was when Henry came to Milwaukee and proposed to me; I was twenty-three years old.)

My Visit to Milwaukee and Chicago

I went to Milwaukee, Wisconsin, to see a specialist about my hearing. I stayed with my Aunt Clara and her daughter, Antonio, and Antonio's husband, Dr. Lambert Hargarten. Aunt Clara was the widow of my uncle, Dr. Carl Flusche, who died when he was fifty-two during a typhoid epidemic in 1896. Aunt Clara and Uncle Carl had two daughters, Antonio and Clara; Clara died at the age of sixteen and Antonio married Lambert Hargarten. Aunt clara lived with her daughter and son-in-law and helped him through medical school. [This was Uncle Paul Wiese's buddy back in Iowa.]

My Aunt Clara was really nice and was considerate of my hearing problem. She advised me to learn sign language. She took me to a deaf and dumb home for girls. There were about fifty of them: they would all flock around me, feel my clothes, and make signs. When I went to bed, they would sit on my bed and make signs. It was quite an experience for me. I only stayed there about a week. I told Aunt Clara I was not ready for that yet.

I found out that there was a difference in social classes in America just like the Europeans with their aristocracy. For instance, the two daughters, Clara and Eleanor Hargarten, couldn't date a plumber or a carpenter; it had to be a doctor or a lawyer, etc. They had a wash woman in the basement and I would go down there and help her with the washing and the ironing. Now that was considered out of line because I was a house guest and a relative. I sure felt sorry for the Hargarten girls. They had beautiful clothes but I never saw either one of them ever go to a dance or to a party. Later on, they both went to the convent. Aunt Clara had one son, Carl, who was out of the church. She would get out early each morning and go to Mass to pray that he would come back into the church, but she died before he did. Mama told us that when Robert, Fritz, and this Carl were small in Westphalia, Iowa, Carl had his baby bottle until he was five-years-old. The bottle would break once in a while because he even ran around with it; then he would cry and say Robert or Fritz broke it.

Dr. Hargarten was supposed to take me to an ear specialist, but he never had time for his own family, much less me. His son, Leo, had a boil under his foot and he limped around for days. Finally, his mother opened it and doctored it. Dr. Hargarten had all those Polish women for patients who had a baby every year. He would brag at the table that he could go to Mass on Sunday, be called out to deliver a baby and be back in time to finish the Mass. They had a library that was off limits for the family. Dr. Hargarten had his poker games there about three times a week. The whole house smelled like a saloon and a smoke house. Then it was a blessing I couldn't hear everything that was going on. I went to an ear doctor for about a month before the doctor told me he couldn't do anything for me.

From Milwaukee, I went to Chicago to visit the Kohs family. Now this Kohs family had lived in Lindsay about five years and then they moved back to Chicago. They had a girl named Agnes who was my age and we had corresponded together. Mr. Kohs was a brick layer and he couldn't make a go of it on the farm in Texas. He'd say that the only thing he acquired in Texas was two sets of twins. They had about ten or twelve children when he got back to Chicago and he couldn't rent an apartment with that many kids; so, they divided the children among his kinfolks. When he and his wife and one or two of the children were all settled down in an apartment they took the rest of the children back gradually, one by one. When they all got off of the street car, the conductor would ask, "Are they all yours?" Mr. Kohs would say, "Yes, and you are not getting a one of them." The oldest boy, Chris, who was about nineteen, was painting in the hall upstairs on a real hot day. He went across to a saloon and drank a cold glass of beer. This caused him to the street hemorrhage from his lungs. He lived a few years and died from T. B.

When I stayed with the Kohs, we were thirteen in the family. Mr. Kohs would go to the butcher shop and buy one-quarter of a hog on Saturday, and by Monday it was all gone. Mrs. Kohs would be so tired and worn out, she would sit at the table with the coffee cup in her hand and go to sleep. The whole family was just wonderful to me. The oldest girl, Rosa, was twenty-eight. She and my sister, Gusta, were the same age. Like Gusta, she did not get to go to school very long because she had to stay home and take care of the babies.

My money was giving out and I had to look for a job. I was also going to a doctor for my hearing, a Dr. Untereiner; he was German Jew. I took Chiropractic treatments at one dollar a treatment. Rosa and I applied for a job at the Nabisco Cookie factory. The first day, we had to wash the tin cookie boxes. First, we had to empty them, and you have no idea what all was in them. One grandmother who was about seventy-five-years old told me she had worked there for fifty years. The second day, we worked at a cookie escalator. The cookies came down on a large tray, one on top of the other. When they were on the bottom, they flattened out like they were on a table. We had to pick up the cookies and set them up on the side; the next girls would stack them in the box. We had to work fast because when the tray got to the end, what cookies were left would fall in a big box. The tray folded underneath the table and would go back up. If you picked cookies all day and set them up to be packaged, you felt like you did a day's work. On the third day, we worked where the saltine crackers came down. We only worked at this cookie factory one week; we had enough. I believe they paid about twenty dollars a week.

Now this Kohs family consisted of seven boys and three girls. When the boys left the house, Mr. and Mrs. Kohs knew just where they went and what they were doing. I was so surprised; I had to compare those boys with my brothers at home. The upstairs where the boys slept didn't have any heat, so they would say their evening prayers downstairs. They would usually lean by a chair. One time, John went to sleep leaning over a chair. Mr. Kohs got a chair next to him and pretended he was the priest in the confessional. He asked John, "What else did you do?" John made a full confession in his sleep. We sure did tease him about that. Nearly all the boys brick layers too. A brick layer made about ten-twelve dollars a day then already. One of the girls, Agnes Kohs, was married and had three children. One time, she and I went downtown to shop. She took the baby along. She took a handkerchief, placed a sliver of bread with a teaspoon of sugar on it in each corner, and made four nipples by tying each one off. When the baby cried, she would stick the nipple in its mouth. She carried the baby around all day. I couldn't see how she could hold out in that mob of people on the street and in the crowded street car.

Rosa Kohs would take the twins, Frank and Tony, downtown to buy them a suit; they were fifteen years old then. The clerk would tell the boys to go and ask their mother how she liked the suits. It sure made Rosa feel bad. [The twins were her younger brothers.) Later, when she was thirty-eight years old, she married a man ten years younger than she was. She wrote me of her marriage. She said she wanted somebody to take care of her when she got a tinsmith with a good job. When they were married about twenty years, something happened to him. He lost his mind and Rosa had to take care of him until he died in 1976.

One of the Kohs boys, Robert, had taken a business course and was employed in the office of a railroad. Now there was a girl in this office that he wanted to date, but she wouldn't have anything to do with him. He played a trick on her by placing a dead mouse in her desk. His employer called Mr. Kohs to come to see him and he told Mr Kohs that they had to fire Robert without a recommendation paper. The poor boy couldn't get another job without those papers, and he had to do all the dirty work at home like mopping the floors and washing the dishes, etc. He did all these chores without any grumbling.

The Kohs sure were a happy family. When I was in Chicago working downtown, I spent Sundays with the Kohs family and Joe would take me back where I was working. We had to change streetcars two or three times and I was scared at night. When I went back home and told all of the Kohs family goodbye, Papa Kohs [as I called him], said to me that I should stay and marry Joe. He said he would build us a house next door. They really were a remarkable family, and I can never thank them enough. When Henry and I went to Chicago to see his brother, Joe, we went to see the Kohs family. Joe Kohs was there too with his wife. When we got ready to leave, Joe gave me a big hug and a kiss. He died not long after; he was a good old soul.

My next job after staying with the Kohs was to keep house for a man and his five children while his wife was in the hospital. He had a good job, and as a side-line he was raising carrier pigeons in his attic. It was during the war and the carrier pigeons were in demand. This job only lasted until his wife came home from the hospital. I got five dollars a week.

When I was keeping house for Otto and Robert, they couldn't pay me much but I got five acres of cotton. They planted and cultivated it for me but I had to chop it and pick it. I sold one bale before I went on my trip, and I had Otto to sell the other one. I got $75.00 for it. I bought myself a pretty fall outfit. It was a gray suit with a mink collar on it. I bought gray, high topped shoes that went nearly half-way up to my knees. I always kept $35.00 in case I had to go home. I had promised Gusta I would be home by April when she was expecting Elfrieda.

Papa Theisen had a brother in Chicago by the name of Peter Theisen. He was a street car conductor whose working hours were from one P.M. until twelve P.M. I went there to visit his family; they only lived about six blocks from the Kohs. Mrs. Theisen was Polish and was a very beautiful woman with dark, curly hair and large brown eyes. They had a three-story, brick house with a basement in what they called two flats. It was very elaborate. The Theisens lived in the top flat, a six room apartment. Her brother, a widower with three children and a nursemaid lived on the lower floor. I never saw Mr. Theisen until dinner; he slept downstairs. Peter Theisen did not look like Papa Theisen. He had red hair and a red beard. He was really nice to me what little I saw of him.

Their daughter, Clara, looked just like her father, and their son looked just like his mother. Mrs. Theisen was ailing already when I was there because she was in bed most of the time. But when she came to the table to eat, she was always dressed just so.

Clara Theisen couldn't hear either--just like me. She worked like a slave. She wouldn't eat in the dining room with the rest us. They had adopted a boy, Mike Carey, when he was real small; he was a mail carrier. Mrs. Theisen's brother, Mr. Clivekowsky, Mike Carey, Peter Theisen, Mrs. Theisen and I would eat dinner in this fancy dining room. The nurse maid, the three girls, and Clara would eat in the kitchen. There was a lot of work to do and Clara never got through with it. I never saw her dressed up or go anywhere. I slept in her room and the closet was full of nice clothes.

In 1925, Mama went to Germany for the second time, and when she came back, she went over to Chicago and visited with the Peter Theisens. She learned that Mrs. Theisen had died and that Clara and Mike Carey had been married already in 1918 when I was visiting with them. That's why I couldn't figure out where Clara slept since I was in her room; they slept downstairs.

This Mike Carey was quite a character. One day while we were eating, he said to me, "Elsie is so innocent, she still believes the myth about Adam and Eve eating the fruit from the wrong tree," and he'd laugh like it was a big joke.

The first Sunday that I was at the Theisens, Mrs. Theisen asked me to help Clara with the wash. I told her I never in my life washed clothes on a Sunday. I noticed none of the household went to church. I think they didn't even know where one was. So I dressed up and went out to hunt a church. After asking a few people, I found one. I became real attached to their two-year-old twins and their three-year-old girl. I sewed each one two or three dresses. I'd go into the basement and help the wash woman with the laundry. She came once a week but there was so much to wash that Clara would Wash too yet. One time, I was with this wash woman and she told me that it was getting to be too much work for Clara, and that they were trying to palm me off on Mrs. Theisen's brother, Mr. Clivekowsky. I thought his wife had died when the twins were born, and I had had a few dates to go to the show with him. He was real nice looking was about twenty-eight years old. He had good job in the insurance business. Now this wash woman told me that he had been married twice and that his first wife was still living. She also said that his wife was in show business somewhere and had married again. Of course, when I found that out, I did not go out with him again. That cooled the friendship off considerably. I notice the silver dresser set was gone. It looked as if they thought I maybe would steal it. I had also had some dates with Joe Kohs. One time we were eating and Mike Carey looked at me and he said, "When a man marries, he wants a wife and no flirt." That did it. I packed my suitcase and put it under the bed. I left and went back to the Kohs. Later on, Joe went to the Theisens and got my suitcase. Then I had Frank Kohs to go the employment agency with me to find me a job. I found a job downtown on the Lake front. It was a nice, large, four-story building. My job was to take care of an eighty-five-year-old blind army captain. He couldn't see, couldn't hear. He was a perfect gentleman. I told him I was scared in that big house since I couldn't hear. He told me not to worry, he could hear everything that went on in that house. My room was right over his room. He said he could hear every move that made me feel secure. My work was to keep his room in order. He would shave himself every morning. When I cleaned the bathroom, I had to lay his shaving things on the same place all the time. When the laundry came, I had to see that he got his clothes, and I put clean sheets on his bed. I had to take him downstairs to the dining room and place him at the table. He was living with his only son and his son's wife. You might say they were living with him since he owned the house. His son was real nice to him, but his wife was hep-cat. She would give her father-in-law a big bowl of oatmeal three times a day. Every chance I had, I'd sneak him something else on his plate. She told me he didn't know the difference in what he was eating. There were about four or five roomers in this house, and I had to take care of their rooms too. One of these roomers took care of the money for this grandpa, because he did not trust the grandpa's daughter-in-law. They would go to Florida ever often and they wanted me to go there with them. I was there about three months.

This stay in Chicago was quite an experience for me. It was such a cold winter; the people would shovel the snow off the side walk and pile it up on each side until finally it was higher than me. Most of the people in a city like Chicago never see daylight. They go to work in the dark and come home in the dark. They couldn't hang their clothes outside because of the coal soot. All the factories burned coal; the sky was dark even in broad daylight. Before I went back to Texas, I did go back to see the Theisens off and on. I especially went to see the three little girls. [I've forgotten their names.] I told the Kohs good-bye too before I left. Those days in Milwaukee and Chicago seem so far off when I sit and reminisce about them.

On the way home to Texas on the train, there was a young man sitting next to me. We got to talking, and he said he was on his way to Fort Worth to the Fat Stock Show which had just started. He noticed that I was traveling alone and asked me to go along with him. I saw how easy it was for some girls to fall into a trap. of course, I refused. Shortly after I got home, Elfrieda was born and I took care of her and Gusta. Jake Bezner and I were Godparents for Elfrieda when she was baptized. I couldn't hear anything so I kept my mouth shut. Jake got stuck while reciting the Apostle Creed; we were supposed to pray it together. Nobody knows how embarrassed I was.

The Tornado of May 1917

A tornado struck Lindsay in May 1917. [I was twenty-four years old.] As I remember that evening at sundown, the sky and everything looked fiery red. The tornado struck about 9 P. M. I was keeping house for my brother, Robert. He had just built a new bungalow as they called that style at that time. Robert had a negro couple working for him and he had built them a two-room cottage just northwest of his house. The garden was between their cottage and Robert's house. When the tornado struck, Robert, the hired man we had then, and I stood in the middle of the room and held hands. It's impossible to describe the force and the roaring noise that accompanied it. The whole house moved everytime it struck. We thought now it's going off of the foundation but each time, the house came back. This happened three times and then it rained just each time, the something fierce. All at once we heard Will, the colored man, call out, "Mr. Robert, Mr. Robert." We opened the north door and let him in; he was holding his wife in his arms. She was struck on her head had a deep gash on one side; blood was all over her face. It seemed that the tornado had lifted their house up and made it turn two summer-saults over our garden. At the southeast corner of the garden, we had a gate with two long posts. Now the post knocked the door of the cottage open. The negro couple was thrown before it hit the northwest corner of our house and knocked a hole out just in our roof. There was nothing left of the cottage but a pile of kindling wood. Then it rained in on our kitchen ceiling. The canvas and the wall paper just hung there and filled with water. All at once, it burst and the kitchen was full of water--about three six inches deep. I had to walk through it to get the stove started to heat water so I could wash the negro woman's bloody face. I had put her in my bed. About twelve o'clock the storm was over, and it was bright moonlight outside. The highway was covered with telephone wires and trees. The only one who could travel was a man on horse back. There were no casualties. One Mexican man had an ear cut off when the boxcar he and his family were living in at Lindsay turned upside down on the railroad tracks. We heard our new-born calf bawling about a mile west of our place on the highway, but it wasn't hurt. Robert had a nice new buggy in a shed; it was lying in the yard upside down. We had a large wood pile north of and the chicken house with about one-hundred chickens was north of the wood pile. There were many chickens beatened into the wood pile, dead. The chicken house was also gone and most of the chickens were dead. The next day, the colored couple went to her folks in Gainesville. I washed out all of the bedding that I could. I even hung the mattress outside; but when I went to bed the next night, my bed was so full of fleas. I couldn't sleep in it. I walked a half-mile to Sturms and slept there. Everybody you talked to had a different story to tell about the tornado.

Our church in Lindsay was destroyed by the tornado. The west end was still standing, and so was the east side with the tower. In between everything was rubble. The priest had to crawl over this rubble in order to get the chalice which held the hosts. The golden crucifix on top of the steeple was found sticking in the ground north of the Neiser's house. Now this Neiser family had had some misunderstanding with the parish priest. There were six in family and three would go to one mass and the other three would go to the next mass; that way, they were only going to pay for in church. When the priest told them they had to pay for six rest of their pews pews, they went to church in Gainesville the rest of their lives--and they lived one block south of the church. This caused the people of the parish to wonder how strange it was that the crucifix from the church landed in their yard.

The tornado also struck Mama's place. We had a large hay barn. It was on the same place where Mr. Schroeder lives now. I don't know just how big this barn was. It had a little tower on top with air vents on all four sides of it. We played in this barn as children. We kids had a initiation code: we had to be able to crawl into this little tower or house on the top of this barn. I made it one time. It was quite a job to get there. The two-by-fours were all a certain distance apart. Now Clara wanted to make it up there too, but her legs were not long enough. She fell down on a bale of hay on her stomach and had the wind knocked out of her. She was plumb out for awhile but she came to gradually. Mama never did find out. Well, the tornado flattened this barn completely, and the whole barn hit the windmill. It was a wonder it did not fall on the Summer kitchen. This was the first of several catastrophes: the first windmill was gone and then the well went dry.

My Trip to San Antonio in 1919
(Written in March 1985)

San Antonio was my last bus stop in search of getting back By hearing. I had had the flu in 1918. I was helping Gusta with five flu patients including Gusta when I also got it. I wasn't quite over it when I learned Carl Wiesman, a cousin in the army in San Antonio, was going to San Antonio on the train right after Christmas, 1918. I went with him, and he took me to Sister Christina, my half-sister, who was in the convent of the Sisters of Divine Providence. She was teaching in a large school in downtown San Antonio, right next to the famous Alamo. Sister Christina also had a hearing problem just like mine and she had told me about this Dr. Moss, an eye, ear, nose and throat specialist; I just had to find out if he could help me. So I went to see him right after New Year 1919. He examined me and the first thing he said was that I had to have my tonsils out. Now, I must go back to the year 1906 to provide the whole story of my tonsil operation in San Antonio.

Mama had taken me to Dr. Rice, an eye, ear, nose and throat specialist in Gainesville. I was twelve years old. He wanted to take out my tonsils. His tools were real primitive. He had a long scissor that was as thin as knitting needles but was as sharp as a razor and was very long. The doctor gave me a shot in my tonsil, but he didn't give me no chloroform, no nothing. I had my white first communion dress on. I had to open my mouth real wide and the doctor clipped off one tonsil with this scissor. Blood shot all over my white dress. He was going to clip out the other one, but I had enough for that day. Mama was with me. I never went back for the removal of the other tonsil. The tonsil that Dr. Rice had clipped off in 1906 had grown back and Dr. Moss removed both my tonsils then in San Antonio, 1919.

After Dr. Moss removed my tonsils, he sent me to St. Rosa's hospital for surgery on my nose. The doctor said that air wasn't being ventilated through my nasal passages like it should and he chiseled some bone off up in my nose--again no chloroform, or no ether. It was the most painful thing I ever went through, and so soon after he had removed my tonsils. I was in the hospital about ten days. My face swelled up twice its normal size, and I had ice packs on it. When I got back to Sister Christina, she said to me, "Why didn't you stay at home if you weren't over the flu?" I did not blame her for telling me that. My room at the school was three stairs up, under the roof. She came up three times a day to look after me, and she was teaching the second grade class during that time.

My burden to Sister Christina was relieved by an incident that had happened in 1915 in Lindsay. The Catholic State League had been held in Lindsay in a three day celebration. We had had five houseguests: among them were Mrs. Dittlinger from New Braunfels, and Henry and Anna Dielman from San Antonio. As always, Mama had written to them about my stay in San Antonio. While I was recuperating from my surgery, Anna Dielman came to see me and she invited me to go and see her. The Dielmans were just wonderful to me. My big problem then was that I couldn't sleep. My doctor gave me shots but it took weeks before I could sleep. After I was with the Dielmans a week or two, I went to the employment agency and I got a job as a cook for a place--I forget the name. There were about twenty girls rooming at this place who had some kind of a job. I liked it just fine but I still couldn't sleep, and I had to go back to the Dielmans.

In the meantime, Fanny Dittlinger, a friend of Anna Dielman, came to San Antonio and took me along to New Braunfels and I was a houseguest there. This Dittlinger family owned a flour mill, a lime kiln, and I don't know what else. Mrs. Dittlinger had been a schoolteacher. Mr. Dittlinger was still at home when I was there and they had a male nurse for him named Alfred Liebscher; he was twenty-one. Their daughter, Fanny, was about twenty-eight. The Dittlingers had another daughter who had married some big shot in Houston, and they had a son who was a mental case in a Chicago private institution. I did not know while I stayed there that Dittlinger had educated his nurse, Alfred Liebscher, to take over the firm. When Alfred and Fanny got married, Anna Dielman told me all about that.

There were four Flusche nuns in and around San Antonio; I would visit with them. Three were in San Antonio and one was in New Braunfels. I got to eat in the parlor where the table was covered with a white tablecloth. These nuns were the same girls that had catered to me in Tioga, Texas, when I was three years old: A small world.

I had made a promise if ever I got so I could sleep again, I would take whatever came my way. Finally, I made it. I was nursemaid for a three-year-old boy. There were five women in this household and no one to take care of him. They had a large, brick house somewhere in San Antonio. I would take the streetcar to get there. The streets were laid out like a big wagon wheel. The hub was the center of downtown; the spokes were the streets. If you wanted to get anywhere, you had to start downtown. I guess I was at this job about three months; it was easy. I had to wash and iron the little boy's clothes--even his diapers. They had large fig trees that were as big as a house. I had to take the boy outside and he would walk right under a fig tree. There were a million bees in those trees, and I had to crawl under the trees and get him quickly before he got stung. One time, two bees stung me on my face and I was all swollen up. The boy's Mama took him in her arms and kissed him and was so glad he wasn't stung. There was not one of sympathy for me.

I stayed with Sister Christina awhile before I went home about in May. I had bought myself some material for a pink, linen dress, and I sewed it while I was with her. I had a new, white staw hat and got home just in time to can peaches, cook for thrashers, etc. I don't know if anyone missed me?

The Cotton Crop in 1919-1920

In 1919, Mama and Alex had a good cotton crop on Lindenau the price was also very good--forty-two cents a pound. He called up Mama at Lindsay and asked if he should sell her share too. Mama told him, "No, I'm going to hold it till I get fifty cents a pound." Just one year later, cotton sold at eight cents per pound and Mama still held her cotton. In 1920, Mama and Alex had about fifty acres of cotton on Lindenau. It rained so much, the cotton was as tall as I and the boll weavel was in it. All fall, Charlie Huber, an orphan boy Mama had taken in, and I drove up to Lindenau to pick the cotton. Alex couldn't get any colored people to pick it. I had to work hard to pick one hundred pounds. I often felt to the farm like giving up, but Mama would cry and we would go to

the farm again. We took our lunch along, and one day a
dog ate our lunch up. think Mama made about two to three
the whole bales from fifty-acre crop and then it sold for
eight cents per pound.

Clara and I had our own experience with cotton in
1919 and 1920. In 1919, Clara got five acres of cotton. The
five acres was on Lindenau and Alex farmed there then.
With cotton bringing forty two cents a pound, Clara made
$500. [I don't remember if clara ever chopped or picked
cotton; I guess Alex did it for her.] I had to stay at
Gusta's and I wasn't able to get five acres of cotton,
so I told Mama that I wanted five acres too. Then Clara
had to stay with Gusta. When I got my five acres in 1920,
and cotton was eight cents a pound, I got one bale; it
would have amounted to $40. Mama got Clara a $50 purple
coat. I borrowed the coat from Clara and gave her the $40
bale of cotton. [The purple coat was part of my wedding
trousseau). Later when Clara was in Iowa, John sold that
bale, cotton for $75 and sent her the $75. The reason the
cotton prices dropped in 1920 was because WWI had just
ended and there was a severe recession.

How I Got Head Lice

This Charlie Huber worked for us in 1920, the fall
before Henry and I got married. One time he went to the
barber to get a hair cut. The barber chased him out
because he had his head full of lice. We all used the
same comb and I discovered I had my head full of lice;
that was about the time I was expecting Henry to come.
Mrs. Hoelker told me what to get in the drugstore to
put on my head. Thank heaven I got rid of the lice just
in time. Henry with the small pox and I with head lice;
wasn't that a nice beginning for our romance!

Mama's Last Years

Henry and I got married March 29, 1921, and moved to
Iowa. Fritz had died in February, a month earlier. Max and
Beulah had married in 1920. When Clara came to Iowa, met
and married Hubert Becker in 1923, Alex and Lindenau were
Mama's sole means of support. When Henry and I moved back
to Texas in 1924, that was when Alex was celebrating with
his five good friends. Mama wanted us to buy Lindenau.
It was a good idea, but Alex came to me and wanted said

that he just found out that we were going to take his farm away from him. When Henry heard that, he wouldn't have anything to do with it. It sure would have made Mama's old age a lot easier. Alex couldn't make a go of farming and Mama had hard times. When Clara left Hubert Becker and came back to live with Mama, Dorothy wax five and Mildred was six. Mama had support Papa Theisen. She couldn't get old-age assistance because she had too much property. She struggled with her poverty and disillusionments until she died of a stroke in 1940. So ended life with Mama.

CHRISTMAS AT HOME

It all started shortly before December 6th, St. Nicholas day. Mama had the full costume of a bishop: the miter headpiece and outfit made of white silk and gold trimming. A few days before the 6th of December, if anyone of us did something wrong, St. Nicholas would appear at a window or the glass door. It sure did make us behave. On St. Nicholas eve, he and St. Rupreckt would come: St. Nicholas brought a sack of goodies: St. Rupreckt brought a bunch of switches. We had to kneel say our prayers; then we sang a special song in German. Max and I were so scared, we'd sit behind cookstove and peek out on the side. This was when St. Nicholas appeared before the 6th. Now, Christmas was something else. We had a nice, big tree and two, three-foot tall angels were in kneeling position on each side of the tree. The sisters had made the angels out of cardboard and shining tinsel. They were painted just beautifully in gold and blue. I often wonder what became of those angels. We had candles all over the tree and had lots of trimmings. For days before Christmas, we were not allowed to peek in the parlor where the tree was or St. Nicholas would appear again. The night before Christmas, we lined up chairs around the room: each one of us had a chair with a plate and our name on it. Christmas morning finally came; we could smell the tree, the apples and oranges. But Mama's slogan was. "Auf zum Gott zum koffe pot." This meant, "Up to God and then the coffee pot." So we'd fo to mass first. Of course, we had to walk about four-five blocks to church. Sometimes it rained or snowed or something, but we'd all go. After mass, we had to sit down and eat. Mama made some kind of sweetbread with raisins and served it with coffee, etc. Mama would sit and talk about everything under the sun. We kids were sitting on needles and pins, waiting to see what the Christ-child had brought us. Finally, after an eternity, Mama would reach for the match box and go into the parlor to light the candles on the tree. Then we were allowed to come in. But alas, Fritz and Herman had to play us about ten songs on the piano, four handed. Of course, we would all sing these songs. Finally we each were allowed to go to our chair. We'd have a big plate full of candy, nuts, cookies, apples, and oranges. We'd always have some gifts which were appropriate for each. All in all, we always had a nice Christmas.

PAPA'S LETTER TO HIS BROTHER AUGUST

(Translated by Elsie Flusche Fuhrman,1985)

In 1900, two of August Flusche's boys from Oklahoma stayed with us. Clara was born in February, 1900. Papa was sick and we were living in the new house even though it was only half finished. The upstairs walls and the ceiling were slatted but not plastered. Mama finished the plastering a couple of years after Papa died in 1901. Before the upstairs was plastered, we'd play there, running back and forth through the framed walls. Papa kept a copy of this letter that he wrote to August, Christmas, 1900.

I will now try to translate a letter from Papa to his brother, August. It seems like Uncle August complained about the treatment of his two sons, Leo and Otto. Papa was kind enough to take in August's two sons and treat them just like his own. He sent them to school, etc. without any charge. He wrote August saying:

We did not want the two boys because I have six of my own. We have three babies and five in school. It was my understanding that it would be for a short time and as it appears now, it will be year or two. Aunt Anna offered to take the strongest one to do some work for her but she wouldn't send him to church and school. I advised you at that time that the best place for the two boys would be in your own home or with their grandmother. I said before, with three babies and five in school and with yours, two more in school. It's understandable that with so many, it can't always be the best care with a sickly wife and a six month-old-baby. Your children talked about your bad luck in school. I understood that they should help us with chopping cotton and thereby help to pay for board and clothing. I was glad that you finally came to the conclusion that you were going to take care of your family again. They did not miss one day in school or church. I bought eacha new suit and everything for their first holy communion. I had to pay $162 for interest on the farm in Muenster. After the fire, I had to buy fifteen pairs of shoes, bedding for four beds, and when the house is finished, there won't be much money left. I deeded the farm in Muenster over to Willi. He had to promise that he would stay home long enough until Robert could do the work. When Sister Christina went to the convent, it cost me $200 for her dowery. I wanted Willi and Sister Christina taken care of before I die. I'm leaving nine small children with a $1,000 debt on the farm. I paid insurance for my brothers and when I got around to getting life insurance on myself, it was too late because my health was so bad. [Papa lived fifteen months yet after this writing.]

AND NOW ABOUT OUR
TWO HIRED MEN

Arthur Galasky

Arthur Galasky worked for us five years at $30 a month and his room and board. He was a good and sober worker, but once a year, he would get on a binge when he got his pay check. Arthur's father had the first cotton gin and the molasses press in Lindsay. In those days, we would take a big load of sugar cane to Galasky's press. He would press out the juice and boil it in a large kettle and make the molasses. twenty-five-gallon barrel We would get about cane. The fried-out bacon grease and the molasses were good eating of molasses out of one load of sugar for breakfast.

Now this old Galasky, Arthur's father, would get on a drinking spree, and beat up his wife. On many occasions, she would run off and hide until he was sober again. At one time, she came to us and she asked Mama if she could stay. We had a big household and Mama was always glad to get help. Mrs. Galasky stayed with us about six weeks. Arthur went to her home when he was sure that his father was not there and got her her clothes. Once, she came down from upstairs, scared to death. She had seen old man Galasky coming to our house. Mama told her to go up to her room and not to worry. She would not tell him where she was. I don't remember too much of Mrs. Galasky, but I remember we had chairs that had twelve round spools on the spokes in the lean-back of the chairs. Now Mrs. Galasky would be churning butter with one hand and with the other, she would finger those round spools as if she were praying the rosary.

As for Arthur, he was engaged to Annie Block. Her father had opened another saloon in Lindsay on the place where the Schuetzen Hall now stands; he called it the Lindsay Beergarten. Mr. Block had planted about twenty trees on the north side; and in time, he intended to make an outdoor beergarten out of it. Now, ever so often, he would get on a binge and had to go home to bed to sleep it off. Annie had to take care of the saloon alone until all hours of the night. It wasn't long and she became pregnant. It nearly killed Arthur. All at once, Annie was gone and not long after, Arthur also was gone. Arthur had paid Annie's ticket to Kansas City where she had the baby. She gave the baby up for adoption and she and Arthur were married and lived somewhere in Oklahoma. Years later, we heard that he was an invalid in a wheelchair and Annie was running around with other men. All at once, she disappeared completely and Arthur's mother went to take care of him. They had no children.

Willi Muller

How about Willi Muller, our other hired hand. He wasn't with us very long. It seems he bought himself a nice spring wagon in Gainesville at Kennerly and Spragons and charged it. He also got himself a nice team of horses and harness on credit; then one night, he was gone and so were several of Mama's hams out of the smokehouse and some loaves of bread. We never heard of him again.

ONE OF PAPA'S STORIES

It seems Tommy Galasky was mass server and the priest was going to give Benediction after mass. The priest asked in the same tune as the hymn, Tantum Ergo, "Whst did you do with the incense pot?" Tommy answered to the same tune, "I left it outside; it was too damn hot."

FAMILY PORTRAITS AND NARRATIVES

(Written in 1985)

Robert
1886-1974

Robert was the oldest of us children. When Papa was gone, he felt the responsibility of taking care of us, but he was not old enough. When Robert was eighteen, there was a typhoid epidemic in Lindsay. Of the five in our family who got the fever, Robert had it the worse; his fever went so high! Soon after this, he got a spell of mental illness and Mama had to have him committed to the Terrell seemed to come in cycles of Institution in 1904. His illness four-year intervals. In between these spells, he would come back to Lindsay and farm. He had horses, machinery and even a new Buick car [one seated]. He told me the car cost $600 and the battery for it cost $600. I could hardly believe it!

When Robert was twenty-six, he met Mary Endres from Wisconsin and dated her. In 1913, Robert and I went to Wisconsin to visit this girl. He told her he didn't think he should marry because of his problem. She said then she wouldn't marry either. When he was in Terrell, she sent him magazines to read, etc.

Eventually, Robert stayed at Terrell and rented out his farm. Al Bezner was renting his farm when the government took his land for the air base in 1942: Robert got $65 per acre. The state kept the money for his expenses at Terrell. Robert worked in the laundry at the hospital for twenty years. He lived in a nursing home near Terrell before he died in 1974; he was eighty-eight years old. Each of his brothers and sisters received $250 after his estate was settled. (A response to a letter of inquiry by Robert's guardian, Max, and later, Max Paul Flusche, into the financial status of Robert during his treatment and his final years as a dependent at Terrell. The letter was sent to Mr. Claude C. McMillan, Assistant claims Officer for the State Hospital in Terrell, Texas, Power, Field Representative. According to the letter, Robert paid from Andrew J. $45 per month after January, 1949.)

Dear Claude,

The guardian of Mr. Flusche is incorrect in his assumption that a suit is about to be file against him. The only letters which have come out have been the regular form letters with a bill attached. I note the two letters from Mr. Janeke of January 19, 1949 and February 9, 1949.

You know we will make no attempt to press payment for any amount due prior to January, 1949. I have made note for no bills to be sent for this amount to the guardian, and the amount accrued during these years be taken off the books by general voucher.

I note from the folder that there were two prior admissions on which nothing has been paid or set up. Unless I hear from you, I will assume that no further action on these two entries should be made.

I note from the file that the patient has $6,500.00 in his guardianship fund. It would seem to me that due to Mr. Flusche's age of 63, that the rate of $45.00 a month would be justified. This charge carries him through ten years with enough left over to bury him.

Yours very truly,
/s/ Andrew J. Power Field Representative

After Mama died in 1940, we put a double tombstone on Papa and Mama's grave. Papa's tombstone was supposed to be for Herman's grave. It stayed in Ella's garage from 1940 to 1970, the year Ella's house burned. Before all the stuff in her house and garage was hauled off, Carl and Clara got Papa's monument and put it on Robert's grave in the Lindsay Cemetery. Clara bought letters and numbers and glued Robert's name on the stone. In time, the letters faded. During the fall that Elizabeth stayed with me, Elizabeth painted over the letters and the numbers with black paint. Aunt Clara sent Elizabeth a thank you note.

Fritz
1887-1921

When Papa was still with us, he and Mama had planned that Fritz should be a priest because of his exceptional learning ability. In the end, this gift caused his downfall. Before he was fourteen-years-old, our pastor had taught him Latin. He started his studies at Subiaco when he was fourteen in 1902. That year, Subiaco had a big fire that nearly burned it down completely. Fritz carried his new trunk down the steps on his back; in time, this strain shortened his life. The students were sent to different Benedictine Colleges and Fritz was sent to Conception, Missouri. He was studious and he made two years of study in one. He was also an accomplished musician. During the vacation in the summer, he would go to Mass every morning and would walk to the farm. He would then do the work of two because he felt that he had to make up for the of us had done while he had been at Mass. He would have been the youngest priest that was ever ordained, but at the age of twenty, he collapsed. He had already taken his first vows and was called Frater William. He came home, but he did not fit in anymore. Mama had to have him committed at Terrell when he was twenty-three-years old. This period between Fritz's nervous breakdown and his admittance to Terrell was a tragic and traumatic period for all of us. He died at the age of thirty-four. Mama always said his death was caused by the back injury he received always said his death during the Subiaco fire in 1902.

Gusta
1988-1960

When Mama had us children, she seemed to have spaced us to her advantage: first were my brothers, Robert and Fritz; my oldest sister Augusta in 1888; my brothers, Herman and Otto; me in 1894; then my brothers, Max and Alex; and last, but not least, her "nesthackechen," Clara, in 1900. We three girls were all six years apart.

Gusta, the oldest girl, had it pretty rough. She didn't get to go to school half of the time. When Papa got sick with T.B. of the throat, they quarantined our place. Mama was taking downstairs in the east room of our house. Clara was six-months-old and Mama had to wean her. Gusta had to take care of Clara and practically raised her. Mama said she could hear Gusta and Clara both crying upstairs; their room was right over her's. Gusta was only twelve-years-old then. Papa died the twenty-sixth of March,1901. In 1902, Mama had a serious operation. All the work rested on Gusta's shoulders. At about the age of fifteen, sixteen, Gusta had Malaria fever. She would start washing the clothes of twelve people; the pile was higher than she was. When she got a spell of fever, she'd lie down on the pile of clothes until she got over the spell and the she would continue washing. She even helped out with the field work on our three farms. We had a hired hand besides our own six boys. All the work, yet Gusta never was very strong.

Gusta went with John Bezner as long as I can remember. She was lucky to marry her first love; not everybody can do that. John and Gusta married August 8, 1908; she was not quite twenty. When I think back now, it seems like she was not much better off then. She had eight boys and two girls; one baby was stillborn. I worked for her nearly everytime she had a baby. John had to build on to the house upstairs. He added a room like a dormitory for the boys, and also, as we called them, for the "stray dogs and cats" that needed a place to stay. If there was a boy out of luck, John would take him in sometimes for days at a time. One thing I will say about John, he was a good provider. They always had a plenty to eat and drink, and Gusta, always had a girl to help her. John passed away real suddenly in 1953 at the age of sixty-seven. He managed everything. He did not let Gusta write checks and she had to learn how to manage a big farming enterprise like theirs. Gusta was seventy-two-years-old when she died on May 1, 1960. The last four-and-a-half years, she suffered with cancer. It was a sad ending for two people so full of life. May they both rest in peace.

Otto
1891-1976

I think Otto was the best brother I had; he wouldn't hurt a fly. When we batched on Lindenau, he always had to walk home every night and milk the cow. In the morning, he would bring milk, eggs, bread, etc. for us.

The most memorable incident with otto was when he ran into the barbed-wire fence in 1905. He had the scars from that accident the rest of his life.

Because Herman could pick 300 pounds of cotton a day, and Otto could only pick 200 pounds, Otto had to do all the plowing. He had four to six horses and since Mama had three farms, otto plowed all the year around unless it got too dry to plow in the summer. He also had to take care of his horses.

Otto married Lillian Goike in 1916 and they lived on his farm out of the sod land Mama bought from Bailey. Otto lost his farm in the mid-thirties and lived on Lindenau. Then, he and Lillian lived in Mama's house in Lindsay after Mama died in 1940. When the government took our farm in 1942, Gusta and Clara said Henry and I could move in Mama's house until Henry found another farm. So, otto and Lillian found a nice, red-brick home in Gainesville where they lived out their lives. In later years, otto lost his hearing and wore a hearing aid. He developed heart trouble and had to have a pacemaker implanted. Lillian became nearly blind and Otto took care of her: they became very dependent on each other. Otto died in 1976.

Herman
1893-1941

Herman could have been a genius if he had gotten the right education. When he was about twelve-years-old, he walked fourteen miles to Muenster to take music lessons; he walked as the crow flies through Ball's pasture. Ball had two sons that were alcoholics. Herman had a gunny sack over his shoulder and he would collect the beer and whiskey bottles he found along the way; he got a penny for each bottle.

Herman had skunk traps set all over the picnic park. He made a lot of money from his skunk hides. Our whole place smelled like skunks. One time, we kids bought Mama a birthday ring, and Herman had the most money.

Herman could hear a new song one time and he could sing it and play it on our piano. When there wasn't much doing on week-ends, we'd go to our place and dance to Herman's music.

Herman ran off from home one time; he was about fifteen then. Mama didn't worry. She said he'll be back. He was gone about three months. He had been in Wichita, Kansas, working in a lime kiln where they make lye. He claimed he had a lot of money that he had put in his shoe on the train ride home. He said he went to sleep and when he woke up, the money was gone. At any rate, after that, he was a lot wiser and more contented.

I could write a book on Herman. All the girls fell for him; he was the sport of the family. One time he had a date in Muenster and he was afraid of her father; he wanted me to go along with him. I told him I had to mop the upstairs. He said he'd help me. He got a twenty-foot water hose, screwed it on the kitchen faucet, laid it up the steps, and was going to wash the floor like that. He sure would have ruined our ceilings downstairs. Well, I went with him to Muenster.

Ella and Herman

The Schniederjans came from Teutopolis, Illinois, with five girls and two boys. Mr. Grube got a hold of him; he could smell it a mile off if anyone had money. Mr. Schniederjan had had a butcher shop in Illinois and Mrs. Shniederjan had been a dressmaker in a millinery shop. They were city people. There they came to Texas. Grube took them out in the sticks east of Gainesville and sold him a farm. They had $4,000. They paid Grube $4,000 for the farm and they didn't have a dollar left to buy horses, machinery or cows to make a living and they had to borrow money right away. Then the house only had two rooms and a shed along the south side of it. They had a kitchen and a bedroom for the boys in this shed. When there was something in Muenster, they would drive all the way East Gainesville to Muenster for a dance--Mr. and Mrs. and as many of the children as the buggy could hold. They'd stay two days there. Mrs. Schniederjan's sister was living in Muenster. The sister's husband was also a Schniederjan but they weren't brothers; they were cousins. Pretty soon, they went broke; then, they rented a place. Mr. Schniderjan never was a farmer.

Ella was just seventeen when Herman came home and told Mama that he and Ella were getting married. Mama said to him (in German), "What do you want with that 'pipchin' (little doll)." He said, "I have to take her away from those other girls so she would learn something." Herman and Ella married in May 1916. Everything went alright. Herman and Ella had two boys already and he'd go with the two boys and buggy and go to church on Sunday. Then, he'd go down to Mama. Mama would ask, "Where is Ella?" Herman said, "I got up, I fed the horse, I milked the cow, I fixed breakfast for the two boys, I dressed the boys and I hitched the horse. Ella still wasn't dressed yet, so I went without her."

Herman was cutting sugar cane at the end of a field when he saw that little Richard had followed him. He picked Richard up and took him back to the house, and then went back to mowing down the cane by hand. He saw something moving under the cut cane and there was Richard again. Herman saw that he had cut off Richard's foot; only the tendons at the heel were not cut. Herman grabbed the boy, jumped on his horse, and rode to his neighbor, John Schmitz. John had a car and drove Herman and Richard to Dr. Whiddon in Gainesville. The doctor wanted to amputate the foot, but Herman absolutely insisted that he try to save the foot. The foot healed and when Richard was older, he only had a slight limp from the accident. One thing I will say for Herman, he was good to his boys.

When we were all together, each one had a certain thing they did on the farm, but when each one had to do everything on their own, they just couldn't make a go of it. So Herman sold his farm to Max and moved to Gainesville and started a produce house on the square. [1922] Later, Max sold his farm to Joe Neu and moved to Gainesville and worked for Herman. They both nearly starved. Herman and Ella separated. Herman just couldn't make enough money for her. Herman left Gainesville and lived alone, ill and destitute. He died of bleeding ulcers in 1941. He and Ella were never reconciled.

Max
1896-1970

Max was a year-and-a-half younger that I. He was very handsome and was very kind to me when I lost my hearing. He never would let me know about my handicap like some of the others did. One time--I was about ten, and Max was eight--we had a bushel of grapes in the cellar. Mama had warned us that God could see everything, that we shouldn't snitch any grapes. The next day, Max and I sneaked into the cellar and got us a bunch of grapes. When we wanted to leave, there was a big snake on the steps. We were so scared: we hollered and screamed. Mama came with a hoe and killed the snake. We then believed that God could see us at all times.

One time, Max had a big boil under his foot. Mama took him out to the cowlot and stuck his foot in a pile of cow manure. Max was always so neat and particular. When Mama did this to him, Max had to vomit.

Another time, Herman and I had Max between us at the table. Now, Max couldn't eat herring. He had a big pile of mashed potatoes on his plate. I kept him busy in a conversation while Herman slipped a big piece of herring under his potatoes. No sooner had he swallowed the potatoes, he ran outside and vomited. We knew then that he couldn't eat herring.

Max and his cousin, Leo Wiese, were big pals. One morning, I was the only one up, Aunt Anna Wiese came in all out of breath and asked me if Max was there. I said I didn't know. I called upstairs to Herman and asked if Max was in bed and he said no. Aunt Anna said to Mama in low German, "They left to 'hope'." This meant Leo and Max ran off together. They got as far as Thackerville, Oklahoma, in a thick timber where they had to chop wood for their beans and sow-belly bacon. Now the couple they worked for lived in a run-down shack. In the middle of the night they would get in a big fight. One night it got so bad, Max and Leo went in to separate them. That was their downfall. They got their walking papers. They came home much wiser.

Max and Beulah

During WWII, everybody hated the Germans—especially the McKays, Beulah's folks; they also hated the Catholics. Max only had a few dates with the girl. Beulah was a telephone operator. Max was with the horse and buggy and he was taking her home one night. There came Mr. McKay with the shot gun and Beulah's brother with the butcher knife. Mas was out of the buggy and she was still sitting in the buggy. When they came out, Beulah jumped out real quick and threw herself between her folks and Max. Max picked her up and put her back in the buggy, drove off and took her to her girl friend. The next day, they went to the J.P. and got married. That was in June. Then, they lived on Robert's place. Gusta didn't rest until they had the marriage blessed in church; so about in August, they were married again in church. Max had his draft call for the army in WWI. He was a clarinet player in his company band. At that time, the wives and girl friends were not allowed to go on the army camps. Beulah had to stay in San Anronio and Max was at the army base; he could only see her on week-ends. Beulah had a room there and she did baby sitting. Max had his heavy clothes ordered already, waiting to be shipped out. Then, an armistice was declared on November 12, 1920. They thought now they could go home, but Max was detained another year because he was with the band and they were sent to New Mexico. There were so many of the soldiers gassed in the war, and they had a camp in New Mexico for them. I guess she stayed with her folks. Max didn't have any money saved up. He only got a ollar a day in the army. When he was discharged, they lived in Robert's farm; then with us in Lindsay. Lindenau was standing empty, so then they moved in there--poor as church mouse. Paul was born on Lindenau. Max sold his 100 acres in the south farm to Joe Neu and bought Herman's farm when Herman moved to Gainesville in 1922. Herman's farm had a house, barn and a well on it, and Max's 100 acres did not. Max then sold the rest of the south farm to Joe Neu and moved to Gainesville and worked for Herman in the produce house. They barely made a living. Later, Max and Beulah moved to Denton, Texas. Max died of a heart attack in 1970.

Alex
1898-1980

Mama often told us what a beautiful baby Alex was. She would walk down the street in Gainesville with him and the people would stop and admire him. After our house burned down in 1899, we lived in a three-room house on Lindenau. Mama put mustard on her breast because she wanted to wean Alex. Max, Otto, Herman and I watched to see what Alex would do when he wanted to nurse. Lo and behold, he liked it. When he got older, he always liked sour pickles and strong flavors--even snaups and beer. He knew Mama liked fish. When he played hooky from school, he'd go fishing in the Elm creek. He would give Mama a batch of fish and he wouldn't get a scolding. He and Fritz shared a room upstairs. Of course Fritz was gone most the time to the seminary. Alex would slide down a post from of upstairs and would stay out all hours. We'd tell Mama that Alex was gone again. We had real heavy quilts on the beds. One time, Mama got her broom and went upstairs to really give it to him. It happened Alex was in bed under the quilts, laughing. Mama hit on top of him so hard, she broke the broom handle. A person just couldn't stay mad at him. He had so many friends. There was George Pitner, Joe Hofer, Ben Stoeck and Nick Mosser. I believe they would have gone through fire for him.

Alex married Emma Hunt in 1925. He was supposed to farm his 100 acres in Lindenau which was promised to him by Mama and he was supposed to work the remaining 77 acres for Mama. First, the well went dry and then the barn burned down. Alex and Emma had Delores and Pat on Lindenau; then they had to move in with Emma's parents, the Barney Hunts. Jeanette was born while Alex and Emma were staying with Barney Hunt. Alex just couldn't make a living as a farmer. They moved to Gainesville and had a service station. Alex and Emma followed the oil company he worked for until they moved to Corpus Christi, Texas. While in Corpus Christi, Alex got a job with Pittsburg Glass Co. and worked there for thirty-seven years. When Alex got away from his buddies in Lindsay, he did well. Alex died in 1980.

Clara
1900-1984

Clara was only one-year-old when Papa died and Mama was partial to her. She never had to go to the farm like the rest of us did. She always stayed in town with Mama. Mama called Clara her "nesthackechen" which meant nesthook in German. She and I didn't get along too well. When she knew Mama was gone, we got along fine, but when Mama was around, she would squeal even if I didn't touch her. I got lickings on account of her. When Mama went to Germany, she said to me, "I want to find Clara alive when I get back." While Mama was gone, Clara and I got along just fine. I was eighteen and Clara was twelve at that time. Clara was a blond and I was brunette and there was as much difference in our personalities as in our coloring. I could have done her sewing but it never was good enough for her. She had exquisite taste with everything. I never had time to get dressed for church or anything else. When Gusta got married at the age of twenty, I was fourteen years old, and all the household chores fell on my shoulders. I worked in the field all week until Saturday. On Saturday, I would go home to clean the house, and iron some white shirts for the boys to wear Sunday. Clara was at home with Mama all week, but Mama wouldn't tell her to do anything.

When Clara was about fourteen, she got a postcard from Gussie Schmitt. The card said, "Are you looking for a beau. I'm the guy." We sure teased her a lot about that.

When Clara came to Iowa, Mama wrote me that we should see that Clara stayed in Iowa long enough to find herself another boyfriend. Mama didn't want her to marry that bum, Joe Hofer. Clara fell for Hubert Becker in Iowa, but Henry and I did not feel we should tell her what to do. When Clara went back to Texas on a visit, Hubert were she and engaged to be married a year later. While Clara was home, Mama wrote me all that she was going through with Clara and Joe Hofer. It looked like they too up again where they left off.

Clara and Hubert married in 1923. It turned out that Hubert was a bigger bum than Joe Hofer. When Mama went to Germany in 1925, she went to visit Clara on her way home; Dorothy was six weeks old. One night, Mama slept with Regina, Hubert's sister, upstairs. Regina jumped up and said, "Now he's coming home." It was three A.M. Mama asked, "Who is coming home?" That's when she first found out what Clara had been going through with Hubert. Clara had never written a word to Mama about Hubert. When Mama got home, I was at her place to welcome her home. Before she even said hello, she started to bawl me and Henry out. She wanted to know where we had our eyes, etc. I could write a book on that subject.

Clara, Dorothy and Mildred came back to Texas in 1931 and lived with Mama: Dorothy was five and Mildred was six. Life with Mama was hard times then. Her land empire had dwindled to Lindenau and Alex was not a successful farmer. After Mama died in 1940, Alex settled, Alex forced a sale of the estate. He wanted to see how much he could get for his 100 acres in Lindenau. When the estate was settled, Alex got $800 for his 100 acres in Lindnau, and Clara got $1,500 for her 77 acres which was to be part of the $2,000 Mama had promised each were sold in of us girls. When Mama's house and the twenty acres were sold in 1942 to John Bezner, Clara and I each got $600.

After Mama died in 1940, Clara took care of Papa Theisen until Sept. 1941; then she married Carl Gimple. Carl was good to her and Clara no longer had financial worries. Carl died of heart trouble in November 1983 and Clara died after a lingering illness because of stroke in August of 1984. God rest her soul.

My Half-brother, Willie

Papa had provided for my half-brother, Willie, by giving him 100 acres of land, where his son Willie Jr. lives today. Papa didn't want any friction between the children. Willie was twenty-five-years old when Papa died. We were all living together. Clara, my half-sister, entered the convent of Our Lady of the Lake in San Antonio in 1898; she lived to be ninety-four-years old. Willie thought he was going with a girl named Maggie Schmitz. He told Mama to buy a birthday present for her. So Mama bought a nice silk parasol at Zackarias in Gainesville. Willie had a nice new buggy and horse. So he spruced up and went to see her. When he got her house, he noticed a horse with saddle was tied up at the to front. He entered in the back and found her mother and father sitting in the kitchen. He asked, "Where is Maggie?" They pointed towards the parlor. Willie opened the door and there sat Maggie and Joe Bezner on the sofa, arm in arm. Poor Willie left as fast as he could with his parasol. Mama said he went to his room upstairs and stayed there for days. He then swore off women.

Henry Fuhrmann in Lindsay would drive to Gainesville on business and sometimes he would take Mama along to do her business. A few years after Willie's affair with Maggie Schmitz, Henry Fuhrmann sent one of his children to Mama to see if she wanted to go to town. Mama said yes. On the way to Gainesville, Henry told Mama his daughter, Anna, was going with Ignatz Zimmerer and he didn't want her to marry him because all the Zimmerers had rheumatism. Natz, as they called him, had it real bad. Then Mama and henry Fuhrman made out a plot to get Willie and Anna together. There was going to be a big wedding at Loerwalds. Mama should see that Willie was there and he was going to have Anna tehre; then they would all leave so Willie would have to take Anna home. It worked and they started dating—this was about Thanksgiving. By May, they were to be married. They were published from the pulpit for the first time. Willie thought he did not have to date anymore. Willie was living on Lindenau and Anna lived about a mile north as the crow flies. Anyway Willie walked across the field to see Anna. He looked through the window and there sat Anna with Natz on the sofa, arm in arm. Willie turned around and walked all the way to Lindsay. Mama was in bed already. He say by her bed and told her to go to Father Bernard; he said there wouldn't be a wedding and that Father did not have to publish them anymore. Mama said in German, "You dumb young one, what's wrong now?" Alright, Mama told Father Bernard and they weren't published that Sunday. Uncle Henry said he was going to get to the bottom of it all. Mama should have Willie at his place and he would have Anna there. Okay. Willie went to Mama and together they walked to Uncle Henry's place. Mama said Willie would take two step forward and one steps backward before she got him there. Then Uncle Henry asked Anna what was the matter; why they weren't published last Sunday. Anna said she did not know. Mama then asked Willie. At first he hedged around, but finally he told what happened. Anna laughed and said, "oh, was that all." She and Natz were taking farewell for a lifetime since she was getting married soon.

Everything went well; they got married on May 1, 1906. At that time, a wedding was always on a Tuesday and at the bride's home. Willie and Anna had a large wedding. They had tents outside to eat under and a big wooden platform to dance on. The orchestra would sit alongside the platform. Sometimes they would have a piano on the wagon for music. The dancing usually would start about four o'clock in the afternoon. Now Willie could square dance alright but he couldn't waltz or two-step. In order to dance the first waltz, Mama had practiced with him for days so he and Anna could dance the first dance together. When they started to dance at their wedding, Mama was in the kitchen. Aunt Anna came in all excited. "Augusta," that was Mama's name, "Come, you've got to see this, you won't believe it until you see it." So they went to the platform outside. There was Anna and Natz dancing the first waltz and Willie standing there as white as a ghost. Mama grabbed Willie and danced with him. Anna thought he couldn't dance. Anna danced with Natz most of the evening. At ten o'clock, Willie went to Mama and said, "Let's go home." Mama said, "You have to stay here with Anna." He said, "No, I'm going home." He and Mama went home to our house. That's how he spent his wedding night.

After the stormy beginning, it seemed as though this marriage turned out pretty good. They had five children and both were hard-working and saving. At first, they lived on Lindenau until their new house was finished. He had the hundred acres Papa had bought Willie and in time, they bought another hundred from the from the Ball's ranch in west. Willie had the two-hundred acres all paid for and cash money in the bank. About that time a real-estate the valley and Gulf of Mexico to promote the sale of land by what company out of St. Louis organized an excursion railroad trip to is now Harlingen and Mission, Texas. Now Willie and Anna had never taken a trip or a vacation anywhere. Joe Schmitz of Lindsay was in cahoots with these agents from St. Louis; he knew who had extra money lying around. He talked Willie into taking this free trip and all expenses paid for a whole week, etc. So Willie and Anna went. I stayed with the children: Celia, 12, Paul, 10, Willie, 8, Christina, 6, and Zita, 4. We drove a two-seated buggy with a tame horse to school in the morning and at four o'clock, we drove home to their farm. Celia said I had to mop the floors upstairs and downstairs everyday. Zita wasn't in school yet. When Willie and Anna got to the valley, all the tourists had to stay together. This real-estate firm had everything spruced up with orange trees full of oranges. But Willie got out of the line and asked a colored man who was watering the trees and flowers, how old those orange trees were. The man answered, "We planted them yesterday." That made Willie suspicious of the whole scam. It turned out that Willie and Anna paid dearly for their free trip to the valley. On the way home, these agents took Willie alone in one car and Anna in another. They made it so hot that there was no way get out of it. They ended up with fifteen acres of citrus land for $12,000. For the first time in his life, Willie got into debt and he worried so about it that it was the beginning of his ailment. Eventually, he was paralyzed and completely helpless and was in a wheel chair for five years. Anna and the children did all the work on the farm. Anna told me that they borrowed six thousand for that land in the valley and that she paid off the debt. She never went to see where her fifteen acres were. Some agent went to her and talked her into exchanging that land for some in Oklahoma. She never looked at that land either. The irony of the whole thing was that the land in the valley would have been a good investment if she had paid the taxes on it. Further irony with Willie and Anna was that Willie died at the age of fifty-two, and Ignatz Zimmerer, her old boy friend, was a hundred and one when he died.

Charlie Loerwald was a neighbor to Anna and Willie. While Willie was still an invalid in the wheel chair, Charlie and Anna fell in love. Charlie had been a widower for twenty years. He had couple of daughters who ran around with Willie and Anna's two girls. When Anna needed some help, she would call on Charlie Loerwald: that's how their love affair got started. Willie was completely helpless and could do nothing about the situation.

Tanta Mari

Tanta Mari was six years older than Mama and Mama had been her bridesmaid when she got married to Franz Loerwald in Attendorn before Mama came to America. The Loerwalds came to Iowa in 1890; they had two or three children already when they came. In 1895, they also came to Lindsay, Texas.

The Loerwalds always had so many big weddings and since Tanta Mari, as we always called her, was Mama's sister, we were always invited. When my sister, Gusta, got married in 1908, Mama was determined that Gusta's wedding would be bigger and better than the Loerwald's. A year after Gusta's wedding, William was born was customary, my Tanta Mari went to visit Gusta and the baby. Mama too and the two of them compared every item Mama had bought for Gusta's dowery. Mana would say, "And the stove cost so and so much." Then Tanta Mari would say, "Is that all? I paid so and so much for my Mary's stove." That would go on with every item until finally they nearly had a hair-pulling squabble. Tanta Mari would go home and the two wouldn't talk to each other for years. But the biggest squabble they had happened later.

One day, Mama told me to tell the Loerwald children in school to come by our house; she had something for them to take home to their parents. Well they came by. Pauline and I were the same age and Clara was two years older. Mama had a flower bouquet and a poem she had made up herself as a congratulation for silver wedding which was at that and that date. Now it happened that their their wedding had been a shotgun wedding as we call it and they had changed the wedding date so Franz Jr. would not know about it: Mama's flowers and poem were out of order. Tanta Mari came to Mama and the fur really did fly that time. I don't think they ever did make up again that time. Tanta Mari had a gall stone operation later on and she died on the operating table; she was sixty-nine years old.

I must tell of the day of my wedding when I visited Tanta Mari. Tanta Mari and Mama never visited each other after they moved to town, but when one of them had a letter from Attendorn or a newspaper, I was the go-between and I had to go to Tanta Mari and deliver the paper or letter. Somehow, Tanta Mari liked me. Now when I got married, Mama made me go to Tanta Mari with Henry. She wouldn't go to the wedding but I had to go there; Mama figured she would give me a present. Well she did give me a nice piece of crocheting and $5.00. Now when Clara married Hubert Becker two years later, Mama made Clara go to her too. Clara didn't want to go but Mama insisted on it. So and Clara and Hubert went to her. The first thing Tanta Mari said to Clara was, "You ain't going to get nothing. You don't deserve it." The reason because she said that was some years before, Clara was going with Joe Hofer and Joe and some more boys would go to the picnic park and spread a lap robe on the ground and sit around it and play poker. Tanta Mari was snooping around there and saw them. She went to our house and told Clara that she should go and make Joe quit playing poker. Clara told her she should go and tell him herself.

Tanta Anna

Tanta Anna was Mama's younger sister; I would call her a saint. When Tanta Anna came from Germany, she had a good education, but she could not speak English. She went to school in Harlan, Iowa, the country seat, for three months. She became a school teacher in Westphalia, Iowa, and she also was a dressmaker. She fell in love with Uncle Paul Weise who was a bartender and a gambler. Her parents was opposed to him and did not want her to marry him. One time while Tanta Anna, Grandpa and Grandma Steinmetz were still living in with my parents in Westphalia, Iowa, Mama and Tanta Anna were waiting by a window which faced the house where Uncle Paul was staying. The law was after Uncle Paul for playing poker. All at once, Uncle Paul crawled out of a small attic window, jumped to the ground, and ran with the law in pursuit; Tanta Anna fainted into the arms of her mother. Mama told her Mama, "There is no use to stop her. It's gone too far." Tanta Anna and Uncle Paul married in Westphalia, Iowa, in 1892. When they got marries, he had to promise he would never open a saloon in Iowa. They lived on a farm there with Grandfather and Grandmother Steinmetz. Now Uncle Paul was no farmer; I think it was Grandma Steinmetz and Tanta Anna who kept the wheels turning. Uncle Paul would haul a load of hogs to the market and stay all night and play poker until the money was gone.

They moved to Texas in 1895. Grandpa Steinmetz built the house in Lindsay with his money and when Grandma Steinmetz died, he continued to live with Uncle Paul and Tanta Anna. They had a large front room where the saloon was and the living quarters were on the back. Uncle Paul would drive to Gainesville twice a week to buy supplies. Tanta Anna would hitch up the horse to the buggy and bring it up to the front of the house. Uncle Paul was always dressed in his Sunday best; he'd sit in the buggy and drive. Most of the time when he got back from Gainesville, he was in no condition to stand at the bar. Tanta Anna would take the horse and buggy back to the barn and unhitch it, then stand behind the bar after putting Uncle Paul to bed. In between times, she'd have to run in the back to look after the baby, etc.

Grandpa Steinmetz was always fussing and yelling at somebody. We kids all scrambled when we saw him coming. He had it in for my brother Alex especially. Alex would crawl under the table and Grandpa had his walking cane and would try to get at him.

One time, Tanta Anna had to fill a gallon jug of shnaups for a customer. They had a ten-gallon barrel of whiskey in their bedroom. She'd take a short hose and syphon it in the jug. She was in a hurry and forgot to pull the hose out and all the shnaups ran out on the bedroom floor. Tanta Anna said it was expensive that she did not tell Uncle Paul. She took a clean towel, soaked it all up, and put it in a crock and sold it.

Uncle Paul made out real good with his first saloon which was on the corner where Ewald Hoelker now lives. When the business site was established downtown by the post office and the grocery store, Uncle Paul built a saloon there. He also had a bartender and life was easier for Tanta Anna. Uncle Paul bought the farm about two prohibition era came and Uncle Paul had to close his saloon. He still catered to special customers on the farm. Now Bill Loerwald, Tanta Anna's own nephew, was determined to turn Uncle Paul in for bootlegging. He'd come to Tanta Anna and make out like he was real sick and that he needed shnaups for a toddy for his stomach. Tanta Anna did not trust him and she turned him down several times but one time she gave in and sold him a pint. Now this stinker took the pint to turn Uncle Paul in. It was in the court for a long time and it cost Uncle Paul $600.

About this time, Frankie, their oldest son, was attending school in Milwaukee, Wisconsin. He wrote his parents that there a saloon on every corner there and that they should come Milwaukee and run a saloon. So they thought this was a good solution to all their problems. They had all the necessary machinery on the farm, a nice new home and everything completed for farming; however, none of their six boys wanted to farm. So they held a sale and sold everything except the farm. There were ten the family and they left for Milwaukee in November of 1916. When they got there, they found out they had to be a citizen for three years before they could get a license. Uncle Paul weighed about two hundred pounds and was plagued with the gout; he couldn't even walk. There they were, eight kids to feed. They thought this Dr. Lambert Hargarten who had been a buddy of Uncle Paul back in his heyday in Westphalia, Iowa, would come to the rescue, buy the saloon in his name, and let Uncle Paul run it. But Dr. Lambert Hargarten was a different man now from what he was when they were poker playing buddies in Westphalia, Iowa.

Well there was Uncle Paul and his family in Milwaukee. Tanta Anna did not have any experience in the grocery business but she soon knew she had to do something. She then bought a grocery store and she would send her little boys around the neighborhood solicit her some customers. But most of them did not know her, she did not know how to keep the store warm so the bottles on the shelf would not burst and the vegetables would not freeze. So she sold out and by February, they were all back in Lindsay, about four thousand dollars poorer and a lot wiser. Since she did not have any horses, cows, chickens or machinery left, she then opened a grocery store in Lindsay. One after another, the boys went to Detroit to work in the Buick factory there. Uncle Paul was still plagued with arthritis in his legs. Tanta Anna was too good-hearted and gave her customers too much credit in the store. So in time, she sold out to Mr. Casper Hoelker and Uncle Paul and Tanta Anna settled back on the farm. About in 1927, Uncle Paul died suddenly from a kidney ailment. Tanta Anna then soid the farm and went to live in Lindsay. She died at the age of ninety.

ANCEDOTES AND REMEMBRANCES

When Lindsay and I were Young. Written, June 7, 1978

The J. M. Lindsay log house on Elm Creek was one of the first homes in Cooke County. At the time of the founding of Lindsay, a family by the name of Ruppaner was living there. There was a big flood in Lindsay and the five-year-old daughter of Ruppaner went to get the cows. She never made it back; the Elm was so high that she drowned. Her funeral was one of the first to be held in Lindsay. Ironically, one of the other first funerals in Lindsay was also a young girl of twelve by the name of Theresia Gieb. (Mama always called her Appolonia.) Her older sister, Mary, was dating a young Iman by the name of Stephen Geray. Incidently, they were the first couple to get married in Lindsay. Now this Mary Gieb was tired and sleepy from previous date. She told her younger sister to cook the breakfast. There still were some coals in the wood stove. Theresia poured coal oil on them. It exploded and she caught on fire. She ran outside and rolled on the ground. Mrs. Stoeck, who lived about one mile west of us, came by our house with a pound of butter. She hollered at us to tell Mama to come at once with butter, that the Gieb girl was burned. At that time, the Giebs lived about where the Metzler brothers are now located, only further back in the field. They rubbed Theresia with butter. She lived about two or three days and suffered terribly.

The Catholic parish of Gainesville was founded about in 1883. There were quite a few Catholics in town, but only about three in the rural areas. The August Pulte family had settled close to Myra in 1877. For three months, they had lived in a tent across from the southwest corner of the courthouse in Gainesville before buying 100 acres of land about nine miles southwest of Gainesville on the Hood road. They lived on a rented farm near Myra while he broke the sod on his farm and put a barbed wire fence around it. In addition to farming and cattle raising,

August and his wife, Carloine, started a wagon yard, a general store, and a post office. The wagon yard was on the Butterfield trail to California and travelers would stop there and spend the night.

August Pulte was instrumental in helping to interest the Flusche Brothers in founding Muenster. In 1889, August wrote a number of letters to a German Catholic newspaper in St. Louis called "Amerika" telling about the opportunities of new settlers in Texas and urged german Catholic families to move to the area. This was how the Flusche became interested in Texas. On the Flusches' third trip to Gainesville, they obtained an option on 22,000 acres of ranchland and staked out the townsite cf Muenster. For August Pulte's efforts, the Flusches deeded a residential lot and an additional two acres. Later, August built a home on the lot in Muenster. After August Pulte died in 1911, his widow, Caroline Pulte were the parents of Emma (Joe Fisher) and Mary (John Knauf), and Joe, Charlie, Alex, Matt and Walter of Gainesville and August of Grand Rapids, Michigan. August and Caroline Pulte are buried on the Sacred Heart Cemetery in Muenster.

The second family by the name of Frank Dudenhoeffer settled about three miles southeast of Lindsay. At the time they came to Cooke County, they had to go to church in Sherman. So they would only go once a year to make their Easter duty. Now, the Lindsay town's people weren't sure whether their marriage was blessed so the Dudenhoeffer's were married again. They had a big wedding. Four or five of their children were running around. Everybody had a big time.

The third family was the Adam Castor family. They lived north of Lindsay, close to the Loerwalds. One cf the Castor girls married Frank Loerwald, Jr. Mrs. Castor died before the family moved to Lindsay. Her tombstone on the muenster cemetery is dated 1895. I don't know very much about this family except that they were real pocr and that they made beds like our bunk beds. The beds were built one on top of the other out of boards like an oblong box; the side boards were about a foot high. They filled these boxes with cotton seed and then covered the cotton seed with a sheet. This was their bed. A daughter, Lucy Castor, was a good dressmaker. She would sew for us about a week or two every summer. She got her room and board and $1.25 per day. She was a nice, pleasant person to have around. She did not marry until later in life.

Now there was a little one-room, red Public School house at Lindsay when the town was organized in 1892. Many children of the first settlers attended this school. I can remember it well. For instance, Anna and Caroline Dudenhoeffer, Celia Mosman, Emilie Flusche, Lizzie and Mary Sandman and Mary Loerwald attended this public school until a Catholic school was started. My father was one of the first school teachers at the Catholic schoo. Now Emilie, my cousin, was brought up as what we would call a sheltered city girl. In her youth, there was a new sporty school teacher and Emilie fell in love with him, but she found out that he had a wife and children somewhere else. She then swore off of men until she was about thirty-two. There was a widower by the name of Joe Hundt had been married for fifteen years and never had any children. Emilie got a letter with a marriage proposal from him. My aunt, Tanta Mari, just so happened to be in the post office when Emilie got this letter with the proposal. The post office and drugstore the east side of Uncle Tony's house, and the living room was on the west side. Tanta Tonchen, we all called her, and Emilie were debating the pros and cons of this proposal while Tanta and Mari was at other side of the door, listening. Tanta Tonchen told Emilie that she thought the marriage was a good idea because there surely wouldn't be any children. Joe Hundt was forty-two and Emilie was thirty-two. Well, they were married in 1914. My brother, Otto and Ella Hundt were best man and bridesmaid. And would you know it! They were blessed with five children, yet.

The John Stoeck Story

And then there was this John Stoeck family who came from Chicago. Mrs. Stoeck did not like living in the country or any work connected with it. Mr. Stoeck had a bad heart and he was advised by the doctor not to do any hard work. The oldest girl, Mamie, was fourteen-years-old but she was not allowed to milk the cows, so Mr. Stoeck had to go to the barn and milk the cow. It was a hot day in August. He made it back to the porch and died. We were the only ones who had a bath tub so the Stoecks borrowed it, filled it full of ice, and lay Mr. Stoeck's body in it. This way, they did not have to embalm him. After he was gone, Mrs. Stoeck was scared to be alone at night. she hired John Kupper, who was still single, to sleep in their house until Mamie, the oldest girl, got married to Tony Loeffelholtz. They built a two room house right by her place. Now Aggie, the second girl, later married Victor Phillip. They lived on a rented farm where they had to pump the water up by hand. Aggie hit her forehead with the pump handle, a lump formed and sometime later, it turned into a growing tumor. When it was about the size of an egg sliced length-wise, they went to a doctor. He said it needed to be operated on at one, but Mrs. Stoeck yammered that she could not pay for it. The young couple had two small children and could not afford it either, so they decided against the operation. When the tumor grew larger, her mother got scared, and offered to pay for the operation but alas, it was too late. It grew so big, it covered her whole face. She could only eat out of the side of her mouth. I never saw it but Mama and Gusta both would go there to help out. I think in time, it weighed fifteen pounds. She suffered several years with it. Her husband, Victor, only had certain days that he could visit her. Aggie and the two children were staying with her mother. When Victor came to visit, he had to bring the feed along for his horse. He also was not allowed to stay overnight in the beginning. They were both young and very much in love. Her mother figured she had enough trouble without adding some more to the family. I don't remember just when Aggie passed awasy. She starved to death.

Mrs. Stoeck also did not like the German names. Now Manie married a Loeffelholz which meant a wooden spoon in German. Aggie married a Phillip; that was okay. Clara, the third daughter, married a Rauschuber. "Huber" in German is about as common name Jones or Smith is in English, but the name "Huber" when used to form the name Rauschuber meant someone who had celebrated a little too long and got tipsy, or worse. Now the fourth daughter, Lucy, married a Gremminger which was also a good German name. Anna, the youngest, married a Sandman which is good in German and English.

The five girls had one brother named Ben. He was sorta in the middle of all the girls. He was what one calls in German "mond suchtig." It meant a moongazer. He would do this in his sleep. He'd crawl on top of the windmill to be closer to the moon. As long as he was in a trance, he wouldn't fall down. But if anyone would have called to him and awaken him, he would have fallen down.

Joe Fuhrmann and Carrie Mueller

Next, there was the Fuhrmann family, Henry's uncle. One of his sons, Joe, was going with a girl named Carrie Mueller. They were to be married soon, and the two families were busy slaughtering a beef. It was to be a large wedding. All at once, the bridegroom was gone. No one knew when or where he had gone. Someone claimed that he saw him walking west through Ball's Ranch with a flour sack over his shoulder. Mr. Mueller and Uncle Henry went to Muenster in search of the illusive bridegroom. They stayed overnight at the Stelzer Hotel. Now Mueller had a little too much of this drink that Muenster was famous for in the year of our Lord, 1904. He dreamed he was in pursuit of his future son-in-law. He stepped out of an upstairs window and broke his big toe. Joe Fuhrmann was not heard from for four years. His bride, Carrie, had a picture taken of herself in her full bridal attire: dress, wreath and veil. A few years later she received a postal card. The picture and its verse was about a woman with sharp tongue. After four or five years, Joe returned and married Mary Orth, a girl of few words.

The Eikof Story

And now there was the Frank Eikof family. It seems he had left Germany under somewhat cloudy circumstances and had changed his name from Schalte to Eikof. They only had one daughter, Ella. Mrs. Eikof was a nice, friendly person and was a very hard worker. Mr. Eikof had a terrible temper and so did Dr. Zell, an artist he worked with Dr. Zell and his wife were living with their son and our pastor, Father Bernard. Eikof was an artist with concrete and Dr. Zell was an artist with the easel and the brush; together, they a pair. Often the sparks would fly. Together they built the four Corpus Christi Chapels on the Church grounds. Eikof did the concrete structure and Dr. Zell would do the painted pictures; he was a real artist. They also built the fourteen stations around the cemetery and the Grotto behind the church. The Grotto was really a concrete water tank about ten to twelve feet deep. One day, Dr. Zell was working on top and he fell down in it. He was a short stocky man and he couldn't get out. His wife, Augusta, happened to and be close by when she heard his call. She just let him sit in there until she got ready to help him out. Incidentally, there was no water in it yet.

Eikof did a lot of concrete work around Lindsay. Everybody had a concrete water tank that he made. He was also a cobbler by trade, and would repair shoes at night. He came to Lindsay three times flat broke. The first farm he had was the place where Jake Bezner now lives. The Elm creek runs right through the middle of it. Once, the Elm was high and Eikof came from the south side in a wagon with a team of horses and tried to cross the creek. But the water was so high and swift, it took him downstream. He called out in his German: "Come Devil get Eikof, get horses and get wagon." But he low got out alive. When he had the farm all paid for, he'd get the "wunderlust" and sell out. This time he moved on and lived in Muenster several years on a farm. The family was out picking cotton. and Ella, his only child, would stand up and jabber too much to suit him. He went up to her and hit her on her back; she hemorrhaged and got T.B. They traveled all over to find a cure even took her. They even took her to Europe to world famous doctors. They then settled in Fredericksburg, Texas, in what is called the hill country. That is where Ella died at the age of eighteen, and that is where her grave is.

That was the second time they came back to Lindsay flat broke. They started all over again. Mrs. Eikof was a good mid-wife. She would attend at the birth, stay on and do all the house work and take care of the mother and child day and night, all for five dollars a week. Mr. Eikof would rent a piece of land and plant cotton on it. Together, they would walk to this cotton field maybe three to four miles out and chop the the cotton and later on, pick it. At night, he'd repair shoes. Soon, they had enough to build themselves a nice house and plant trees and shrubs and made a show place out of it. But when he had it all paid for, he got the "wunderlust" again. There was a real estate man here by the name of Grube. He talked about ten families of Lindsay to move to Colorado and buy land. Eikof was one of them. He sold out and went to Colorado. In Colorado, everyone of them had to leave the land go because they were starving to death. The only one that stayed was Christ (Christoper) Neiser, Grube's son-in-law; he was too ashamed to come back.

That was the third time Eikof came back to Lindsay to start all over. One time, they rented land for cotton from my half-brother, Willi. The other time, they rented from Mrs. Hinzman, about three miles south of Lindsay. I don't remember where they lived until he got his house built. This time, he built the nicest house of all. It was built on the main street of Lindsay and was made entirely of concrete; it still stands today. In no time, Eikof had the house and the beautiful landscaping all paid for. When he had it all finished, Mama said to him in German that it was a real paradise. Eikof answered, "Yes, and the devil sits right in the middle of it." The Eikofs adopted a boy who became a priest at Subiaco, Arkansas. We all called him Eikof's Sepp (Joseph).

At that time in Lindsay, they would have a fish fry once year on the Elm creek and Eikof was always chosen to fry the fish. About the last time he did it, he got finished frying and asked if there were any fish left. Just as a joke, Father Bernard told him that there was enough for a poor sinner. Eikof got one of his hot temper spells. He ran up the creek, pulled a piece of wire out of fence and went to hang himself. His wife followed him. He was already dangling from a tree when she pulled him down. He got so mad at her that he bit her on her finger and she had to go doctor. He then became a recluse and didn't show himself anymore. They sold out and went back to Germany to live. When Mama went to Germany in 1925, she visited them. They lived in the same county as that of Attendorn. He had built a house out of concrete almost like the one in Lindsay. It had a nice big yard and had lots of trees and shrubs. When Mama saw him, he was in a wheel chair. He had a heart condition, and died after that.

After World War II, everyone in Germany had to take in refugees. Mrs. Eikof lived alone in the big house and had two or three women living with her. She had many friends in Lindsay who sent her packages of food. One day, Mrs. Reinart, who had sent her a package, got a letter from one of Mrs. Eikof's refugees which said Mrs. Eikof had more packages than she needed. This refugee wanted Mrs. Eikof's friends to send packages to her. The German government went by the people, and decided how many refugeesthey could take care of. The owner was not asked if he wanted them or not.

The Pittner Story

The Pittner family who bought the Eikof farm consisted of Mr. and Mrs. Pittner, Adolph, Fred and George. Mr. Pittner would tell about his wife always having to have the last word. He said if he I threw her into the water and the water went over her head, she would still insist on the last word by holding up her hand and by signaling with her fingers. Now, Adolph and my brother, Otto, were good friends. Also good friends of Otto were Christ Neiser and Butch Dieter. The four of them would sit on our long gate, spit tobacco and watch the people go by. None cf them ever went to a dance. They would debate how foolish and time consuming it was to dress up and jump around all night, not counting the money it cost. And worse cf all, first thing you knew, you'd get hooked and then what would you have. Mama always said that otto never would get a wife and we would have to hunt him one. Then she mentions different girls for him. One was Annie Neiser. Otto answered her by saying that if he wanted a milkmaid to milk his cows, he'd hire her. After many years, otto married Lillian Goike, Adolph Pittner married Annie Wreck from Iowa, Butch Dieter married my cousin, Clara Wiese, and Christ Neiser married Anna Grube. Another son, Fred Pittner, was in the army in 1918 in San Antonio. He gct the flu really bad and it left him partially paralized. He married a Lueb girl and they are now living in Hereford, Texas.

Then there was George, the youngest. He was going with a girl by the name of Mary Geray. He gave her permission to write checks on his name. Everything was okay until the money gave out. Mr. Pittner had bought quite a lot of war bonds during World War II. He did nct trust the banks so he put them in a fruit jar and buried them in the cellar. But he made the mistake of telling his wife where they were. In the meantime, he died. All at once remembered those war bonds. Mrs. Pittner became very nervous that she she might have told George where the bonds were hidden. She dug in the cellar, but George had beatened her to them. All she found was the empty jar. It was getting to be rough going for them. George did not farm much because it looked like hard work to him. He did not have enough credit to buy a loaf of bread stealing from Fritz Mosman's store. Everytime he stole a ham and the stuff to go with it, he would throw a party for his pals on the Elm Creek. Now this Fritz Mosman suspected who was stealing his hams. He had a certain brand of chewing tobacco that no one but George would buy. Fritz planned to catch George. He put a mark on his ham because he had to have proof of guilt; otherwise, it wouldn't stand up in court. In order to get to Fritz's supplies, one had to crawl under a set of double doors on his stomach. So George crawled under these doors and a plug of tobacco fell out his shirt pocket. Now Fritz Mosman knew for sure it was George. The next time Fritz's ham was gone again and there was a party on the Elm Creek, Fritz Mosman got a Sheriff from Gainesville to raid the party. He showed the Sheriff his mark on the ham. George was arrested and put in the clink. Jake Bezner went to see George and went bond for him. Jake had George make out the Pittner farm to Jake at sixty dollars an acre. It joined Jake's farm to the east. That is where Jake and Lizzie are now living. George got out of jail and disappeared. Poor Adolph paid for the diamond ring that George bought for Mary Geray. Mrs. Pittner did not know where George had gone; she would ask in church, "Have you seen my George?" Mary Geray never married. She died at the age of seventy-two a few months ago.

The Nick Mosser Story

Nick Mosser's first wife had died leaving him with three small children. He married again and his second wife became Mama's best friend and neighbor. We had many pleasant visits together. They had a daughter named Regina who was about my age. One evening, we all were together at the post office, our stomping ground. I told her a party at so and so's place and I asked if she I wanted to go along. She said that she had to ask her father first was afraid to ask him. He was one of those what you call a block-headed Dutchman, so I went with her to her home. I was scared too. When we got to the living room where he was reading the paper, I asked him if Regina could go with me to this party. He didn't look up from the paper and said in his German, "Da wirt nicks draus." It meant nothing doing. Regina had just told him she was going to the convent in San Antonio.

Now the Mossers had a son named Joe who had just got out of the navy. Mrs. Mosser was going to help him to find a wife. She was an expert in quilting and had a big chest full of quilts upstairs. She invited a whole lot of women over one Sunday for a party including Katie Wendel, our priest's cook, who was about Joe's age. Now along the middle of the afternoon, Mrs. Mosser took Katie upstairs to show her all her pretty quilts. It just happened that Joe was also upstairs. He came to where his Mama and Katie admiring the quilts. Mrs. Mosser quickly left them alone and came downstairs. It was no time that Katie came downstairs and went out of the front door, red as a beet in her face. That was the end of that. Mrs. Mosser was a tall, heavy-set woman and whenever the usually reticent Mr. Mosser got to feeling pretty good, he had a song he would always sing in German. It meant this: the large woman may be loved and adored but he would always love and adore the small one. The small woman was so patient and cuddly all the while, etc. Mr. Mosser's song in German is: "Das grosa mag sich laben n lieben jeder mann/ Ich aber lieb das kleina So lang ich lieben kann/ Das kleina ist gedulig u lieben allzeit." That's all I remember of this song.

In the afternoon at about four o'clock, the men would come from all directions to Uncle Paul's saloon. When they came from the north and east, they had to come by our house. There was Mr. Krebs, Mr. Hofer with his white horse and Mr. Mosman. Of course, Mr. Metzler came in from the west; Mr. Schmitz came in from the south, etc. Mr. Kuhn had a beer song he would sing when he felt good; it was about a boat that wasn't there at all. Then they would all go in this boat and cross the river, etc.

The Frank Mages Story

And now about the family of Frank Mages. The Mages and the Rueschenbergs all came from the Westphalia, Iowa. Mrs. Mages was a Rueschenberg. The Flusches and the Rueschenbergs were neighbors in Wamge, close by Attendorn, Germany. The Frank Mages were real well-to-do in Iowa. He was a carpenter and he also owned a farm. They had about six to seven children when he sold out and moved to the western part of Oklahoma. There were droughts and dust storms there just like in West Texas. Mrs. Mages told me that three years in a row they didn't even raise potatoes, much less anything else. That nice big house didn't keep them from starving. Now the Casper Hoelker family had lived there in Oklahoma and had come to Lindsay: so, the Mages also came to Lindsay a few days before Christmas, They had rented a farm from a Neu about five miles south of Lindsay, but the freight car with all their belongings did not come yet. So about three of the boys stayed with us, some stayed with Uncle Paul Wiese, and Mr. and Mrs. and their two little girls, Dora and Celie, stayed with the Loerwalds.

One of the boys who stayed with us was Joe Mages who was sixteen years old. On Christmas Eve, Mama got everything ready like we always did. We would place the chairs around the walls, each one plate on it with his name on it. Now with the three Mages boys, we just put out three more chairs with a plate and their names on them. Mama was debating how much of this she would put on it and how much of that: she just stretched it out a little further. Now Joe was sixteen-years-old and he still believed in Santa Claus.

Now Mr. and Mrs. Mages with the two little girls stayed by the Loerwald's. One day, Mrs. Mages heard Mrs. Loerwald tell Mr. that they nearly ate up a whole hog already--meaning the Mages. Mrs. Mages dressed the two little girls up real warm because it was very cold. She went to church first and prayed a rosary. Then she went to the railroad depot where it was warm and waited. She told me this many years later. She said she couldn't eat another bite by the Loerwalds. When Mr. Mages came that night, he asked Mrs. Loerwald where his wife was. She motioned towards the depot. He went there and Mrs. Mages told him what Mrs. Loerwald had said. The Mages then drove to the place where they were going to live. They did not have any beds nor bedding, only the clothes they had on. The freight with their belongings finally came. Mr. Mages did carpentry work and also farmed. A few years later, they were living right north of the church. They had a big garden and the crows would eat everything up. So Mr. Mages told the boys if the crows came again, they should shoot them. The gun was hanging on the wall right over the north door, and it was loaded. There were about three or four boys, each trying to get to the gun first. Tony, who was about fourteen-years-old, got there first. He got on a milk can and as he stepped down, the gun went off hitting him right in his stomach, killing him instantly. Mrs. Mages was sewing in the next room. When she saw what had happened, she said she was so excited she couldn't move. She told Joe to get Mr. Mages and tell him Mama wanted him to come. Mr. Mages was working somewhere south of Lindsay as a carpenter. She was expecting again real soon. When Joe went to get him, Mr Mages thought her time had come. He hurried home and had to step over the body of his son who was lying right in the doorway.

They were still living on the same place when in 1918, the cyclone struck Lindsay and destroyed the church. They lived in a big, two-story house. It was a landmark since it was already there when Lindsay was founded. It stood right north of the church on the Adolph Fuhrmann farm. All of the family was in it when the house was totally destroyed by the tornado. They all crawled under their table along the wall; that wall fell over the table. Mrs. Mages held the baby in her arms. When a jolt threw the baby out of her arms and in between some two-by-four boards, she pulled it out. The baby didn't have a stitch of clothes on, but it was not hurt. Some of their bed sheets were hanging on some trees in the Elm Creek. The shoes were knocked into the ground. Everything was gone. Mama put an ad in the Gainesville paper for clothing and bedding for them. The Mages moved into a house where Ewald Hoelker now lives. The people responded to Mama's ad and the Mages had more of everything that they had before. Soon after that Jane (Augusta—Mama was her baptismal sponsor) was born.

The Mages family then moved to the Jagelky farm. When we lived on the French place, we were neighbors to them. The day our twins were born, it was real cold. We did not have a phone. I knew my time had come so Henry got Mrs. Mages to come and stay with me while he went to town to see the doctor. We had just moved to this French place. We had re-decorated the whole house and I was going to have my baby at home. While Henry was gone, Mrs. Mages and I were sitting there, waiting. All at once, the stovepipe fell out on the floor. The stove was red hot and I knew the pipe had to be put in the wall again. Mrs. Mages said she couldn't do it because she had never done it before. So I got on a chair and placed the pipe in the wall. That evening, the twins were born in a Gainesville hospital. Since I never went to a doctor, I did not prepare for two babies. Henry bought some flannel for diapers and gowns; Mrs. Mages served them for me.

Mr. Mages was a small man; he never weighed more than 135 pounds. He was a very religious man. They lived five miles from church but he often walked there on Sundays to attend two masses. He never neglected his work on the farm. If he didn't have nothing else to do, he chopped out Johnson grass or cockleburs. Now there was a Slim

Jirasek who wanted to get this farm away from Mages. He told Jagelky that Mages was sitting in church instead of farming. Well he succeeded in getting Mages off of his farm. Because Mages had four grown sons, he needed a larger farm. He finally ended up in Era, about twenty miles from church. There were seven hundred acres in this farm and each one of the boys rented one hundred acres from it. Each boy had a car and there was only one barrel of gasoline. They all tapped this barrel but it was Mr. Mages who payed for it. One after another got married and they would just move in with their parents until they found a place of their own. It looked like it all worked out alright. Mr. and Mrs. Mages finally found a house close to the Lindsay Church where they lived out their old years. The fourteen children all made out alright with very little help from their parents.

The Hoelker Story

The Hoelkers lived in Anton, Oklahoma, the place where the Mages family nearly starved to death. Mr. Casper Hoelker owned the grocery store in Anton. He was a good friend of William Schmitz in Lindsay. When Uncle Paul and Aunt Anna decided to sell their grocery store and move back on their farm, William Schmitz wrote Casper Hoelker that the Wiese store and house were for sale. That's how the Hoelkers came to Lindsay. The family consisted of Mr. and Mrs. and ten children: six of the children were from Mrs. Hoelker's first marriage to John Weiss; three were from her second marriage to Casper Hoelker. Mr. Hoelker had been a fifty-two year old bachelor. I think he married the widow Weiss more out of sympathy than affection. Mrs. Hoelker's six children were Katie, Rosa, Mary, twins, Louise and Louis and Johnny, and one child before she married Weiss: the three Hoelker children were Ewald, Albert and Laura. Katie, the oldest, entered a convent; she was the prettiest of all the girls. Louise and Louis worked for John and Gusta. They were very handsome, especially Louis. All the girls fell for him.

One of Louis' girl friends was a girl by the name of Louisa Phillips, a real Jezabel. Louis was working on a road gang by Myra when Frank and Louisa Phillips were getting married. That night at the wedding dance, Louisa danced all night with Louis and even left the hall with him. Anna Mages was keeping house for her brother. She told me that Louisa and Frank went home together that night, lived together for awhile, but Louisa left him. Frank got his marriage straightened out with the church and later, he married Leona Mosman, an old flame of his. I don't know what became of Louisa Phillips.

There was another girl, Maggie Bezner, daughter of Albert Bezner, who Louis wanted to date, but Albert wouldn't allow him on his place. But where there is a will, there is a way. Somehow, Louis and Maggie were together in his car. There was accident, but It looked like she nobody ever found out what really happened. tried to jump out of the and that Louis grabbed her. It appeared that she had a head concussion--as though she fell out of the car, head first, and that she was dragged awhile. Louis did not Want to take Maggie to her home so he took her to her sister, Mrs. Rosa Wolf, in Muenster. Maggie died the next day. Albert had Louis arrested and put on trial. He was in jail when John Bezner went bail for him. Louis was released and he skipped and went to Anton, Oklahoma. Later, he married a childhood sweetheart. He never went back to Lindsay. He died in 1984. Three of the Weiss girls, Louisa, Mary and Rosa all went back to Oklahoma. Johnny is living in Gainesville.

Mr. Hoelker was suffering from asthma when they came to Lindsay. One Sunday, Mrs. Hoelker had Laura to stay with her father. He had a terrible spell of asthma. Laura was supposed to give him a shot, but she dropped the needle. Mr. Hoelker went a terrible shock. Dr. Whiddon from Gainesville gave him a shot, but Casper never regained consciousness. Mrs. Hoelker then ran the store until the boys, Ewald and Albert, were old enough to take it over. Mrs. Hoelker and I became good friends about the time Henry and I got married. She came to visit nearly everyday. Mama didn't get along with her very well. Mrs. Hoelker wasn't very friendly with her customers for one thing. Also, I think Mama was jealous of her because she always had candy or something in her mouth.

In WWII, Albert was drafted, but Ewald was spared because of ill health. Albert and Helen Laux were engaged to be married. When Albert left for the army, he told Ewald to take good care of Helen which he did by marrying her. Poor Albert married a red-head with one child and they had three children of their own; then, she left him.

Mrs. Hoelker was chopping weeds in her yard on a very hot day. She went into the house and drank a cold bottle of Coca Cola. Three hours later, she died. She was sixty years old.

The Elm Creek Flods

I remember that the Elm Creek bridge washed out twice. The first time was when my sister, Gusta, was about twelve-years-old. She had to take a flour sack with the bread to the boys on the south farm. She came to the bridge and when she saw that she could not cross over on the bridge, she walked about a quarter of a mile east of the bridge; she thought she could jump across the creek. The creek was swollen from the flood and the water was very deep. When she jumped, she didn't make it. She told me that she never hit bottom and that she didn't know how she got out. Of course the bread was all soaked. When she got to the boys who were waiting for the bread, she got a bawling out yet on top of it.

The second time the bridge was washed out, there had been another flood. We were all up on the south farm picking cotton when we had one of those sudden thunder and lightning showers. We all sat under the cotton wagon. Lightning and thunder was all around us and rain poured down by the bucket full. When it was over, we learned that Mrs. Grimm, who was about one mile south of us, was killed by the lightning. She was on top of the wagon trying to cover the cotton with a wagon sheet. The lightning also killed three horses about one mile west of us; the horses were standing along a barbed-wire fence. When they brought the coffin of Mrs. Grimm to the Elm bridge, they could't cross it, so they lifted the coffin from the south side of the creek and some men on the north side took it.

HOW THE SIX FLUSCHE BROTHERS ACQUIRED THEIR WIVES

My father, Wilhelm, was the oldest of the Flusche brothers to come to Iowa to make his fame and fortune in America. Papa came to Westphalia, Iowa, in May 1873. After he was established in Westphalia, he went back to Germany to get his bride, Christina Plucht. Because they were cousins, they were not allowed to get married in Germany and so they got married in Westphalia, Iowa, in 1875. There was a typhoid epidemic and Christina died in 1881. After a courtship by correspondence, Mama left Germany and married Papa in Westphalia, Iowa, in 1895.

Uncle Joseph was the second oldest. He came over from Germany with his brothers Carl and Emil in May, 1872. They had a girl working for them named Anna Dressman, and Grandma Flusche decided she should marry Joseph. It wasn't considered proper for her to stay there with so many men in the house. She really wanted Emil, he was nice looking and younger. Uncle Joseph was the only one of the Flusche brothers who didn't have an education because he had poor eye sight. Well, they got married, October, 5, 1872 in Dunlap, Iowa.

Uncle Carl, the doctor, had gone to Westphalia, Iowa, also to make his fame and fortune before going back to get his bride. In the meantime, his fiancé died in Germany. Uncle Carl then married her sister, Clara Feldman, who was quiet a bit older than Carl, in May, 1873, in Westphalia, Iowa. Clara had come to America with Grandma Flusche, Papa, Aunt Anna and August. Unknown to Tanta Clara, Uncle Carl had had an illegitimate child in Germany whom he was supporting. He did not want Tanta Clara to know about it so he had Papa to send the monthly payments to it. When Mama and Papa got married, Tanta Clara found out about it. Mama and Tanta Clara weren't on good terms so Mama told her about this and the lid nearly flew off.

Then, there was Uncle Anton. He was the first of the Flusche brothers to come to America. He came to the

United States in 1871, and became a druggist. Antonia Feldman, a sister to Clara, Carl's wife, was staying with her sister but was working for somebody on the farm. She had been brought up in the convent shere her two older sisters lived. While on a visit to Westphalia, Iowa, Uncle Anton found Antonia sitting under a tree, crying. She had to carry the lunch out to the field and it was hot. She was not used to rough farm work. Uncle Anton married her on the spot and catered to her ever after.

Grandmother Flusche, Aunt Anna, Emil and August had moved to Kansas where Anton, Emil and August organized Westphalia, Kansas, in 1880. Grandmother Flusche died on May 21, 1881, and was the first to be buried in the new cemetery. That same year, Uncle Emil married Anna Heese on November 23, in Kansas City, Missouri. Uncle Emil met his future wife on the ship on his way back from Germany. He was walking around on deck when he saw a girl sitting there, crying her heart out. Emil asked her what was the matter. She said reading the paper with the address of her relatives where she was supposed to go in America and the wind blew the paper away. Now she didn't know where to go. Uncle Emil brought her along to Iowa with him and later married her. Anna's mother married a man much older than she. She was pregnant and had asked her husband to crawl up an apple tree and get her an apple. She shook the tree. He fell off and broke his neck and died. She was accused of murder and her child was born in jail. That child was Anna Heese, Uncle Emil's wife.

Now there was Uncle August, the youngest. Grandmother Flusche of Bertha was still there yet. They had a girl working for them by the name of Bertha Hoschulte. Now Uncle August took Bertha to a dance. In those days, nobody but the rich people wore fancy underwear. Bertha wore real heavy muslin and dancing so much made her hot. She pulled off her muslin underwear and wrapped them in newspaper. On the way home from the dance, she lost them and somebody found it the next day. Grandmother Flusche made Uncle August and Bertha get married right away.

MAMA AND THE MAJOR
HERMAN VONSTAHOW

As a young girl, Mama worked for this Major Herman vonStahow family for five years. They had two daughters born to them while Mama stayed there; one in 1882, and the other in 1884. Their names were Margo and Elli. These vonStahows were very wealthy and Mama kept in touch with them all through the years she was in America. In 1914, she and Max visited them in Berlin. They had a beautiful town house there and they had a large country estate in East Prussia called Blumenfeld; the whole village worked for them. I don't know how many hectare was in this country estate. (What we would call an acre here is called a hectare there.) The name Blumenfeld means "Field of Flowers" in German. When Henry and I were living in Iowa in 1921, I got a ten page letter from Mama in which she tried to explain to me the things that were going on in Blumenfeld. It seems like the caretaker of Blumenfeld wrote Mama about the rumors going on there. They also had a stud farm on this estate with fancy riding horses and they had hired a riding master to take care of the stable and the horses. He also had to escort the vonStahow daughters when they went riding. Margo was about thirty-eight by then and Elli thirty-six. They had never married because they were afraid a man would only want them for their money. Since they were getting up in age, they still wanted an heir. Now this riding master had a family in Berlin and he and his wife were in cahoots to get Blumenfeld. Mama would get postcards from Margo and Elli from every summer resort all over Europe where Mama thought they were traveling together. But they were with this Herr Kruger. Neither of the sisters wanted the other to have an heir. So Herr Kruger would travel with one to a certain resort and maybe a half-a-year later, he traveled with the other one. In time, they each had a boy but the boys died soon after birth. Again, they each became pregnant at half-a-year intervals. But the second time, first one of the girls and her baby died because she had kidney poisoning. A half-a-year later, the other girl and her baby died also. This caretaker had drawn a sketch of the cemetery in Blumenfeld where the whole family of Herman vonstahow were then buried: Mr. and Mrs. vonStahow, Margo with her two sons, and then Elli with her two sons. This Herr Kruger had it all sewed up. The court couldn't do anything about it because he had married both of them. Mama sure had some sleepless nights when she got all of this information. She had always thought maybe she would get something from that estate. Mama went to Father Bernard and told him this whole sordid story. Father Bernard's only comment was, "If the two ladies were that ugly that they couldn't get them a man. Ha! Ha!"

Me (Elsie), twenty-years-old: 1914

Early Lindsay, Texas

Mama and Max on steamer to
Germany, 1914

A tornado destroyed the
church in 1917

Mama in her later years

My home, built in 1901

Henry and I beside
Uncle Henry's car

Girls on horses: Ella Hundt,
Clara Flusche and Emma Hundt

The cook shack for the threshers

Robert on the horse, Willie. On top:
Max and Alex. Below: Gusta, Clara and Elsie.

Thrashing in the "olden days"

MAMA'S GERMAN SAYINGS

1. Fine Schnecker - Is somebody who loves gourmet food.

2. Schivefel Hannes - Is someone who is very finicky with his meals.

   Uncle Pauls motto was:
3. Besser einmal Wohlgelebt als inner so gestumpelt
   Better to have lived well once, then to have lived a little bit at a time.

   Mama's slogan was:
4. Bescheidenheit ist eine zier doch weiter kommt man ohne ihr
   Modesty is a virtue but you get further with out it.

5. Morgenshtund hat gold im Mund
   The morning hour has gold in the mouth.

   Mr Kohs - Chicago - Morgenshtund hat blei an arsch
   Morning hour has lead on your butt

6. Warum halten offne Tafel Kluge Leute Speitzen drau
   Fools serve lavish meals; smart people take advantage of them.

   To the sound of taps: Mama heard this at the Kaserne (Military camp) in Berlin.

7. Zu Bett zu Bett, var eine hat, War keins hat, muss auch zu Bett.
   To bed, to bed, who has one; who has none, must also go to bed.

8. Arm wie eine Kirchenmaus
   Poor as a church mouse

9. Der Telfel scheist immer auf dem Hochsten haufen
   The devil always shits on the biggest pile.

10. Gibts man jemand den kleinen Finger dann will or die gause Hand.
    Give someone your little finger; he'll take your whole hand.

11. Der packt sich nicht, fur nichts am Hintern.
    He won't reach to his butt for nothing.

12. Wer jemand eine grube grabt, Fallt selbst hin ein
    If someone digs you a grave, he'll fall into it himself.

13. Beer auf Wein, das lass sein, Butt Wein auf Bier, das rat ich Dir.
    Beer on wine avoid, but wine on beer I advise you.

14. Die Musik spielt Lustig und in Freud. Der Bass spielt Kummer und verdruss.
    The first violin plays happy and in love; the bass violin answers, disappointment and sorrow.

15. Gottes Muhlen malen langsam aber sicher.
    God's mills grind slow but sure.

16. Die Liebe fallt oft auf einen Mist Haufen und nicht immer auf ein Rosenblat.
    Love does not always fall on rose pedals: it sometimes falls on a manure pile.

17. Es ist nicht immer gold was glanst.
    It isn't always gold that glitters.

18. Ei genlob stinkt.
    Self-praise stinks.

19. Wenn es den Esel zu gut geht, geth er aufs Eis Und bricht sich das Bein.
    If a mule's life is too pleasant, he will go skating on the ice and break a leg.

20. Freunde in der Not. Ein Hundert auf ein Lott.
    Friends in need. One hundred on a load.

21. Lugen haben kurze Beine.
    Lies have short legs.

22. Komm ich nicht Heute, Kommt ich Morgen.
    If I don't come today, I'll come tomorrow

23. Wer einmal lugt den glaubt man nicht, Auch wenn er die
    Wahrheit sprichet
    If he tells a lie once, you don't believe him even
    though he tells the truth.

24. Nie soll wieter in das Land - Lieb von Lieb sich wagen
    - Als man Bluhend in der Hand - Kann die Rose tragen.
    Two lovers should never part longer then you can carry
    a blooming rose in your hand.

25. Bekannte Sellen Treffen sich, zu wasser und zu Land.
    Acquainted souls often meet on water and on land.

26. Wie Du mir so ich Dir.
    As you do unto me, I will do unto you.

27. Es ist nichts so fein gesponnen, Es kommt doch an die
    Sonne.
    When planned yet so carefully, truth will come out in
    the end.

28. Heile, heile Katzen Dreck, Morgen ist es wieder weg.
    Hail, hail cat's dirt, tomorrow it will be gone.

29. Sage mir mit wenn Du u gehst, Und ich sage Dir was Du
    bist.
    Tell me with whom your freinds are, and I'll tell you
    what you are.

30. Ich habe die alte Frau gefragt, wie gehts? sie hat
    geantwortet gut, aber sie hat doch mit einem Auge
    geweint.
    I asked the old lady how are you? She answered good,
    but she did cry with one eye.

31. Ein gutes gewissen ist das beste Ruhekissen.
    A clean conscience is the softest pillow to sleep on.

32. Morgen morgen nur nicht heute, Sagen alle faulen Leute.
    Tomorrow, tomorrow, not today: is what all the lazy
    people say.

33. WennDu ein Madchen hast, dann hast Du eins - Wenn Du
    zwei hast, dann hast Du ein halbes - Wenn Du drei
    hast, dann hast Du keins. If you have one girl to help
    out, you have one; but if you have two girls, you only
    have a half of one, and if you have three girls, you
    have none.

34. Viele Hande machen schnell ein Ende.
    Many hands will bring the job to a quick end.

35. Der Apfel falt nich weit vom Baum.
    The apple doesn't fall far from the tree.

36. (Father Bernard said this one on the pulpit) Eine
    richtige bescheidene person im Kloster ist so wenig in
    finden wie ein Weisser Rabe.
    A real pious, modest person in a religious order, is
    as scarce as a white crow.

37. Reiche Leute haben feine Sachen, Was Sie nicht haben,
    das lassen Sie sich machen.
    Rich people have beautiful things. What they don't
    have, they'll have manufactured.

38. Viele Kochen verderben den Brei.
    Too many cooks ruin the stew.

39. Mitten im Leben sind wir von Tod ungeben.
    In the midst of life, we are surrounded by death.

40. Ye mehr er hat je mehr er will, Nie stehen seine
    wunsche still.
    The more he has, the more he wants. His wishes are
    never all full filled.

41. Jede Mutter labt Ihre eigne Butter.
    Every mother brags on her own "butter."

42. Je naher bei Rom, je lauher der Christ.
    The closer to Rome; the weaker the Christian.

43. Ein geschencker gaul, guckt man nicht im Maul.
    You don't look into a horse's mouth that was given to
    you as a gift. (Don't look a gift horse in the mouth.)

44. Viel geschrei und wenig Wolle.
    The lamb that makes the most noise has the least wool.

45. Warum macht der Hahn die Augen zu, wenn er kraht? Weil
    er es aus wendig weiss.
    Why does the rooster shut his eyes when he crows?
    Because he knows it all by heart.

46. Ein blindes Schwein findet auch als mal ein Eichel.
    Even a blind hog finds an acorn now and then.

47. Kleine Kinder, kleine Sorgen, Grosse Kinder, grosse
    Sorgen.
    A small child, small worries; a grown up child, large
    worries.

48. Wenn das Kind klein ist, dan tretet es die Mutter auf
    den schos, Aber wenn es gross ist, dann tretet es die
    Mutter auf das Her
    When the child is small, it steps on the mother's lap.
    But when it's grown, it steps on the mother's heart.

49. Das passt wie die Faust aufs Auge.
    It fits like the fist on your eye.

50. Kurz gebgt und lange Knackwurst.
    A short prayer and a long sausage.

51. Ewn ich den niemand finden kann.
    If I could get a hold of that nobody. (When I tried to
    find out who broke my nice dish!)

52. Die einzage Zeit das Kind kann sprechen warend der
    Mahlseit, ist venn die Katze die Treppe rauf lauft nit
    denn Ofen auf denn puckel.
    The only time a child may talk during a meal, is when
    the cat runs upstairs with the stove on its back.

53. Wer es nicht inkoph hat, Mus sie den fuss Haben.

If you don't have it in your head, you better have it in your feet.

54. Jades Toephchen hat sien Deckelechen.
Every pot has its lid.

55. (Papa theisen had to eat a lot of humbel pie, living with Mama.)
Jeh Hocher er steht, Jeh neldriger der fall.
The higher he stands, the further the fall.

56. Frauden des Labens.
Joys of life.

57. Geld wachst nicht auf den Baumen.
Money don't grow on trees.

58. Las nicht die Linka hand wessen wis die rachts hand tot.
Don't let the left hand know, what the right hand is doing.

59. Er traugt auf Baeda Schultern.
He carries on both shoulders.

60. Wenn das Madchen sahr auf geputzt war, dann wird die sanne duster.
If the maiden is all dolled up, the sun will get dark.

61. Gott sorgt das die Bauma nicht in dan Himmel wachsen.
God sees that the trees don't grown into heaven.

62. Ein Klatchwieb hat harra auf dea zahne.
A gossiper has hair on her teeth.

63. Wasser est Gansa wine.
Water is goose wine. (Mr. Bauer's saying)

64. Wenn du grauchi fulst, dann lauft die laus uber die Leber.
When you feel grouchy or ill humored; a louse crawled over your liver.

65. Ich hatte katzenjammer.

I had a hangover.

66. Du hast grosse rosinen in dienen koph.
    You have big raisins in your head. (Have big ideas)

67. So klat, Mann yaqt kein Hundt aus.
    It's so cold a person wouldn't chase a dog outside.

68. Jes Ma Jo
    Jesus Mary Joseph

69. Schreibt es un Kamin
    Write it in the chimney.

MY MORNING AND EVENING PRAYERS (GERMAN AND ENGLISH)

My Evening Prayer
(Translated from the German by Madeline Zimmerer)

Weary AM I, going to rest,
Closing both my eyes.
Father, let those eyes of Thine
Hover over my bed.
If today I have done wrong,
May You, Dear God, overlook it, because
By Your grace and Jesus' blood
All wrong is turned to good. Amen.

My Morning Prayer
(Translated from the German by Madeline Zimmerer)

O God! Throughout this night You have
With fatherly care watched over me.
I praise and honor you for it,
And thank You for all that is good.
Protect me on this day
From sin, death, and all misfortune.
And what today I think, say, and do,
Please bless, oh best of fathers, do!
Protect me, also, I beg of you,
O holy angel of God.
Mary plead at God's throne
For me with Jesus, your son.
May He be praised at all times,
From now on, and for eternity. Amen.

Abend Gebet - Evening Prayer

Mude bin ich, geh zur Rurh,
Schliesse beide Auglein zu
Vater, lass die Augen Dein
Uber meinem Bete sein Sie es Lieber Gott nicht an.
Deiner Gnad' und Jesu' Blut Macht ja Alen Schalden gut. Amen.

Morget Gebet - Morning Prayer

o Gott Du hast in Dieser Nacth
So Vaterlich fur mich gewacth.
Ich lob und preise Dich dafur
Und dank' fur alles Gute Dir!
Beware mich auf diesem Tag,
Vor Sunde, Tod, und jeder Plag'
Und was ich heute denke, red' und treh
Das segne bester Vater, Du.
Beschutz auch, ich bitte Dich,
o Heiliger Engel Gottes mich.
Maria, bitt' and Gottes Thron,
Fur mich, bei Jesus, Deinin Sohn,
Der hoch gelobt sie aller Zeit
Von nun an bis in Ewigkeit. Amen.

PART II

Maternal and Paternal Family Records

Elsie Flusche Fuhrman

WILHELM FLUSCHE FAMILY RECORD

Maternal Family Record
of
Elsie Flusche Fuhrman

Wilhelm and Elizabeth Walter Steinmetz as written by Mrs.
Paul Weise Sr. nee Anna Steinmetz

William Steinmetz	Married	Elizabeth Walter-Steinmetz
Born: 1821	Sep. 14, 1847	Born: 1827
Died: Nov. 8,1910		Died: Jan. 2,1896
Buried: Lindsay, Texas		Buried: Lindsay, Texas

Sep. 14, 1847, we were married by the Rev. Fr. Pastor
Greve.

Aug. 10, 1848, we moved into our home which we had purchased
from the Widow Peter Hesse.

Oct. 13, 1848, at 6:30 A.M., our first child was born. We
named her. Maria, Anna, Theresia, Elizabeth. Sponsors
were Mayor Arnold Becker and Elizabeth Schrage (born
Zeppenfeld our mother).

Mar. 24, 1851, at 9:30 A. M., our second daughter was
born. Her name was Maria Anna, Wilhelmina. Sponsors were
Eberhart Sommer (a tailor) and Wilhelmina Kraft.

Jan. 15, 1854, at 8:30 P. M. our third daughter was born. Her
name vas Maria (Mrs. Frank Loerwald), Anna, Ferdinandina.
Sponsors were (Carpenter) Ferdinand Becker and Miss Anna
Maria Merteus, a local school teacher.

Jul. 19, 1856, our first son was born at 4 P. M. We named him Englebertus Robertus. Sponsors: Engelbert Ispharding and Mrs. Maria Kutsch.

On St. Barbaras, 1858, our second son was born named Joseph who died at birth.

Apr. 2, 1860, at 10 P. M. our fourth daughter was born: Josephina, Emma, Auguste (Mrs. Theisen). Sponsors: Nephae, Joseph Rall and Josephine Halver (born Walter) at Boschum.

Apr. 6, 1860, on Easter morning, our mother Elizabeth Schrage (born Zeppenfeld) died form T. B.

Sep. 18, 1862, at 11 A. M. our fifth daughter was born. Theresia, Josephina. Sponsors: Joseph Walter and Miss Theresia Neukirch.

Mar. 8, 1865, at 4 A. M., our oldest daughter, Elise, sixteen years of age, died.

Grandpa and Grandma Steinmetz and "Drei alten hounder," taken about 1905

Standing from left to right: Tanta Mari (Mrs. Frank Loerwald), Tanta Anna (Mrs. Paul Wiese) and Mama (Augusta) (Mrs. Wilhelm Flusche).
Seated: Grandpa (Wilhelm) and Grandma (Elizabeth) Steinmetz.

My mother, Augusta Steinmetz, and my father, Wilhelm Flusche.
Married, Oct. 29, 1885

Mama's second marriage to John Theisen, 1905

The Flusche family picture, taken in 1905. Back row: Robert, Fritz, Gusta and me (Elsie). Front row: Max, Herman, Clara, Mama (Augusta Theisen), Alex and Otto.

My half-brother, Willie, and Anna Fuhrman Flusche:
Married, May 1, 1906

My half-sister, Clara, before she entered
the convent of the Sisters of Divine
Providence, 1897

She took the name of her mother, Christina

Mar. 24, 1865, at 2 P. M., our third son was born. Peter, Adolph. Sponsors: Peter Adolph Dingerkus (shoemaker) and Mrs. Bernhard Schneider, both from here.

Dec. 27, 1865 at 3:30 P. M., our youngest son died of scarlet fever.

Nov. 1, 1866 at 6:30P. M. our sixth daughter was born. Anna, Maria, Josephina, Hedwig. Sponsors: Joseph Neukird and Anna Maria Rall.

Sep. 28, 1869 at 8 months, ur youngest daughter, Hedwig, died at age two years, eleven months. Cause of death, pneumonia.

Jan. 24, 1870, our Aunt Josephina Walter died form consumption at Boschum.

Jan. 24, 1870 at 5 A. M., our seventh daughter was born. Anna, Katharina, Ferdinandina. (Grandna Wiese) Sponsors: Ferdinand Bishop and Engelbert Ispharding both from here.

Mar. 25, 1870, our Aunt Josephine Walter died from consumption at Boschum (a repeat) Recorded as January 24, 1870 in record.

Family Record
Of
Paul and Anna Steinmetz Wiese

Paul Weise	Married:	Anna Steinmetz
Born: Jun.1,1866	May 10,1892	Born: Jan. 24,1870
Died: Aug. 8, 1926	Died: Mar. 2,1960	

Children:	Born:	Died:
Frank	Apr. 28, 1893	Jan.16, 1874
Anna Maria	Jul. 28, 1894	Sep. 14, 1895
Leo J.	Dec. 4, 1895	Aug. 17, 1963
Clara Wilhelmina	Dec. 14, 1897	Sep. 21, 1966
Elizabeth Katherine	Feb. 2, 1899	
Wilhelm Anton	Aug. 11, 1901	
Paul Robert	Sep. 10, 1903	Sep. 10, 1971
Albert John	Sep. 30, 1905	Aug. 8, 1948

Vincent Ignatius   Dec. 15, 1907
Cecilia Elizabeth   Sep. 22, 1913

Frank Wiese   Married: Clara Margaret Schad
Born: Apr. 28, 1893   Jan. 10,1922   Born: Jul.28, 1903
Died: Jan. 16, 1974   Died:
Son of Paul and Anna Wiese

Leo J. Wiese   Married: Lorie Wilson
Born: Dec. 4, 1895   Feb. 12, 1921
Died: Aug. 17, 1963
Son of Paul and Anna Wiese

Clara Wilhelmina Wiese   Married: Wilhelm A. Schmitz
Born: Dec. 14, 1897   May 8, 1917
Daughter of Paul and
Anna Wiese
                                             Died: Nov. 27, 1918
Clara Wilhelmina Wiese   Married: Valentine John Dieter
2nd Marriage   Nov. 16, 1920   Born: Oct. 27, 1891
Died: Sep. 21, 1966   Died: Sep. 20, 1960

Elizabeth Wiese   Married: Jacob Robert Bezner
Born: Feb. 2, 1899   Feb. 17, 1919   Born: July. 1, 1892
                                             Died:

Vincent Ignatius Wiese   Married: Florence Zettler
Born: Dec. 15, 1907   Oct. 25, 1927
Son of Paul and
Anna Wiese

Cecilia Wiese   Married: William Joseph Schmitz
Born: Sep. 22, 1913   Born: Jul. 19, 1910
Son of Paul and Anna
  Wiese
                                             Died: Aug. 12, 1968

Family Record
of
Frank and Mari Steinmetz Loerwald

Frank Loerwald	Married:	Mari Steinmetz
Born: Jul. 29, 1850		Born: Jan. 15, 1854
Died: Nov. 1, 1939		Died: Jul. 23, 1923
Children:	Born:	Died
Frank August		
Joseph	Apr. 22, 1878	Mar. 13, 1957
Robert Joseph	May 19, 1881	Sep. 10, 1962
Charles	Aug. 11, 1883	Dec. 6, 1940
Mary	Nov. 2, 1885	Feb. 4, 1960
William Julius	Aug. 11, 1887	Oct. 2, 1957
Annie	Sep. 23, 1889	Nov. 25, 1974
Clara Elizabeth	Dec. 5, 1891	Jan. 1, 1948
Pauline	Dec. 28, 1893	Feb. 6, 1926
Elsie	Mar. 21, 1896	Feb. 5, 1899
Anton	Nov. 21, 1898	Feb. 10, 1899

Frank	Married:	Mary Castor
Born:	Oct. 30, 1900	
Died:		

Robert Loerwald	Married:	Clara Lueb
Born: May 19, 1881	Oct. 9, 1906	
Died: Mar. 13, 1957		

Charles Loerwald	Married:	Magdalina Kempf
Born: Aug. 11, 1883	Nov. 14, 1905	
Died: Dec. 6, 1940		

Mary Loerwald	Married:	Adam Beyer
Born: Nov. 2, 1885	Nov. 9, 1907	
Died: Feb. 4, 1960		

William Loerwald   Married: Clara Hofer
Born: Aug. 11, 1887   Oct. 26, 1909
Died: Oct. 2, 1957

Annie Loerwald   Married: Joseph J. Schmitz
Born: Sep. 23, 1889   Jan. 14, 1908
Died: Nov. 25, 1974

Clara Elizabeth Loerwald Married: Aloys Kuntz
Born: Dec. 5, 1891   Jan. 16, 1812
Died: Jan. 1, 1948

Pauline Loelwald   Married: Theordore H. Schmitz
Born: Dec. 28, 1893   Feb. 13,1912
Died: Feb. 6,1926

Paternal Family Record
of
Elsie Flusche Fuhrman
Family Record

Earliest Flusche recorded, is about Johann Eberhardt Flusche. His parents moved from Attendorn to Neger about 1690.

Johann Eberhardt Flusche Married: Christina Ackerschott
of Rhode Parish, Neger   in 1710

Johann Adolf Flusche   Married: Elizabeth Andres
Born: About 1715   in 1739   of Neger
Died: Jan. 27, 1786, age 71

Farmer, Tailor, and provisor of Chapel. He also was of Rhode Parish, Neger, Germany

Peter Flusche   Married: Elizabeth Hebrig
Born: Feb. 1, 1742   in 1771
Also of Neger, Germany
Son of Johann Adolph

Johann Adam Flusche   Married: Elizabeth Gante
Born: Apr. 6, 1774   in 1801
Son of Peter
Died: Aug. 16, 1844

Stephan Flusche   Married: Catherina Flucht
Born: Jun. 2, 1805   Sep. 11, 1838   Born: Sep. 2, 1815
at Attendorn   in Attendorn
Son of Johann Adam
Died: Mar. 22, 1867   Died: May 21, 1881

Stephan Flusche, was father of the Flusche brothers.

Catherina Flucht Flusche was the daughter of Johann Wilhelm Flucht and
Elizabeth Hitze of Hanemicke. She was from Wamge, Germany, and died
in Westphalia, Iowa. Stephan was a schoolteacher in Liesterscheid, a
village near Wamge, from about 1830 until his death on March 22, 1867
of pneumonia.

Children of Stephan and Catherina Flucht Flushce

1. Wilhelm Flusche   First Marriage: Christina Flucht
Born: Aug. 9, 1839   Jun. 24, 1875
Wamge Germany
Son of Stephan
Died: Mar. 26, 1901   Second Marriage: Augusta Steinmetz
Buried: Lindsay, Texas   Oct. 29, 1885

2. Joseph   Married: Anna Dressman
Born: Dec. 21, 1840   Oct. 5, 1872
Died: Oct. 22, 1895   Died: Aug. 20, 1912

Buried: Muenster, Texas   (At the time of her
                                        death she was second wife of Conrad
                                        Walterscheid of Muenster

3. Carl (Doctor)	Married:	Clara Feldman
Born: Jan. 13, 1843	May 1873	Born: Mar. 13, 1846
Died: Dec. 7, 1896		Died: Jun. 25, 1918

4. Anton	Married:	Antonia Feldman
Born: Feb. 12, 1847		Born: Oct. 16, 1860
Died: Jan. 25, 1925		Died: May 2, 1923
Buried: Lindsay, Texas		Buried: Lindsay, Texas

5. Emil	Married:	Anna Heese
Born: Feb. 10, 1849	Nov. 23, 1881	
Died: Jan. 24, 1930		Died: May 15, 1895
Buried: Mount Carmel,		Buried: Pilot Point,
Texas		Texas

6. August	Married:	Bertha Hoschulte
Born: Jul. 23, 1853		
Died: Feb. 28, 1928		
Buried: Crekola, Oklahoma		

A daughter died at the age of 11 months on June 21, 1856. (Would have been born, September, 1855. Emil remembers the birth and baptism of August and the death of his sister.)

Wilhelm Flusche Family Record

First Marriage of Wilhelm Flusche

Wilhelm Flusche	Married:	Christina Flusche
Son of Stephan	Jun. 24, 1875	
Born: Aug. 9, 1839	in Westphalia, IA	Born: 1852
Wamge Germany		Nierst Germany
		Died: Aug. 11, 1881
		Westphalia, Iowa

Children:	Born:	Died:
1. William Joseph	Apr. 17, 1876	Jul. 24, 1928
2. Clara Christina	Sep. 11, 1877	Oct. 23, 1972

Became Sister Christina of Divine Providence in San Antonio, Texas

3. Maria Anna	Sep. 22, 1879	May 13, 1880
4. Anna	Aug. 9, 1881	Sep. 21, 1881

William Flusche Family Record

Second Marriage of Wilhelm Flusche

Wilhelm Flusche	Married:	Augusta Steinmetz
	Oct. 29, 1885	Born: in Attendorn
	Westphalia Io.	Germany
	Apr. 1, 1860	
Died: Mar. 26, 1901		Died: Feb. 28, 1940
Buried in Lindsay		Buried in Lindsay

Children:	Born:	Died:
1. William Robert	Aug. 1, 1886	Apr. 25, 1974
2. Frederick Robert	Oct. 2, 1887	Feb. 22, 1921
3. Augusta Mary	Oct. 27, 1888	May 1, 1960
4. Otto Stephan	Aug. 18, 1891	Jan. 22, 1976
5. Herman Joseph	Dec. 20, 1892	Nov. 23, 1941
6. Anna Elizabeth	Oct. 22, 1894	
7. Max Paul	Apr. 3, 1896	Jun. 6, 1970
8. Anton Alex	Nov. 24, 1898	Aug. 25, 1980
9. Clara Antonia	Feb. 28, 1900	Aug. 27, 1984

From the Journal of Wilhelm Flusche
Westfalia, Shelby County, Iowa.
Written In German; Translated by
Elsie Flusche Fuhrman, June, 1985

Baptismal Record of the Decendants
of
Wilhelm and Augusta Flusche

1886, August 1, Wilhelm Robert was born. Baptized, August 8, by Father Brommenshenkel in Westphalia, Iowa. Godparents: Wilhelm Steinmetz, and Frau Anna Flusche nee Heese (Emil Flusche's wife).

1887. October 2, Friederick Carl baptized 3rd October by Father Brommenshelkel in Westphalia, Iowa. Godparents: Carl Flusche, and Elizabeth Steinmetz nee Walter.

1888. October 27, Maria Augusta was born. Baptized, 29th October by Father Brommenshenkel in Westphalia, Iowa. Godparents: Anton Flusche, and Maria Loerwald nee Steinmetz.

1892. December 20, Herman Joseph was born. Baptized on 1st January 1893 by Father Bardenhewer, Lindsay, Texas. Godparents: Joseph Becker (Augusta Flusche Theisen's cousin) and Frau Antonio Flusche nee Feldman (Uncle Anton's wife).

1894. October 22, Anna Elizabeth (Elsie) born. Baptized 31 October by Father Weber, Lindsay, Texas. Godparents: Emil Flusche, and Anna Flusche nee Dresmann (Uncle Joseph's wife).

1896. On Good Friday, 3rd April, Maximilian Paul was born. Baptized, Easter, 5 April. The first child baptized by Father Mielinger, Lindsay, Texas. Godparents: Paul Wiese, and Elizabeth Flusche nee Hofschulte (Uncle August wife).

1898. 24 November, Anton Alexander was born on Thanksgiving Day. Baptized November 27. Godparents: Uncle Anton Flusche, and Frau Anna Wiesman nee Flusche (Uncle Joseph's daughter).

1900. February 28, on Ash Wednesday, Clara Antonio born. Baptized November 27. Godparents: Willy Flusche, and Antonia Hargarten nee Flusche (Uncle Carl's daughter).

Family Record of the Descendants
of
Wilhelm Flusche

William Flusche Jr.	Married:	Anna Fuhrmann
Son of Wilhelm	May 1, 1906	Daughter of Henry Fuhrmann
Born: Apr. 17, 1876		Born: Sep. 22, 1885
Died: Jul. 24, 1928		Died: Mar. 14, 1974

Children: Born:
1. Cecilia   Dec. 17, 1907
2. Paul F.   Sep. 6, 1909   (Unmarried)
3. William   May 15, 1911
4. Christine   Feb. 1, 1913
5. Zita   Jan. 2, 1917

Family Record of
Julius and Cecilia Hermes

Julius Hermes Sr.   Married: Cecilia Flusche
                            Feb. 15, 1927   Daughter of William
                                                Flusche Jr.

Children: Born
(1) William   Feb. 13, 1928
(2) Julius   Mar. 14, 1929
(3) Richard   Sep. 5, 1931
(4) Walter   Feb. 24, 1933
(5) Marcella   Dec. 20, 1934
(6) Patrick   Apr. 4, 1945
(7) Patricia   Apr. 4, 1945
(8) Mary Ann   Nov. 4, 1946

---

(1) William Hermes   Married: Mary Evelyn Hofbauer
Son of Julius Hermes Sr.   Feb. 13, 1953   Daughter of Clem

Children: Born:
[1] Debra Louise   May 17, 1953
[2] Alyce Marie   Aug. 23, 1954
[3] Cheryl Ann   Apr. 10, 1957
[4] Denice Marcel   Mar. 11, 1958
[5] Gary Wayne   Nov. 25, 1959
[6] Laura Jean   Apr. 25, 1961
[7] Timothy Lynn   May 15, 1962
[8] Glenn Joseph   Sep. 7, 1963
[9] Pamela Kay   Mar. 15, 1966

---

(2) Julius Hermes Jr.   Married: Clara Annette Flushce
Born: Mar. 14, 1929   Oct. 12, 1954   Born: Sep. 21, 1936

Son Julius Hermes Sr.

Children: Born:
[1] Bobby Joe   Jul. 13, 1955
[2] Kenneth Ray   Apr. 22, 1958
[3] Stephen   Apr. 1, 1962
[4] Carol Ann   Aug. 28, 1968

---

(3) Richard Hermes   Married: Edna Hoenig
Born: Sep. 5, 1931   May 30, 1956
Son of Julius Hermes Sr.

Children: Born:
[1] Ronnie James   Dec. 14, 1956
[2] David Lee   Feb. 18, 1958
[3] Eugene Paul   May 14, 1959
[4] Larry Joe   Nov. 23, 1960
[5] Shirley Ann   Apr. 6, 1962
[6] Dale Francis   Dec. 22, 1963
[7] Gayle Marie   Dec. 22, 1963
[8] Beverly Sue   Jan. 4, 1966
[9] Leroy Jerome   Nov. 28, 1967

---

(4) Walter Hermes   Married: Joan Wolf
Born: Feb. 24, 1933   Nov. 21, 1959
Son of Julius Hermes Sr.

Children: Born:
[1] Dwayne Jospeh   Aug. 18, 1960
[2] Sharla Catherine   Jul. 6, 1963
[3] Dennis Julius   Oct. 5, 1967

---

(5) John Dave Fleitmann   Married: Patay Hermes
Born: Apr. 4, 1945   May 29, 1965

                                                      Daughter of Julius
                                                        Hermes Sr.

Children:	Born:
[1] Douglas John	May 8, 1966
[2] Samuel Julius	Aug. 20, 1969

Billy Zimmerer | Married: | (6) Marcella Hermes
| | Oct. 12, 1955 | Born: Dec. 20, 1934
| | | Daughter of Julius
| | | Hermes Sr.

Children:	Born:
[1] Barbara Marie	May 1, 1958
[2] Michael James	Oct. 30, 1959
[3] Janet Patricia	Jul. 10, 1962
[4] Nancy Sue	Sep. 29, 1964

Family Record of
William and Elvira Eberhart Flusche

3. William Flusche | Married | Elvira Eberhart
Born: May 15, 1911 | Aug. 27, 1938
Died: Oct. 23, 1972
Son of William Joseph

Children:	Born:
(1) Imogene Mary	Aug. 2, 1939
(2) William Edward	Jul. 13, 1940
(3) Robert James	Aug. 9, 1943
(4) Mary Catherine	Sep. 2, 1946

Albert Zimmerer | Married: | (1) Imogen Flusche
| | | Daughter of William
| | | Flusche
Born: Jul. 15, 1935 | Dec. 28, 1958 | Born: Aug. 2, 1939

Children:	Born:
(1) Albert Joseph Jr.	Sep. 17, 1958
(2) Deryl Joseph	Oct. 9, 1959
(3) Deboran Ann	Jan. 17, 1961
(4) Gary Joseph	Feb. 26, 1962

[5] John Joseph	Jul. 25, 1963	
[6] Shelly Marie	Jan. 10, 1965	
[7] Carl Joseph	May 17, 1966	

---

(2) William Edward Flusche	Married:	Vivian Harrison
Born: Jul. 13, 1940	Sep. 8, 1962	Born: Jan. 9, 1942
Children	Born:	
William Jr.	Apr. 3, 1968	

---

(3) Robert James	Married:	Medders
Born: Aug. 9, 1943		

Hess	Married:	(4) Mary Catherine
		Born: Sep. 2, 1946

John Voth	Married:	(4) Christine Flusche
	Nov. 29, 1936	Born: Feb. 1, 1913
		Daughter of Willie & Anna Flusche
Children:	Born:	
(1) Alyce Evelyn	Aug. 26, 1939	
(2) Lorena Mary	Apr. 2, 1943	
(3) Dolores Cacilia	Jul. 13, 1946	

Robert David	Married:	Alyce Evelyn Voth
		Born: Aug. 28, 1939
		Daughter of Christine Flusche Voth
Children:	Born:	
[1] Pamela	Oct. 12, 1965	
[2] Tammy	Aug. 26, 1966	
[3] Russell	Mar. 1, 1969	

Frank Sandman	Married:	Lorena Mary Voth
Apr. 26, 1962		Born: Apr. 2, 1943
		Daugther of Christine
		Flusche Voth

Children:	Born:
(1) Robert	May 29, 1969

---

(2) Jimmy Zimmerer	Married:	Dolores Cecilia Voth
	Aug. 21, 1965	Born: Jul. 13, 1946
		Daugther of Christine
		Flusche Voth

Children:	Born:
[1] Jeff	Sep. 6, 1966
[2] Jenifer	Jan. 22, 1968

Alfons Fleitmann	Married:	(5) Zita Flusche
Died: Feb. 27, 1957	Oct. 24, 1939	Born: Jan. 2, 1917
		Daughter of Willie &
		Anna Flusche

Children:	Born:
(1) Melvin Henry	Aug. 15, 1942
(2) Robert Wm. Nick	Dec. 5, 1944
(3) Clarence Joseph	Jan. 16, 1946
(4) Doris	Jan. 23, 1953

Family Record of
John and Auguta Flusche Bezner

John Bezner	Married:	Augusta Flusche
Born: May 12, 1885	Aug. 20, 1908	Born: Oct. 27, 1888
Died: Jan. 25, 1953	St Peters, Lindsay	Died: May 1, 1960
		Daughter of Wilhelm &
		Augusta Flusche

Children:	Born:	Died:
William John	Jun. 16, 1908	Jul. 4, 1979
Hugo Albert	Mar. 8, 1911	
Son Born Dead	Jul. 22, 1915	Jul. 22, 1915
Walter Robert	Jul. 27, 1916	
Elfrieda Elizabeth	Apr. 2, 1918	Nov. 22, 1965
Raymond William	Nov. 7, 1919	Jul. 11, 1949
Herbert Joseph	Jan. 27, 1921	
Ralph Max Leonard	Jan. 30, 1923	
John Rufus	Nov. 20, 1924	Apr. 29, 1984
Mary Louise	Jan. 13, 1928	

William Bezner	Married:	Margaret Meur
Born: Jun. 16, 1909	Nov. 17, 1937	Born: Jul. 10, 1911
Died: Jul. 4, 1979	in Michigan	

Children:	Born:	Died:
Marlene	Nov. 13, 1938	
Joseph	May 22, 1940	
Rose Mary	Dec. 25, 1941	
Michael	Jul. 3, 1943	(Unmarried)
Bernadette	Nov. 26, 1947	
William	Aug. 29, 1950	
David	May 18, 1954	Aug. 18, 1956

James Bass	Married:	Marlene Bezner
Born: Jun. 17, 1936	Jul. 9, 1960	Born: Nov. 13, 1938
	In Lindsay	
		Daughter of William and Margaret Bezner

Children:	Born:
Carolyn	Apr. 21, 1961
Mary Margaret	Mar. 27, 1962
Paul	Jul. 16, 1963
James	Oct. 4, 1966

Will Bezner	Married:	Catherine Bogner
Born: Aug. 29, 1950	Apr. 22, 1978	
Son of William and Margaret		

Children:	Born:
Abbie	Jan. 3, 1980
John	Jun. 5, 1981
Ellen	Nov. 21, 1982

Francis J Schindler	Married:	Rose Mary Bezner
Born: Jul. 10, 1937	Aug. 12, 1961	Born: Dec. 25, 1941
	In Lindsay	
		Daughter of William
		And Margare Bezner

Children:	Born:
Steven	Jul. 8, 1962
John	Aug. 29, 1963
Kathleen	Feb. 28, 1965
Douglas	Oct. 28, 1967
Jennifer	Nov. 6, 1980

Joseph Bezner	Married:	Marliese Kleinknecht
Born: May 22, 1940	May 15, 1962	Born: Jul. 12, 1941
	In Germany	
Son of William & Margaret Bezner		

Children:	Born:
Andrew	Apr. 1, 1963
Marliese	Sep. 9, 1966

Bernadette, daughter of William & Margaret Bezner, entered the Congregation of Sister of Divine Providence in San Antonio, Texas- Sep. 5, 1965. Made First vows, Aug. 2, 1966.

Hugo Albert Bezner	Married:	Florence Mozella Jirasek
Born: Mar. 8, 1911	Sep. 22, 1962	Born: Feb.23, 1919
Son of John and Augusta Bezner		
No Children:		

William Bomar Woods	Married:	Elfrieda Elizabeth Bezner
Born: Mar. 19, 1921	Nov. 30, 1945	Born: Apr. 2, 1918
		Died: Nov. 22, 1965
		Daughter of John & Augusta Bezner

Children:	Born:
Don Michael	Mar. 30, 1947
Lonnie Ray	Feb. 15, 1950

Don Michael Woods	Married:	Sandra Kaye Miller
Born: Mar. 30, 1947	Don is Divorced	

Lonnie Ray Woods	Married:	Jannie Spires
Born: Feb. 15, 1950		
Children:	Born:	
Sally		

Raymond William Bezner	Married:	Oleta Rosson
Born: Nov. 7, 1919	Dec. 27, 1943	Born: Jul. 13, 1922
Died: Jul. 11, 1949		
Son of John & Augusta Bezner		
Children:	Born:	
Ray William Buster	Jan. 1, 1945	

Ray William Bezner	Married:	Marcy Neu
Born: Jan.1, 1945	Jan. 29, 1966	
Son of Raymond William Bezner		
Children:	Born:	
Rae Ann	Oct. 19, 1967	
Robert Wayne	Apr. 18, 1969	

Herbert Joseph Bezner	Married:	Ella Pauline Hanson
Born: Jan.19, 1926	Apr. 29, 1946	Born: Mar. 24, 1925
Gainesville, Texas		Johah, Texas
Son of John & Augusta Bezner		

Children:	Born:
Herbert Joseph	Mar. 28, 1947 at Gainesville
Lawrence Jeff	Mar. 6, 1949 at Gainesville

Ralph Max Leonard Bezner Married: Nora Jane House
Born: Jan. 30, 1924   Jul. 13, 1944   Born: Nov. 6, 1925
Son of John & Augusta Bezner

Children:	Born:
John Scott	Feb. 16, 1946
Steven Charles	Jul. 27, 1950
Russel Max	Dec. 6, 1955
Leanne	Jan. 25, 1959
Lori Jan	Jun. 4, 1960
Gary Van	Jun. 4, 1960

Rufus J Bezner   Married: Gladys Wilde
Born: Nov. 19, 1924   Nov. 9, 1949   Born: Jun. 19, 1926
Died: Apr. 29, 1984   in Muenster   Daughter of Joe Wilde
Son of John & Augusta Bezner

Children:	Born:	Died:
Jeffry	Apr. 27, 1951	Jun. 17, 1958
Rickey	Aug. 11, 1952	
Carol	Sep. 28, 1953	
Sharol	Sep. 28, 1953	Dec. 7, 1953
Jay	Dec. 12, 1955	
Mary Kaye	Apr. 11, 1957	

Bernard Duffy   Married: Mary Louise Bezner
Born: Dec. 7, 1926   May 31, 1963   Born: Jan. 13, 1928
                                         Daughter of John &
                                            Augusta Bezner

Children:	Born:
William J Duffy	
(Step-Son)	Jun. 28, 1953
Julie Dian	Feb 2, 1966

Family Record of
Otto and Lillian Goike Flusche

Otto Stephen Flusche Married: Lillian Goike
Born: Aug. 18, 1981 Jan. 11, 1916
In Westphalia, Iowa
Baptized: St Boniface
 Church
Died: Jan. 22, 1976
Son of Wilhelm & Augusta Flusche

Children:	Born:
Gertude	Dec. 7, 1916, in Lindsay
Hilda	May 9, 1918, in Lindsay
Norbert	Jun. 8, 1919, in Gainesville
Otto Stephen	Oct. 24, 1920, in Gainesville
Bernard	Nov. 21, 1925, in Gainesville
Kenneth	Nov. 28, 1930, in Gainesville
Terry William	Sep. 25, 1936, in Gainesville

Earl Kline Married: Gertrude Flusche
  Jul. 4, 1943 Born: Dec. 7, 1916
    Baptized: St Peter's
     Church Lindsay
    Daughter of Otto &
     Lindsay Flusche

Children:	Born:
Earlyne	Feb. 8, 1944

Joseph McCage Married: Earlyne Kline
  Nov. 30, 1963 Born: Feb. 8, 1944
    Duaghter of Earl
     Kline Gertrude

Children:	Born:
Joey	Oct. 28, 1964
Melisa	Dec. 4, 1965
Patrick	Sep. 2, 1968
Chris	Oct. 27, 1971

George Luttmer	Married: Aug. 18, 1937	Hilda Flusche Born: May 9, 1918 Daughter of Otto & Lillian Flusche

Children:	Born:
Barbara	1939

John C Sims	Married: Sep. 14, 1958	Barbara Luttmer Daughter of Hilda Flusche

Children:	Born:
John C Jr	Oct. 23, 1959
Joe	Jul. 8, 1961
Nancy	Oct. 31, 1963
Herry	Jul. 8, 1965

Norbert Flusche Born: Jun. 8, 1919 Son of Otto & Lillian Flusche	Married: Nov. 6, 1941	Wilma Swindle

Children:	Born:
Norbert Jr	Aug. 13, 1942
Linda	Apr. 20, 1945
Mary	Dec. 27, 1952
Louann	Aug. 9, 1955

Edward A Dill	Married: Jul. 6, 1968	Linda Flusche Born: Apr. 29, 1945 Daughter of Norbert & Wilma Flusche

Children:	Born:
Edward D	Aug. 10, 1969

Otto Stephen Jr. (O.S.)	Married:	Una Bill Wille
Born: Oct. 24m 1920	Mar. 31, 1951	
Son of Otto & Lillian		

Children:	Born:
Anthony	Apr. 28, 1952
Beverly	Jul. 28, 1853
Margaret	Dec. 9, 1954
Patricia	Nov. 29, 1961

Bernard Flusche	Married:	Marion Harrison
Born: Nov. 21, 1925	Oct. 10, 1954	
Son of Otto and Lillian		

Children:	Born:
Bernard Jr.	Sep. 30, 1955
Will	Jun. 8, 1958
Paul	Nov. 9, 1960

Kenneth Flusche	Married:	Ruby Whitworth
Born: Nov. 28, 1930	Sep. 28, 1951	
Son of Otto & Lillian		

Children:	Born:
Nancy	Dec. 22, 1952
Kenneth Wayne	Dec. 7, 1953
Sharon	Feb. 9, 1955
Mildred	May 14, 1956
Tarrance	Sep. 27, 1957
Joan	Sep. 17, 1958
Gregory	Dec. 4, 1960
Paul	Sep. 11, 1962

Terry Flusche (Johnny)	Maried:	Annette Everest
Born: Sep. 25, 1936	Jan. 8, 1964	
Son of Otto & Lillian		

Children:	Born:
Terry William Jr	Mar. 17, 1967
Adopted Children:	
Donna	Jul. 1, 1969
Terrie Lee	Dec. 6, 1962

Family Record of
Herman and Eleanor Schniederjan Flusche

Herman Joseph Flusche	Married:	Eleanore Helene Schniederjan
Born: Dec. 16, 1893	May 2, 1916	
Died: Nov. 23, 1941		
Son of Wilhelm & Augusta		

Children:	Born:	
Richard Herman	Feb. 17, 1917	Deceased
Julius Otto	May 25, 1918	Deceased
Robert Lee	Feb. 11, 1921	Deceased
James Max	Apr. 13, 1922	
Herman Joseph Jr	May 8, 1924	
Eleanor Louise	Mar. 30, 1927	

Richard Herman Flusche	Married:	Margie Herman
Born: Feb. 17, 1917	Dec. 26, 1938	
Son of Herman & Eleanora Flusche		

Children:	Born:
Susan Ann	

Larry Turner	Married:	Susan Ann Flusche
		Born:
		Daughter of Herman & Margie Flusche

Children:	Born:
Malissa Daniele	Feb. 6, 1969

Julius Otto Flusche	Married:	Imogene McGough
Born: May 25, 1918	Nov. 7, 1941	
Son of Herman & Eleanora Flusche		
Died in Action in WWII, Jan. 4, 1944		
Over Muenster, Germany		

Children:	Born:
Philip Anthony	Sep. 5, 1942
Frederick Otto	Feb. 12, 1944

Herman Joseph Jr	Married:	Maryjory Ruth Norris
Born: May 8, 1924	Jun. 26, 1943	
Son of Herman & Eleanora Flusche		

Children:	Born:
Dianne Gayle	

David Crawford	Married:	Dianne Gayle Flusche
		Daughter of Herman Joseph Jr & Maryjoy Ruth

Children:	Born:
Tammy Annette	Jul. 20, 1964

Leonard Zwinggi	Married:	Eleanor Louise Flusche
	Jul. 4, 1948	Born: Mar. 30, 1927
		Daugher of Herman & Eleanor Flusche

Children:	Born:	
John Russell	Sep. 5, 1957	Mar. 25, 1967 In Tractor accident
Mark Joseph	Feb. 3, 1961	1980 (Sand cave-in accident at Lake Texoma)

Philip Anthony Flusche   Married: Connie Jean Pine
Born: Sep. 5, 1942   Jun. 17, 1967
Son of Julius & Imogene
  Flusche

Children: Born:
Steven Philip   May 1968

Frederick Otto Flusche   Married: Marcia Mary Hightes
Born: Feb. 13, 1944   May 20, 1967
Son of Julius & Imogene
  Flusche

Children: Born:
Pamela Ann   Jul. 12, 1968

James Max Flusche   Married: Betty Lou Gilliland
Born: Apr. 13, 1922   Aug. 9, 1942
Son of Herman & Eleanora
  Flusche

Children: Born:
Carol Frances   Jun. 13, 1944
Jerry David   Oct. 8, 1945

Joseph Stroud   Married: Carol Frances Flusche
                                                 Born: Jun. 13, 1944
                                                 Daughter of James Max &
                                                   Betty Lou Flusche

Children: Born:
Miler Phedger
Joseph Jr

Family Record of
Henry J. and Elsie Flsuche Fuhrman

(Source: Coralee Fuhrman Pulte)
1416 W Hwy 82, Gainesville, TX 76240

Henry J. Furhman	Married:	Elsie Flusche
Born: Jan. 28, 1886	Mar. 29, 1921	Born: Oct. 22, 1894
At St. Joe, Iowa	at Lindsay Texas	at Lindsay, Texas
Dies: Apr. 6, 1976		Lives in Muenster, Texas
Buried: Muenster, Texas		

Children:

1. Elizabeth Mary (Elsie   Married: Gilbert Frank Endres
Born: Jan. 19, 1922   Jun. 29, 1949   May 14, 1913
Living in Muesnter, Texas 76252 - Budweiser Distributor.

Children: Born:
(1) Lou Ann   Married: David Spaeth
Born: Oct. 29, 1951 nov. 21, 1970   Mar. 5, 1950
Living in Gainesville, Texas

Children: Born:
[1]. George   Nov. 8, 1971
[2]. Brenda   Aug. 31, 1974
[3]. John David   Nov. 25, 1977

---

2. William John   Married: Katherine Eigel
Born: Mar. 10, 1924   Aug. 11, 1956   Born: Jun. 28, 1933
Living in Fort Worth, Texas   Kay is R.N and Adult
Electrical Engineer at   Religious Intructor
  General Dynamics

Children:
(1) Robert William   Single
Born: May 8, 1957
Ph.d in Psychology

(2) Christina Carolyn   Single
Born: Mar. 1, 1961
B.A. R.N. Lives in Denver, Colorado

(3) Katherine Marie   Single
Born: Oct. 30, 1963
Physics Student at UTA, Arlington, Texas

(4) Amy   Single
Born: Oct. 22, 1971
Student at Nolan, High, Forth Worth, Texas

---

3. Alvin Michael   Married: Ellen Grace Friske
Born: Feb. 3, 1927   Oct. 20, 1953   Oct. 26, 1934
                   Living in Muenster, Texas
President and Manager of   Office Manager of Muenster
  Muenster Telephone Corp.   Telephone Corp.

Children:
(1) Kent Michael   Married: Sammye Wibble
Born: Nov. 15, 1960   Jan/ 14, 1984   Born:
Living in Greenville, Texas

(2) Gene Henry   Mar. 27, 1964
Business Compuiter Student at NTSU, Denton, Texas

---

4. Coralee   Married: Robert J. Pulte
Born: Jan. 20, 1930   Oct. 18, 1951   Born: Jul. 20, 1920
Lives in Gainesville, Texas   Died: Mar. 14, 1983

Children:
(1) Michael Joseph   Single
Born: Sep. 12, 1952
Ph.d. Teaches Math at the Univeristy of Arkansas, Little Rock

(2) Christopher   Single
        Charles
Born: Dec. 3, 1953
M.A. Teaches English in Japan

(3) Don Edward   Married: Belinda Donald
Born: Apr. 2, 1956   Sep. 15, 1984   Born: Jun. 13, 1957

M.S. Sys. Ana. Works   Apartment Locator for
  General Dynamics   Realtor

(4) Steven Douglas   Single
Born: Aug. 9, 1960
M.E. Student at UTA Arlington, Texas

(5) Diane Marie   Single
Born: Apr. 29, 1966
Student at NTSU, Denton, Texas

---

5. Rosalee Ann   Married: Robert J. Bayer
Born: Jan. 20,1930   May 7, 1953   Born: Sep. 28, 1927
Living in Muenter, Texas   Died: Dec. 18, 1985

Serving out her husbands term as Commissioner of Precinct 4

Children:
(1) Carl Joseph   Married: Norma Jean Richardson
Born: Mar. 15, 1954   Apr. 24, 1983   Born: Aug. 2, 1960

Living in Muenster, Texas - Works for Valenite Co.

Children: Born:
[1] Robert Travus   Feb. 23, 1983
[2] Mark   Aug. 28, 1985

(2) Carolyn Ann   Married: Charlie Lawrence
Born: Aug. 29, 1966   Mar. 4, 1984   Born: Sep. 2, 1960
Living in Lindsay, Texas

(3) Dolores (Dolly)   Married: Harold Owens
Born: Aug. 10, 1956   Apr. 12, 1975   Born: Oct. 23, 1956
Living in Lindsay, Texas

Children: Born:
[1] Jeremy   Aug. 9, 1975

(4) Betty Lou   Married: Tim Cole
Born: Sep. 7, 1958   Jun. 30, 1978   Feb. 24, 1959
Living in Austin Texas. Tim is law student at UTA.

Children: Born:
[1] Wendy   Sep. 22, 1979

(5) Allen William   Married: Christie Yosten
Born: Sep. 21, 1960   Jul. 12, 1986   Born: May 26, 1967
Lives in Denton, Texas

(6) Henry Louis   Single
Born: Aug. 28, 1962
Lives in Denton, Texas

(7) Susan Marie   Single
Born: Apr. 2, 1965
Lives at home

6. Max Gerald Henry (Jerry) Married: Carolyn Brinker
Born: Dec. 11, 1934   Sep. 13, 1958   Born: Sep. 3, 1937
Lives in Houston, Texas. Jerry works for St. Joseph's Hospital

Children:
(1) Glen Allen   Single
Born: Sep. 23, 1959
M.S. Architecture. Lives in Houston, Texas.

(2) Elizabeth Blanche   Single
Born: Jan. 6, 1962
Lives in Houston, Texas

(3) Mark Christopher   Single
Born: Dec. 16, 1965
Lives in Houston, Texas

Family Record of
Max Paul and Beulah Flusche

Max Paul Flusche	Married:	Beulah Mae McKay
Born: Apr. 3, 1896	Jun. 25, 1918	Born: Sep. 17, 1899

Son of Wilhelm & Augusta Flusche
Died: Jun. 6, 1970

Children:	Born:
Max Paul Jr	Jul. 27, 1920
Harold William	Jan. 13, 1923
Donald Frederick	Feb. 21, 1928
Eugene Thomas	Jan. 29, 1935

Max Paul Jr	Married:	Dorothy Ann Hoch
Born: Jul. 27, 1920	Nov. 23, 1941	Born: Dec. 6, 1926

Son of Max Paul & Beulah

Children:	Born:
Max Paul III	Dec. 15, 1942
Mary Ann	Jul. 6, 1954

Harold William	Married:	Arlie Bell Kithens
Born: Jan. 13, 1923	May 14, 1943	Born: May 11, 1926

Son of Max Paul Sr and Beulah Flusche

Children:	Born:
Harold William Jr.	Sep. 30, 1945
Stephen Anthony	Mar. 27, 1947
Marcia Ann	Oct. 6, 1950
Nancy Louise	Dec. 3, 1952
Melinda Sue	Oct. 29, 1955
Jeff	About 1969

Harold Flusche Jr	Married:	Sherry Jeanette Anderson
Born: Sep. 30, 1945	Jun. 30, 1967	Born: Mar 10, 1948

Son of Harold & Arlie Flusche

Children:	Born:
Marcia Ann	

Michael Lewis Penwarden   Married: Marcia Ann Flusche
Born: Mar. 9, 1951   Aug. 1, 1969   Born: Oct. 6, 1950
                                       Daughter of Harold &
                                       Arlie Flusche

Children: Born:

Donald Frederick Flusch   Married: Jonnie Clyde Mullican
Born: Feb. 21, 1928   Feb. 25, 1950   Born: Mar. 30, 1930
Son of Max Paul & Beulah Flusche

Children: Born:
Donald Frederick Jr.   Mar. 27, 1951
Earl John   Aug. 8, 1955
Michael Edward   Aug. 29, 1961

Family Record of
Alex Anton and Emma Catherine Hundt Flusche

Alex Anton Flusche   Married: Emma Catherine Hundt
Born: Nov. 24, 1898   Feb. 23, 1925   Born: Apr. 7, 1900
In Lindsay   St Peters   in Lindsay
Son of Wilhelm & Augusta Flusche

Children: Born:
Dolores Augusta   Jan. 13, 1927 in Lindsay
Patricia Alice   May 22, 1929 in Lindsay
Jennette Elizabeth   Apr. 20, 1936 in Lindsay
Louise Ann   Sep. 7, 1940 in Corpus Christi

Henry Joseph Majefski   Married: Dolores Augusta
                                       Flusche
Born: Aug. 17, 1925   Jul. 23, 1954   Born: Jan. 13, 1927
                                       In Lindsay
                                       Daughter of Alex &
                                       Emma Flusche
Children: Born:
Carl Henry Majefski   Jun. 20, 1947

Chas Earl Bendfield   Jul. 13, 1947
Sharon Kay Bendfield   Dec. 12, 1949
Debra Lou Majefski   Aug. 22, 1955

Herman Mullinex   Married: Patricia Alice Flusche
Born: Oct. 5, 1926   Apr. 3, 1951   Born: May 22, 1929
In Van Alstyne, TX   in Lindsay
Died: 198?   Daughter of Alex &
                                                 Emma Flusche

Children: Born:
Monty Lee Mullinez   Dec. 16, 1960

Travis Hubert Mullinex   Married: Jeannette Elizabeth
                                                   Flusche
Born: Mar. 10, 1931   May 15, 1954   Born: Apr. 20, 1936
In Van Alstyne Tx   in Lindsay
                                                 Daughter of Alex &
                                                   Emma Flusche

Children: Born:
Charyl Ann   Nov. 6, 1955
William Larry   May 27, 1958

David Greely Hendrix   Married: Louise Ann Flusche
Born: Jun. 12, 1929   Jul. 15, 1959   Born: Sep. 7, 1940
                                                 Daughter of Alex &
                                                   Emma Flusche

Children: Born:
Nori Kay   Jul. 27, 1961
Sherri Lynn   Jun. 26, 1962

Family Record of
Hubert and Clara Flusche becker

Hubert Becker

Died: Cincinnati Ohio
  of Cancer
Buried: Dayton, Ohio

Married:
Jun. 5, 1923
St Peters

Clara Flusche
Born: Feb. 28, 1900
in Lindsay Texas

Daughter of Wilhelm &
  Augusta Flusche

Children: Born: Died:
Mildred Margaret   Mar. 28, 1924   Died: 197?
                   In St Joseph Iowa
Dorothy Augusta   Sep. 25, 1925

Richard Fette   Married: Mildred Margaret Becker
Born: Apr. 3, 1919   Capistrano Chapel   Born: Mar. 28, 1924
                       California

Killed in WWII   Daugther of Hubert &
                                               Clara Flusche

Frank P Swan   Married: Mildred Margaret Becker
                                               Fette
Born: Oct. 3, 1920   St John's   Born: Mar. 28, 1924
                       El Cerrito   Daughter of Hubert &
                       California   Clara Becker
                                             Died: 197?

Children: Born:
William Wallace   Jan. 5, 1946
Robert Clark   Mar. 8, 1948
Janine Clare   Mar. 20, 1953
Sherryl Ann   Mar. 20, 1955

Kenneth H Mitchell   Married: Dorothy Augusta Flusche
Born: Oct. 13, 1922   May 23, 1942   Born: Sep. 25, 1925
                       St Mary's
                       Gainesville
Died: 19??   Daughter of Hubert &
                                               Clara Flusche

```
Children:               Born:
Kenneth H Jr            Jan. 13, 1943


Baptized by Fr Brady, Sponsors Mildred Fette and Chas Mitchelle
```

```
Kenneth H Jr Mitchelle   Married:        Elaine Welch
Born: Jan. 13, 1943      Nov. 27, 1965   Born: Oct. 23, 1946
                                         in Hood Texas
Son of Kenneth Sr & Dorothy Mitchell

Children:               Born:
Charles
Marilyn
Kenneth Jr (Divorced)
```

```
Carl Gimple             Married:        Clara Flusche
Born: Aug. 24, 1901     1941            Born: Feb. 28, 1900
                                        Daughter of Wilhelm &
                                          Augusta Flusche
Died: Nov. 8, 1983                      Died: Aug. 27, 1984
No Children
```

PART III

Biography of Henry J. Fuhrman: Taped
Interviews and Stories

Maternal and Paternal Family Record of Henry J. Fuhrman

Henry's family picture, taken in 1919. Back row: Adolph, Henry, Cecilia, Val, Clara, Joseph, Theresa, Nick and Louis. Front row: Anna, Grandpa (John) and Grandma (Mary Ursula) Fuhrmann and Elizabeth.

Henry's favorite picture: San Francisco, 1906

Henry in his late twenties

For winter travel,
wheel-less wagon with horses

Henry's family home in St. Joe, Iowa

Family members in John Fuhrmann's barnyard

Thrashing on the farm in Iowa

INTRODUCTION TO BIOGRAPHY
OF HENRY J. FUHRMAN

Chronology of Events Henry refers
To in His interview by Jerry Fuhrman

1886, Born

1892, finished St. Joe School

1898, finished fourth grade, left school

1905, Mason City, Engine School

1912, Janitor

1912, Gales, Store

1909, Fargo, North Dakota

1913, Moosejaw, Canada

1913, Came to Galveston

Netherhill, Saskatchewan, 1/2 section

700 acres in Iowa

1915, Trip

1919, Canada

1921, Married

Life Before Marriage

Henry went to engineering school in Mason City at age of nineteen to learn to operate steam tractors, his first time to leave home. He also made some trips to Chicago to sell cattle. As the younger brothers grew up, he more or less started supporting himself and helped his dad by turning over his extra earnings. First he hunted hunted muskrats and sold hides. Then he walked to the church and started the fire in the early morning and did janitorial work. Next, he worked in Nick Gale's store: picked up cars at Livermore and drove them to St. Joe. He taught folks to drive after they bought a car: the women drivers scared him to death. Also, he delivered coffins which leads to his great story about getting drunk and the horses taking him home in a blizzard.

Then he worked on farms in North Dakota where his sisters settled. He broke up prairie at Moosejaw and Netherhill with oxen on his dad's homesteaded land (1/2 section). Made two trips to Galveston. In 1915, he decided to see the world. He went to depot in Bode, Iowa and he had the ticket agent to put an itinerary together for a cost of, I think, $34. He went through Yellowstone Park on horseback for several days (before roads and cars). I think the tape covers the rest.

Taped interview of Henry by his son Jerry in 1968

Jerry: What is your name?

Henry: Henry J. Fuhrman

Jerry: What does "J" stand for?

Henry: John

Jerry: Middle name John?

Henry: No. Because when I moved to Texas, there so many Henry Fuhrman here, I had to put the "J" in there to keep my bank account everything straight.

Jerry: Where were you born?

Henry: In St. Joe, Iowa

Jerry: What year?

Henry: 1886, January 28.

Jerry: What do you remember playing when you were a little boy?

Henry: O boy that's something! All kind of mischief. Climbin trees and stuff. Sliding down the hill by the cemetery there when I went to school. That's when I went to school, but before that, they took me along to town because if they left me at home, I would be climbing the tress, sheds etc.

Jerry: What kind of games did you play?

Henry: Oh, we played all kinds of games--that's when we got bigger.

Jerry: What was your favorite toy?

Henry: We got some toys, but I guess an air gun was the first thing I got.

Jerry: Did you use to have to milk cows when you were small?

Henry: Well, I was pretty young. My Dad never did milk (milk many). My mother milk them; then, when we got old enough, we children milked them. At first, we milked two or three, and after we got big, we milked ten-twelve.

Jerry: How big of a farm did you have?

Henry: 700 acres in all, I think. Two different places.

Jerry: You had that when you were a little boy already--that much land?

Henry: No not all. We just had 160-180 acres. After a while when Uncle Henry moved to Texas, then Dad brought that farm. Then when old man Schreiber died, we bought that farm. I think we had 730 acres all together there. But it was a lot of swamp and slew then.

Jerry: You had to lay tile on it and run canals?

Henry: (Evaded question) There was a lot of hunting. I know a lot of people would come out from Mason City in the fall and shoot ducks.

Jerry: When they (the ducks) migrated through there?

Henry: Yes. The muskrats. I bet there were hundreds of those muskrats who'd build houses out of that slough grass. The muskrats—we're hundreds in there--minks, and everything.

Jerry: Did you do much hunting?

Henry: Heck yeah! We didn't get no money from home and then Nick and Joe, they did the chores. I'd go hunting. I'd get up at four o'clock with the gun and go. Had traps setting. Then I went there. The minks and stuff that I got there; we'd divide the money. One morning, I took a spear from my hay-rack tooth, and had it straightened out by a blacksmith--real sharp. I speared, I think, eighty-two in less than two hours. I'd stick it through their houses, and get two in one (thrust) spear. I sold them for fifteen cents apiece without skinning. That one year, I think we earned eighty-six dollars for trapping. Then we divided with the other brothers because they did the chores. They had money that way though. Prairie chickens--ducks I was no good at getting--but Prairie chickens I could get them good. And jack rabbits. Shooting them.

Jerry: What kind of gun did you have then?

Henry: I had a repeater. Winchester repeater. With ducks, I never was no good with it. The prairie chickens, I could get them. Them ducks, (garbled here) had that more leisure, more competitive, sore slick way.

Jerry: When do you remember going to town the first time?

Henry: I guess I was six. Dad took us to the circus.

Jerry: In Algona?

Henry: Yeah. First time I went to a circus you know. Dad kept me on the arm. Lifted me up to see the (garbled) and stuff. I could write a whole history about--that time, they had it all thought out first you know.

Jerry: When is the first trip you took?

Henry: Well, I went to Chicago a couple of times. That time we kept twenty or twenty-one steers every winter; then, when they were fattened toward spring, then we shipped them to Chicago and I had a free ride. San Francisco world's fair. First, I went to Yellow Stone Park. I went through that-- took a week.

Jerry: How old were you then?

Henry: I guess I was twenty-four that time. I went down
        to Seattle, Puget sound, where they make the
        battle ships. I was in the submarine, the first
        submarines they made that time. Puget sound where
        they built the battle-ships. Seattle, then I down
        to Portland, Oregon, then San Francisco. Well,
        I went to Spokane, Washington, too where they
        grew those peaches and stuff. I stopped off—that
        agent was really good. He knew all the scenic
        points. Mount Glazier, I was on that before I got
        to San Francisco to the fair. (Since there is no
        Mount Glazier listed, daddy must be referring
        to Mount Rainier National Park: "Twenty-six
        glaciers originate in the perpetually ice-clad
        summit . . ") (In the Cascade Range of the state of
        Oregon . . .the Oregon Cascades rise to snowcapped
        peaks: Mt. Hood, . . .and Mt. Jefferson and Three
        Sisters. -- No Mount Glazier in Oregon.?) Then I
        went to San Diego. Bull fights, and prize fights,
        all kind of chicken fights—rooster fights--Tijuana.
        Then I went to Salt Lake City. From there, with
        the Mormon with the temple—every week they got a
        little trouble--went through the temple. They got
        a big monument with the sea gulls there. Years
        ago, grasshoppers got so bad in there, they ate
        the whole crop up. They prayed and prayed, All
        at once, the sea gulls came in by the millions.
        They would just eat and throw-up. They got rid of
        them (grasshoppers) by the sea gulls. That's the
        reason they put that big monument there. Let's
        see, where did I go from there.

Jerry: Went to Colorado?

Henry: Yeah, I went to Colorado. There Colorado Springs-
        -what is that national park? (Garden of the Gods)
        or (Rocky Mountain National Park?) where Pikes
        Peak is, you know. By Colorado Springs, and??
        (Sounds like William's) Cave there, and there were
        thousands of hair pins sticking there. Ladies'
        hair pins. Then, I asked them what that was for,
        and they said the ladies leave their hair pins
        so a man could pick it up; they were looking for
        a husband. I was at Pikes Peak, mushroom garden,
        what then was called William's cave, Indian
        reservation—Heck, where did I go from there then?

I think from there, I went to Kansas City and then home. Including that trip, I made four or five trips. I went twice around the coast. I went twice down to Galveston.

Jerry: That's when you met Mother when you came to Texas? How did you meet Mother?

Henry: First we met down there in Lindsay. Then after a while, we met in Milwaukee. Then, everything was off again until I was up in British Columbia. Then I told her that time we broke up, it was her turn; if she wanted to make-up again, she had to write first. I was way up in British Columbia, and she sent the letter home. She did not know where I was. We didn't correspond anymore. Then they had the letter laying there two or three weeks before they sent it to me, you know. Up in British Columbia, when I got it, then we corresponded. I told her, I met other girls, but I never could find nothing to suit me right. Then, I started on the way down (to Texas) and wrote her I was coming and I sent her a necklace and stuff and wrote her I was coming. When I got down half way between--what is that place yet in there where I had to change--right on the divide, (garbled--where the water goes on bottom this side??) Anyway, I had the fever. A nurse happened to be sitting by me. I told her. She first asks me if she could sit beside me. I had an overcoat on, I was cold--I told her I had fever and chills and I did not know what was wrong. She said she was a registered nurse and she gave me a prescription--some capsules. I think it was three capsules. Before I went to bed, I took one, and then one every hour. Then there was a bottle of mineral oil; I should take that when I first got up in the morning. Boy, when I took that, I slept like a cat that night. In the morning, I took that (mineral oil) --that cleaned me out. Boy, I felt like a spring chicken. Then I had to go to Los Angelos and change there. (Blisters) were breaking out all over me. Boy I was getting those. I went into the barber shop there. I told the barber that I had something breaking out on me: face, body, and all over. He looked at me, and said, "Heck, the barber shop there. I told the barber that I had something breaking out on me: face, body, and all over. He looked at me, and said, "Heck, that's nothing. I can cure that. I went into the barber chair and he shaved me. The massage pulled the skin off all those things, you know. Powdered me up, and I looked good. I felt good too. Boy, when I got to San Francisco, then I had to go to San Diego and change again and there they (the blisters) came out again. From San Diego, I went down to San Antonio. And boy I was so full of them things. Boy I rubbed on them. They'd burst. I asked the fellow what the heck it was; the conductor didn't seem to know what it was. All at once a fellow told me when you get to San Antonio, you buy some fish oil and sulphur. Mix that like butter. And before you go to bed, rub that all over. I busted then--some vere that long, sticking out. I done that. He said I had to do those two nights. Then I changed again in Dallas to come to Lindsay. Then, in Dallas, it did it again. Boy, I smeared it on again. There wasn't as many on there anymore. The next morning, I needed to shave, I got down there, I went into the barber shop.

Jerry: Now we're back in the pest house again.

Henry: Well, I got there. They put me in an apartment with the others. They all looked like they were old men. And face was shining and when they turned to the side of you, and changed the bed sheet, the sheet was all full of blood. All they did was give them a bed--no medicine. And then I got one of those nurses to write to Mama. And she just put on there that I was in the pest house and I had the small pox. That's all she put on. And there was three weeks. Fred Mosman, he called up from Lindsay, and asked about me. I told him I was alright and was feeling good and everything. They didn't have to worry. Then before I went out (garbled) went back to where I stayed overnight in hotels, They had to fumigate everything where I slept and where my clothes were. When I got home, went to Lindsay, and I went to her.

You want me to go back way up for K. C. initiation: Prince Rupert? They started a new lodge and had to get a bunch of members to go up there and to handle the crowd. I went up there. It was twelve hours on a steam boat. I pretty near went up to Alaska that time. That was far off you know. I went back again--that was a different trip though.

Jerry: What did you do in British Columbia?

Henry: First, I worked in a shingle mill where they make shingles, you know. Then after a while, I worked in a lumber mill where they make railroad ties—it was mostly railroad ties that time. Some of the trees, they had to cut lumber off, too, where the trees were too big, you know. Made switch ties (garbled—sounds like brick ties.) In on of the great big ones—I didn't work long in there. Beveled saws where they cut four or five, six inch deep trace, where they cut the boards off. One sawed off on top; just one a little ahead of another, I worked there a long time.

Jerry: What did you do in the saw mill?

Henry: In the shingle mill, I just split the logs. They couldn't take them where they saw the shingles off. They had to be small enough so they could handle them; they had to split them. First when I got there, I worked like a fool to get

Jerry: Did you split them by hand?

Henry: With sledge hammers and wedges. The wedges would kick out--one thing and another. Then had to put them under water too, that came from the lake. After a while, though, I could keep up. I went inside and watched how they sawed then shingles and how they packed them and everything. That man that saws the shingles has two saws. That block, they put that on a carriage that goes back and forth-- a lot of times-- it goes one way. One time, the big end is on the top, the next time, the big end is on the bottom. Then with the other hand, he had a little saw there; he had crack the widths (?). He had to handle two saws. Many lost their fingers in there. I don't remember--I used to know how much they cut a day. It was an awful lot they cut there.

Jerry: What did you do at the second mill? That mill where you cut railroad ties; What did you do there?

Henry: The railroad ties--I stacked them, you know. The railroad ties, I had to burn the slats. They had the carriage where the slats went. I had to take them off, you know. boards, they had cut different sizes of boards off. Some had to come on this conveyer, and some on that conveyer, you know. It kept me busy. Then, after you know it good--the slats were all afire; they kept on burning, you know.

Jerry: Where was that in British Columbia?

Henry: It was in Mission, Chilliwack. I worked for a dairy man. I milked cows, and he worked some land. He cleared off some land. It was all timbers, and they cleared off and right beside us, they cleared forty acres. At that time, it cost $3,000. an acre to clear it, you know. They blast them out with black powder. They dug holes under with their shovels and then put 100, sometimes 200 pounds of powder under. But they wouldn't let them go off except at certain times. In the evening. They just loaded all day. Then they had, what you call them engines--they had no wheels under them. They dragged them with the cable. They had cables, miles long. When they were blown out, split, they put the cables on there, and pull that thing out of there. Take them sometimes a quarter of a mile and then they'd pile them up so they could burn them, you know.

Jerry: You worked in Canada too, one time didn't you?

Henry: Yeah. One time, I—east of Moosejaw, I drove oxen there. For a French Canadian—four miles east of Moosejaw.

Jerry: What province is that?

Henry: It's Saskatchewan, There was where my Dad had a piece of land there in Saskatchewan, but not where I worked.

Jerry: How old were you when you worked up there?

Henry: I think I was twenty-seven then.

Jerry: Did you work there in the summer or all year long?

Henry: Well, I went up there in the mountains; it doesn' get much cold. In Moosejaw, I stayed there in the spring and summer. Ivan Waters, I knew them from Iowa, and they were in North Dakota, and they wrote me that they wanted me to help thrash there. I went there to help them cut their grain, and then, I went with an independent thrasher outfit. The crew I was with got those bumps and everything. (?) I went through that you know. When I got home, after the harvest was over and everything, Henry Faber, and my sister got married. I went home for the wedding. I sent $200. dollars home. Without it, I'd use it otherwise, you know. I sent $200. dollars to Dad, and when I got home, old man Faber said I made more money than Dad did on the farm.

Jerry: You went to Chicago to take a diesel course one time? Engine course?

Henry: That was long before all this here. That was in Mason City.

Jerry: How old were you when you took that?

Henry: I was about twenty. Maybe not twenty. Maybe nineteen.

Jerry: Where did you go to get there?

Henry: Livermore was the place, I think.

Jerry: What do you remember about your father?

Henry: Oh, he was a blacksmith. He always worked in the toolshop. He read quite a bit too. He use to have those old German papers. He was quite a politician. He read a lot. He sold horseshoes. He shelled I don't know how many ears of corn with a power sheller. And they had to shoe the horses you know, horseshoes, and blacksmith stuff--if something broke on the machine and stuff.

Jerry: How did your father come to Iowa?

Henry: His parents moved here. He was thirteen years old when they came. First, they moved to Keokuk, Iowa. Then after awhile, they came to St Joe, Kossuth County. Guysechen came from there too.

Jerry: What year did they come in.

Henry: I really don't know. He was thirteen years old. (John born, December 4, 1857. Would be 1870) He used to hed the cattle then for the neighbors. Then he lived in a sod house.

Jerry: In Germany, where did they come from?

Henry: My grandmother (Engert) was a Bayer, At that time, everybody had to go into the army when that old (certain age). At that age, my grandfather (Engert) didn't want to go into the army. Then, he skipped the country before he was old enough to be conscripted). They got married just before they went on the ship. He skipped the country. He skipped Germany. My Grandfather Engert side.

Jerry: They settled in Illinois?

Henry: Yeah, Wheaton, Illinois (thirty-five miles out of Chicago). Everybody had to go to the army in Germany when they got that old. They didn't want to; so they skipped the country.

Jerry: Did your mother see the Chicago fire?

Henry: Yeah, they were right close there. The railroad went through there land where that happened, you know. That time, the railroad boxes got so hot too. They started burning on the track. She saw quite a few of them. They even had to unload the cattle out of the car. Burned too fast. The cattle were running around there. I remember they telling me (that) they always went to Chicago to get something special. T think even for liquor. Anyway, they bought most of their groceries in Chicago. They took load of grain or stuff to Chicago, and then bought their there groceries. And going home, there always--robbers would always be on the road so much. One time, they had a sausage and held that out with a handkerchief over it you know: had the sausage sticking out and scared the robber away. That time, they know when the farmers came home from Chicago, that they had money. Were a lot of robberies about that time.

Jerry: What do you remember about your mother?

Henry: (Still on Chicago fire topic) She was there at the Chicago fire. I don't remember too much what she said. She was there, though. I don't know much more. You make two, three trips, you get mixed up. I went twice to west coast—three times when I came down to Lindsay.

Jerry: What do you remember about your mother at home?

Henry: Oh! She was a hardworking woman, I know that. She had twelve, thirteen kids. She'd go out and milk cows too yet when we were small. She always had a quarter of an acre of garden. She was a hard worker.

Jerry: That's about all we've got.

Stories Taken from a Taped Interview of Henry Fuhrman Shortly Before His Death by Alvin Fuhrman

How I Lost My Finger

We hauled prairie hay, some 75 tons a year. When prairie hay is dry you know. it is hard to haul, I don't know how that fork was made. It was out of steel, and it was about six feet wide when you had it out apart. When the hay was in the barn, we pulled on the little rope and tripped it; then they pulled it back out again. At this particular time, my sister, Anna, had a horse on the rope and she was leading it. We had a great big fork, (it was before we had slings.) We took a great big bite, and hay got on the pulley. It was right under the wagon and I tried to pull the hay out. (I can barely remember. I didn't go to school yet. I was only 5 or 6 years old). When I grabbed for the hay, I grabbed ahold of the rope and my hand was pulled into the pulley. It took my little finger off-- it was hanging by a thread. It hurt very much. The next finger was badly cut, and the leaders were cut. As you can see, I could never move it very much. The doctor wrapped it bent. If he had wrapped it straight. It would have stayed that way, it is better that it was slightly bent. The middle finger was also cut but not so bad. Years later after I was married, I would dream at night and wake up hollering, "Hold the horses," trying to get them to stop.

How We Used to Catch Muskrats

In the summer, Dad had about 10 or 12 acres of slough (swamp). The slough grass grew up so high-about 6 or 7 feet high. The muskrats would build houses in there out of that slough grass. Some of the houses were 3, 4 feet high and 5, 6 feet wide. The minks would also make holes to get in and hide themselves. The muskrats were about a foot to 16 inches long; the small ones vere a foot had web feet. They would go under the water all the time. I sold hundreds of them one winter. I only got 14 to 15 cents apiece because they were damaged. I had a long spear--it was really a tooth from a hay rake, straighten out with a weight on there; it had a sharp long point. I would run it right into the house. Sometimes, once in a while, I would have two of them. I would have to dig a hole to get them out. And another thing, if you missed them you could hear them spash in the water. You could see them swim and you could hit them right through the eyes. In the winter time, the water would be frozen and you would see them under the ice. They always had a place to go in there. I know our neighbor had a dog and when you took it along, by golly, if there was a mink around there, he had a different bark-always a different bark. Sometimes right out in the slough, he would smell them out while they were sitting in their nest under the ice or under the ground. He could smell them out through the ground. I don't know what the dog's name was.

British Columbia Wood Cutting

There were some big trees; some were two-and-a-half to three feet in diameter. We would cut them down and saw them into 14 feet lengths, put powder into them and strike a match to blow them apart. We had to do that a number of times to get them small enough to handle. I don't know what the man's name was who had a fiddle saw. It had a wire over the top and a saw on the bottom. It was real long, and was like a hand saw only real long--6 to 8 feet long. Then there was a lever on there to pull it up and push it down then, you fiddled. That's why you called it a fiddle saw. He could saw a log 3 feet in diameter. First we hauled the logs home and then cut them up on the place. But after while, he would pull up his machine down in the timber and we would saw them up right down there.

Then we put them on a sled box or wagon box and hauled them up like that and brought it home. (The fiddle saw was horse powered. He had two horses on it. They would go round and round and the saw would go forward and back.)

Breakin Sod With Oxen

My dad got a homestead in Canada. Some fellows from Livermore, Iowa, went there and took a homestead. Dad took a homestead too, and I thought I would go up there too once. It was too early yet for field work so I worked in town for a contractor for about a month. Then I worked for a farmer. I drove four oxen for about three months. I had to get up at four in the morning and hitch them to a plow called a gang plow. You would guide the oxen by hollering gee and haw--no lines or nothing. Their heads were tied together were horse collars but they were turned upside down. No lines, just gee and haw. The furrows were a half-mile long. When we came close to the house, they did not want to turn around to go back. I would have to whip and whip them to make them turn. That was breaking sod.

Daddy and the Undertaker

This Gales that I worked for in St Joe sold coffins. He sold a coffin for a child and I had to drive it up there on a Sunday afternoon. I used a one-seated buggy. It had a place for another seat on it, but when we'd haul a coffin, we'd put the coffins there. I drove this coffin to a place about eight miles northwest of the store where I worked. On the way back, I drove past Hed Lehman. There were three or four men talking outside by the barn on the southside so that the wind couldn't hit them. When I drove by them, they waved to me and I drove in there. I was cold, by dowzy! It was cold-about 30 degrees below zero. They had a whiskey bottle there and they coaxed me to drink from it. By golley! I could have drunk that like it was water. After awhile, I left there and drove about four miles back to St Joe. The horses knew the way home. Then the storekeeper came out and said; "Henry, what's the matter with you?" He took the horses and I went into the store--he told me to stay outside. It was warm by the stove, and then I started to vomit. Then, the storekeeper begged me to go outside. I stayed outside awhile. Later,

I went to bed upstairs over the store and slept; I stayed there overnight.

Church Janitor

I walked from our place more than one winter. I had to be down in St Joe to start the fire in the church at four o'clock in the morning. Most of the time, I stayed overnight at Pete Erpeldings from church (my sister and brother-in-law); they lived about a block or two from church. Then I'd start the fire in church. I was church janitor three or four years or more. I remember a couple of times, I had to fill up the lamps in church. At that time, we had lamps hanging-there was no electricity. There were eight lamps hanging on one string (chandelier). The priest cook helped me fill the lamp. She would stand on the ladder and use a pole to lower them down so I could put coal oil in them. I remember one time when I worked for Gales, there was forty hours devotion. When I came back from Livermore where we traded, it was getting dark in church. A lit candle was always kept on the St Joseph altar so people could see. When I came, I had to light the lamps in church from this candle and then carry the candle back to the St Joseph altar again.

FUHRMAN FAMILY RECORD

Maternal Grandparents Of Valentine VonEngert
and Barbara Koesser Engert (Hohenzoeller)

Valentine VonEngert	Married:	Barbara Koesser
Born: 1819	1835	Born: Aug. 9, 1830
Bavaria, Germany		Bayern (Bavaria), Germany
Died: Jan. 20, 1896		Died: Nov. 18, 1921

Children:
1. Maria Ursula
In Wheaton, Illinois
Died: Jul. 30, 1942
Buried: St. Joe, Iowa

Married
Nov. 27, 1883

John Fuhrmann
Born: Dec. 4, 1857

Died: Feb. 10, 1938

2. Barbara
Born: 1864

Married:
1896
Second Marriage
1905

A Mr. Glad

Jacob Fuhrmann
Born: 1865
In Germany

Died: Dec. 15, 1952
Buried: Assumption
  Cemetery
Chicago Heights. Illinois

Died: Jan. 15, 1954
Buried: Assumption
  Cemetery
Chicago Heights, Illinois

3. Nicholas
Born: Aug. 26, 1866

Nicholas was born
  at Windfield,
    Dupage Co.,
    Illinois

Died: Jan. 8, 1924   Nicholas died at
                              Mexicali,
                            Mexico. Buried:
                              St. Joe, Iowa.

4. Regina   Married: Jacob Fuhrmann
Born: 1868   (She was Jacob's
                            first wife.
Died: Dec. 20, 1904   (He married
                              Barbara
                            After Regina
                              died.)

Children:
(1) Loretta   Born: Dec. 1901
(2) Veronica

Two other children diead
  at birth.

5. Valentine   Married: Mary Lenerz
Born: 1870
Died: 1960
Buried: Fairbault,
  Minnesota

6. Elizabeth   Unmarried:
Born: 1872
Died of consumption

7. Anna Mary
Born: 1874
Died: 1896

Aunt Amanda said one was a nun. It would have to be Mary

   Elsie Flusche Fuhrmann said that Barbara was married
a year or so to her first husband. He was lowered into a
wall in which gas had accumulated, and he was dead when
he was pulled up. Then, Barbara married Jacob in a "*
Joseph's marriage."

About Nick Engert: Nick Engert was considered a lady's man when he was young. He had had a disappointing love affair in Iowa and went to live in California where he worked as a carpenter. Henry J.(Fuhrman) visited him in California when Henry traveled down the west coast on his way from British Columbia to Lindsay, Texas, for his marriage, Grandma Fuhrmann received a telegram that Nick died in a tavern across the border in Mexicali, Mexico. Nick had gone to the tavern over the week-end; someone had slipped something into his drink, and robbed him. (He was rolled.) Grandma Fuhrmann paid all the expenses for his funeral. She had his body shipped to Iowa and laid him out in the Fuhrmann house. Henry and Elsie Flushce Fuhrman went to his funeral when they lived in Iowa after their marriage. (1924)

Valentine Engert was born in 1819, and Barbara (sometimes Spelled Barbra) was born in 1830. Both were born in Bavaria, Germany. In 1861, (other information says 1860), they came to America with their children. The Engerts first lived in Chicago and were there at the time of the great Chicago fire in 1871. The flames could be seen from their home. Later the Engerts moved to a farm near Wheaton, Illinois, and farmed there until 1881 when they moved to St. Joe, on the west side of the present Highway 169. This place was known as the Hiram Howard home, which was used by stagecoaches as they traveled through. The horses were fed and also had a chance to rest. The house had many little rooms so the passengers also had a chance to rest before continuing on their journey. Later the house was moved into the grove to make room for a new residence. The house remained there until the 1930's when it was demolished. The Erpelding family can still remember playing in the various rooms when they were young.

After the death of Valentine Engert (1896), (Grandma) Engert and Elizabeth moved to a home between the Peyson house and Knott home. (St, Joseph's Centennial Book.)

PATERNAL FAMILY RECORD
OF
THE FUHRMANN FAMILY

Peter Fuhrmann was from Gameln, Germany. (No other information.)

(Grandfather of John Fuhrmann.)

Children: Born:
1. Peter   1823 In Gameln, Germany
2. Joseph   1833 In Gameln, Germany
3. Margaret Catherine Lived in Gameln, Germany, after her marriage
4. Anna Gerdruda   Lived in Landkern, Germany, after her marriage.

Family Record of
Peter and Anna Wilhelmy Fuhrmann

Peter Fuhrmann	Married:	Anna Maria Wilhelmy of Kaifenheim
of Gameln	Nov. 4, 1845	
Born: Oct. 18, 1823	in Kaifenheim	Born: May 24, 1821
Died: Dec. 4, 1883	lived in Gameln,	GerDied: Mar. 23, 1889

Peter and Anna Maria moved to Kaifenheim, Germany, April 1853. Came to America, and to Keokuk County in 1869.

Children:
1. Anton
Born: April 20, 1850 at Gameln, Germany
Died: May 11, 1869 at Baden, Keokuk County, Iowa, of pneumonia.

2. Joseph   Married   Catherine E. Stroebele
Born: Oct. 9, 1851   Jan. 19, 1875
At Gameln, Germany   at Gameln, Germany
Died: May 10, 1937   Buried: Livermore, Iowa
in Kossuth, County

3. Henry   Married: Anna Heiderscheidt
Born: May 20, 1853   Nov. 6, 1879
in Kaifenheim, Germany
Died: Sep. 23, 1934
Buried: Lindsay, Texas   Buried: Lindsay, Texas

4. Mathias
Born: Mar. 4, 1855
at Kaifenheim, Germany
Died: April 4, 1869
at Baden, Keokuk County, of pneumonia

5. John Joseph   Married: Anna M. Link
Born: May 31, 1865   Aug. 29, 1887   Lived at Iowa City, Iowa
Died: April 14, 1917

6. John   Married: Maria Ursula Engert
Born: Dec. 4, 1857   Nov. 27, 1883
at Kaifenheim, Germany   at St. Joe, Iowa
Died: Feb. 10, 1938
Buried: St. Joe, Iowa

LETTER OF JOSEPH FUHRMANN
TO ANTON FLUSCHE

Iowa City, January 30, 1935

Dear Tony Flusche and Family:

In answer to yours of the 27th, I will give you a short sketch of our family. The Furhmanns in the old country were very popular in at least six towns or villages. It seems that the town of Duenfuss was the head of all, as half of that town were Furhmanns. I traced many of the Fuhrmanns in other towns who came from this Duendfuss.

Our Grandfather, whose name was also Peter, came from there. He had married a girl in Gameln who had a house there and he settled and lived in Gameln, and raised four children, two sons and two daugthers. The sons were Peter and Joseph; the daugthers names were Margaret Catherine and Anna Gerdruda. When the girls married, the one in Gameln and the other in Landkern, the sons got the house. When our father got married to a girl in Kaifenheim, his brother Joseph was only about ten years old and both stayed in the house in Gameln about eight years. When I was about 1 1/2 years old, we moved to my mother's old home in Kaifenheim. I only remember one thing when we lived in Gameln and that is that Father's brother, Joseph, who was my Godfather, played a great deal with me and carried me round. Now in that old house in Gameln there was an open well, and a stairsteps to an upper room going right past the well. My Uncle Joseph, who was at that time about eighteen years old, had me on his arms, told me to look down into the well, and in fun said, "I throw you right in." When he swung me over the railing, I got so scared that I nearly went into fits. That is about the only thing I remember when I lived in Gameln. When we moved to Kaifenheim, brother Henry was born a short time after we got there. I also faintly remember mother's sister, who lived across the street, took me to her house that night.

Now why and when did we come to America and Iowa. Mother had a half-sister living then near Elyria, Ohio, and we also had some distant relations in Iowa. We had letters from them for several years and when father had to pay $1,300.00 security debt, he decided to go to America.

We came to Ohio about the first of May, 1868. After looking up our friends and relations there we went to Iowa and settled in Keokuk County at Daden, where we bought forty acres farm land, half Improved. As we had not work enough there, we worked out for other farmers; that is, four of us; Anton, myself, Henry and Mathias. John Jos. got a job in a store, and brother John made his frist Communion at Baden. All did well, but alas, the next spring, Anton and Mathias died of Pneumonia, Henry had Typhoid fever, and I froze both feet. Yes, it was a sorrowful time for us all. As my feet were so tender, I went to school (Public School) and the next year, the Priest begged me to teach in the Catholic School until he was able to get Sisters. John Jos. Worked in a drugstore in Sigourney and father sold the farm and moved to Kossuth County. He and mother went on the train and Henry and John went with the wagon while I stayed in Baden and J. J. in Sigourney. I went to help them harvest the first year they were there (63 years ago). Brother Hnery had to come with a lumber-wagon forty miles to Fort Dodge to get me (that was as far as there was a R.R.) Brother John was watching the cattle for the neighborhood.

Now a word about mother. Her name was Anna Maria Wilhelmy. Her father came from Hambuch where many by the name of Wilhelmy lived; he married a girl from Kaifenheim and had only two daughters. Mother's sister was my Godmother and her uncle (her father's brother) was brother Henry's Godfather. Her sister (Mother's) had six children, two sons and four daughters. She had married a young man from Duengenheim by the name of Schwall. She died when I was about five years old, and her husband died after we were in this county five or six years. Now all are in Eternity. Only the widow of the oldest son, Anton is living. She had been a classmate of brother Henry in school.

Best wishes to all,
Your old Uncle,
Joseph Fuhrmann

Family Record
of
John Fuhrmann

John Fuhrmann	Married:	Maria Ursula Engert
Born: Dec. 4, 1857	Nov. 27, 1883	Born: Feb. 14, 1862
Died: Feb. 10, 1938	St. Joe, Iowa	Died: July 30, 1942
Buried: St. Joe, Iowa		Buried: St. Joe, Iowa

Children:

1. Anna
Born: Sep. 24, 1884
Died: Oct. 9, 1974
Buried: St. Joe Iowa
Married: Jun. 4, 1907
Matthew Faber
St. Joe, Iowa

2. Henry
Born: Jan. 28, 1886
Died: Apr. 6, 1976
Buried: Muenster, Texas
Married: Mar. 21, 1921
Elsie Flusche
at Lindsay, Texas

3. Joseph
Born: May 24, 1887
Died: May 1, 1968
Buried: In Chicago
Married: Feb. 26, 1924
Elizabeth Ruf
at St. Joe, Iowa

4. Cecilia
Born: Oct. 19, 1888
Died: May 19, 1959
Buried: Cassellton, N. D.
Married: Oct. 19, 1909
Henry Faber
at St. Joe, Iowa

5. Nick
Died: Jan. 14, 1890
Died: Aug. 1951
Buried: Portland, Oregon
Married: Apr. 10, 1929
Adeline Hathaway

6. Theresa
Born: Jun. 13, 1891
Died: Apr. 15, 1964
Buried: St. Benedict, Iowa
Married: Jun. 3, 1913
John Thill
at St. Joe, Iowa

7. Val   Married: Minnie Bennett
                      Oct. 20, 1919   at Netherhill, Saskatchewan,
Died: Dec. 31, 1983   Canada.
Buried: Calgary, Canada

8. Elizabeth   Married: Peter Erpelding
Born: Aug. 19, 1894   Jun. 8, 1915   at St. Joe, Iowa
Died: Jun. 5, 1921
Buried: St. Joe, Iowa

9. Clara   Married: Charles Plathe
Born: May 26, 1896   Jan. 30, 1918   at St. Joe, Iowa
Died: Jun. 23, 1952
Buried: St. Joe, Iowa

10. Theodore
Born: Dec. 17, 1898
Died: Sep. 1899 (9 months)
Buried: St. Joe, Iowa

11. Louis   Married: Susan Thilges
Born: May 2, 1900   Nov. 26, 1931   at St. Joe, Iowa
Died: Mar. 18, 1963
Buried: In Algona

12. Edward
Born: Aug 26, 1901   He got convulsions when his teeth came
Died: 1914   and caused him to be retarted
Buried: St. Joe, Iowa

13. Adolph   Married: Amanda Kupper
Born: Nov. 2, 1904   Sep. 6, 1933   at Lindsay, Texas
Died: Feb 12, 1972
Buried: Muenster, Texas

Elsie Fuhrman remembers how Peter Fuhrmann died. When John and Mary Engert were planning to be married in November, 1883, (Great) Grandpa, Valentine Engert and (Great) Grandpa Peter Fuhrmann drove to Livermore, Iowa, to get the beer for the wedding. They sat on a spring seat on a wagon and when they hit a big dump, Grandpa (Peter) Fuhrmann fell backward off the wagon and broke his neck. He lived three days and died just before the wedding. Grandma, Anna Maria Fuhrmann, then made her home with Papa and Mama Fuhrmann.

(Biographical information from Adeline Erpelding Wagner)
1621 E. Lucas St., Algona, Iowa 50511

Both the Fuhrmanns and Engerts came to Iowa and settled in Kossuth County, there, John and Mary met and married November 27, 1883, at St. Joseph, and lived on the Fuhrmann farm for fifty years.

John was a prosperous farmer and accumulated many acres of land in the vicinity. This land remained in the family until the great depression and the late 1920's and early 1930's when many banks closed and much land was lost. The original Fuhrmann farm was saved and is still in the Family.

Mary was known for her work outside of the home in spite of her large family. Mary was a "midwife" in the area. The doctors had to travel by horses and buggy, and many times would have been too late for births, so the families called on Mary to come into their homes to help with the deliveries before the doctor arrived. Mary was also known for her handiwork. She mad many quilts and crocheted many bedspreads and dollies besides having a house full of plants and a yard full of flowers.

In 1934 the Fuhrmanns celebrated their Golden Wedding and retired into the Engert home in St. Joe, where they lived until John passed away on February 10, 1938, at the age of 81. Mary Passed away July 30, 1942, at the age of 74.

Family Record of
Anna Fuhrmann and Matt Faber

(Source: Arlene Faber Salz, 1990
E Lucas, Algona IA 50511)

Anna	Married:	Mathias Faber
Born: Sep. 24,1884	Jun. 4, 1907	Born: Apr. 18, 1879
At St Joe, Iowa	at St Joe, Iowa	
Died: Oct. 9, 1974	Died: Jan. 13, 1959	

Children:	Born:	Died:
1. Raymond	Aug. 30, 1908	Jun. 22, 1919
2. Alvina	Feb. 21, 1910	Jun. 22, 1919
3. Lydia	May 21, 1911	Jun. 22, 1919
4. Bernadine	Apr. 11, 1913	Jun. 22, 1919
5. Ernest	Jan. 23, 1915	Jun. 22, 1919
6. Leona	Nov. 18, 1918	Jun. 22, 1919

Anna and Matt's first six children died when the family home burned down June 22, 1919.

---

7. Joseph   Single
Born: Feb. 1, 1919

---

8. Raphael Faber	Married:	Mary Evelyn Bormann
Born: Mar. 4, 1921	Jun. 17, 1947	Dec. 6, 1925

Children:		
(1) Richard Roger	Nov.24, 1947	Verlaine Kay Boehm
Born: Oct. 6, 1948		Born: Jun. 16,1952

Children:	Born:
[1] Brent Richard	Dec. 5, 1975
[2] Kara	May 13, 1978
[3] Anna Elizabeth	Dec. 8, 1985

(2) Robert	Married:	
Born: Feb. 18,1950	Apr. 15, 1972	Divorced, 1984

Children:	Born:
[1] Brea	Jul. 21, 1977
[2] Seth	Mar. 26, 1980
[3] Reed	oct. 11, 1981

(3) Rodney	Married:	
Born:	Jun. 26, 1976	Dovorced 1984

Children:	Born:
[1] Heather	Jun. 3, 1975
[2] Nathaniel	Mar. 12, 1978
[3] Jerod	Oct. 5, 1981

(4) Kay Ann	Married:	Robert Sewell
Born:	Feb. 28, 1976	Born: Jul. 8, 1955

Children: Born:
[1] Lindsay   Jul. 22, 1977
[2] Megan   Apr. 24, 1980
[3] Matt   Jan. 23, 1983

(5) Randy	Married:	Diane Goodman
Born: Feb. 16, 1955	Aug. 13	Born: Jun. 24, 1957

Children: Born:
[1] Ryan   Dec. 16,1979
[2] Jennifer   Oct. 19, 1983

(6) Raymond   Single
Born: Mar. 4, 1956

(7) Mary Ann	Married:	Mike Bormann
Born: Mar. 3, 1958	Aug. 17, 1973	Born: Aug. 3, 1955

Children: Born:
[1] Andrew   May 26, 1981
[2] Charles   Nov. 12, 1983

(8) Julie Ann	Married:	Steve Bowman
Born: May 27, 1963	May 5, 1984	Born: Sep. 20, 1960

---

9. Mary Theresa	Married:	Rieneld Salz
Born: Oct. 6, 1922	Nov. 14, 1944	Born: Jul. 30, 1920

Children: Born:
(1) Juditch Ann   Married: Thomas Gorman II
Born: Apr. 16, 1946   Apr. 29, 1972   Born: Mar. 24, 1946

Children: Born:
[1] Tiffany
[2] Thomas III
[3] Katherine
[4] Another Child   Dec. 1, 1985

(2) Carole Marie   Married: Robert William
Born: Sep. 14, 1949   Apr. 29, 1972   Born: Aug. 1, 1943

  Children: Born:
    [1] Thomas Curtis   Oct. 23, 1974
    [2] Kimberly Marie   Dec. 12. 1977

(3) Larry Dean   Single
Born: Jan. 14, 1953

---

10. Herman   Single
Born: May 11, 1924

---

11. Florian   Married: Margaret Elenz
Born: Feb. 4, 1926   Jul. 14, 1960   Born: Nov. 24, 1938

Children: Born:
(1) Todd Michael   Dec. 21, 1967
(2) Amy Marie   Aug. 13, 1973

---

12. Arlene   Married: Clete Salz
Born: Nov. 6, 1928   Aug. 29, 1950   Born: Apr. 10, 1926

Children: Born:
(1) David Charles   Married: Donna Kellner
Born: Oct. 10, 1951   Mar. 2, 1974   Born: Mar. 18, 1955

  Children: Born:
    [1] Melissa Marie   July. 8, 1975
    [2] Tiffany Adelle   Aug. 14, 1976
    [3] Jeffrey Cletus   Jul. 3, 1978
    [4] Natalie Sue   Oct. 4, 1980

(2) Donald Matthew   Married: Leona Bert
Born: Oct. 14, 1952   Sep. 7, 1974   Born: Feb. 10, 1955

Children: Born:
    [1] Heather Ann   Jul. 3, 1975
    [2] Jeremy John   Dec. 19, 1976
    [3] Joshua Jacob   Oct. 1, 1979

(3) Dean Michael   Single
Born: Aug. 10, 1955

(4) Dennis George   Married: Sharon Briggs
Born: Sep. 25, 1958   Born: Jul. 27, 1961

  Children: Born:
    [1] Tora Christine   Sep. 8, 1982

(5) Dale Joseph Salz   Married: Kathy Ann Jameson
Born: Apr. 15, 1960   Apr. 24, 1982   Born: Dec. 7, 1961
Lives in Raleigh, N. Carolina

  Children: Born:
    [1] Justin William   Nov. 22, 1982

(6) Lori Ann   Single
Born: Dec. 5, 1963
Works in Des Moine, IA

Family Record of
Henry J. and Elsie Flsuche Fuhrman

(Source: Coralee Fuhrman Pulte)
1416 W Hwy 82, Gainesville, TX 76240

Henry J. Furhman   Married: Elsie Flusche
Born: Jan. 28, 1886   Mar. 29, 1921   Born: Oct. 22, 1894
At St. Joe, Iowa   at Lindsay Texas   at Lindsay, Texas
Dies: Apr. 6, 1976   Lives in Muenster, Texas
Buried: Muenster, Texas

Children:
1. Elizabeth Mary (Elsie   Married: Gilbert Frank Endres
Born: Jan. 19, 1922   Jun. 29, 1949   May 14, 1913
Living in Muesnter, Texas 76252 - Budweiser Distributor.

  Children: Born:
    (1) Lou Ann   Married: David Spaeth
    Born: Oct. 29, 1951 Nov. 21, 1970   Mar. 5, 1950
    Living in Gainesville, Texas

    Children: Born:
      [1]. George   Nov. 8, 1971
      [2]. Brenda   Aug. 31, 1974
      [3]. John David   Nov. 25, 1977

---

2. William John   Married: Katherine Eigel
Born: Mar. 10, 1924   Aug. 11, 1956   Born: Jun. 28, 1933
Living in Fort Worth, Texas   Kay is R.N and Adult
Electrical Engineer   Religious Intructor
at General Dynamics

  Children:
    (1) Robert William   Single
    Born: May 8, 1957
    Ph.d in Psychology

    (2) Christina Carolyn Single
    Born: Mar. 1, 1961
    B.A. R.N. Lives in Denver, Colorado

    (3) Katherine Marie   Single
    Born: Oct. 30, 1963
    Physics Student at UTA, Arlington, Texas

    (4) Amy   Single
    Born: Oct. 22, 1971
    Student at Nolan, High, Forth Worth, Texas

---

3. Alvin Michael   Married: Ellen Grace Friske
Born: Feb. 3, 1927   Oct. 20, 1953   Oct. 26, 1934
Living in Muenster, Texas
President and Manager   Office Manager of
  of Muenster Telephone   Muenster Telephone
  Corp.   Corp.

  Children:
    (1) Kent Michael   Married: Sammye Wibble
    Born: Nov. 15, 1960   Jan/ 14, 1984   Born:
    Living in Greenville, Texas

    (2) Gene Henry   Mar. 27, 1964
    Business Compuiter Student at NTSU, Denton, Texas

---

4. Coralee   Married: Robert J. Pulte
Born: Jan. 20, 1930   Oct. 18, 1951   Born: Jul. 20, 1920
Lives in Gainesville, Texas   Died: Mar. 14, 1983

  Children:
    (1) Michael Joseph   Single
    Born: Sep. 12, 1952
    Ph.d. Teaches Math at the Univeristy of Arkansas, Little Rock

    (2) Christopher   Single
      Charles
    Born: Dec. 3, 1953
    M.A. Teaches English in Japan

    (3) Don Edward   Married: Belinda Donald
    Born: Apr. 2, 1956   Sep. 15, 1984   Born: Jun. 13, 1957
    M.S. Sys. Ana. Works   Apartment Locator for
    General Dynamics   Realtor

    (4) Steven Douglas   Single
    Born: Aug. 9, 1960
    M.E. Student at UTA Arlington, Texas

    (5) Diane Marie   Single
    Born: Apr. 29, 1966
    Student at NTSU, Denton, Texas

5. Rosalee Ann   Married: Robert J. Bayer
Born: Jan. 20,1930   May 7, 1953   Born: Sep. 28, 1927
                                              Died: Dec. 18, 1985
Living in Muenter, Texas
Serving out her husband's term as Commissioner of Precinct 4

  Children:
  (1) Carl Joseph   Married: Norma Jean Richardson
   Born: Mar. 15, 1954   Apr. 24, 1983   Born: Aug. 2, 1960
   Living in Muenster, Texas – Works for Valenite Co.

   Children: Born:
    [1] Robert Travus   Feb. 23, 1983
    [2] Mark   Aug. 28, 1985

  (2) Carolyn Ann   Married: Charlie Lawrence
   Born: Aug. 29, 1966   Mar. 4, 1984   Born: Sep. 2, 1960
   Living in Lindsay, Texas

  (3) Dolores (Dolly)   Married: Harold Owens
   Born: Aug. 10, 1956   Apr. 12, 1975   Born: Oct. 23, 1956
   Living in Lindsay, Texas

   Children: Born:
    [1] Jeremy   Aug. 9, 1975

  (4) Betty Lou   Married: Tim Cole
   Born: Sep. 7, 1958   Jun. 30, 1978   Feb. 24, 1959
   Living in Austin Texas. Tim is law student at UTA.

   Children: Born:
    [1] Wendy   Sep. 22, 1979

  (5) Allen William   Married: Christie Yosten
   Born: Sep. 21, 1960   Jul. 12, 1986   Born: May 26, 1967
   Lives in Denton, Texas

  (6) Henry Louis   Single
   Born: Aug. 28, 1962
   Lives in Denton, Texas

(7) Susan Marie   Single
Born: Apr. 2, 1965
Lives at home

---

6. Max Gerald Henry (Jerry) Married: Carolyn Brinker
Born: Dec. 11, 1934   Sep. 13, 1958   Born: Sep. 3, 1937
Lives in Houston, Texas. Jerry works for St. Joseph's Hospital

Children:
(1) Glen Allen   Single
Born: Sep. 23, 1959
M.S. Architecture. Lives in Houston, Texas.

(2) Elizabeth Blanche Single
Born: Jan. 6, 1962
Lives in Houston, Texas

(3) Mark Christopher   Single
Born: Dec. 16, 1965
Lives in Houston, Texas

Family Record of
Joseph and Elizabeth Ruf Fuhrmann

Source: Dorothy Fuhrmann Berte. RR.1,
Box 191, Algona, IA 50511

Joseph Fuhrmann   Married: Elizabeth Ruf
Bron: May 24, 1887   Feb. 26, 1924   Born: Jul. 16, 1904
St. Joe, Iowa   Mertzalben, Germany
Died: May 1, 1968   Lives in Phoenix, AZ
Buried: St. Joseph's Cemetery, Chicago, Ill

Children:
1. Ervin Fuhrmann   Married: Mary Henry
Born: Feb. 2, 1925   Jul. 19, 1952   Born:
Address: 18601 Woolman Dr, Minnetonka, MN 55343

Children:

  (1) Joseph Daniel   Married: Cindy Keers
  Born: Sep. 24, 1953 Aug. 9, 1975 Born:

  Children: Born:
    [1] John   1977
    [2] Catherine   1979
    [3] Michael   1983

  (2) Kurt Gregory   Single
  Born: May 6, 1955

  (3) Francelle   Married: Francis Mora
  Born: Oct. 20, 1956 Jul. 31, 1982

  (4) Beth   Single
  Born: Oct. 6, 1964

  (5) Kathryn   Single
  Born: Mar. 1, 1969

---

2. Lilian   Married: Robert Schaub
Born: May 17, 1926 1947   Born:
  Children:
    (1) Larry
    Born: Sep. 10, 1950
    Died: Dec. 31, 1950

    (2) Gail   Single
    Born: Apr. 27, 1953

    (3) Janet   Married: Michael Hetts
    Born: Apr. 28, 1955 Jul. 4, 1981 Born:

    Children: Born:
      [1] Adam   1982

    (4) John   Single
    Born: Dec. 5, 1963

3. Dorothy   Married: Adam Berte
Born: May 14, 1928   Nov. 18, 1950   Born:

  Children:
    (1) Ronald   Married: Cheryl McDonnell
    Born: Dec. 7, 1957   Nov. 27,1975   Born:

    Children: Born:
      [1] Larry   1976
      [2] Michael   1983

    (2) Allen   Married: Connie Jenson
    Born: May 23, 1953   Jan. 15, 1983   Born:

    Children: Born:
      [1] Adam   1983

    (3) Larry
    Born: Jun. 26, 1957
    Died: Oct. 10, 1976

    (4) Bill   Single
    Born: Feb 12, 1962

---

4. Rita   Married: Edward Ellickson
Born: Mar. 26, 1932   Jun. 16, 1956   Born:
Died: Sep. 23, 1982

  Children:
    (1) Gregg   Single
    Born: Jul. 23, 1957

    (2) Donna   Single
    Born: Sep. 17, 1960

Family Record of
Cecilia Fuhrmann and Henry Faber

(Source: Dorothy Faber Kapaun. Box
432, Casselton, N. Dak. 58012)

Cecilia Regine	Married:	Henry Faber
Born: Oct. 19, 1988	Oct. 19, 1909	Born: Jun. 6, 1881
Died: May 19, 1959	at St. Joe, IA	Died: Dec. 4, 1962

Children:

1. Arthur
Born: Jul. 2, 1910
Died: Mar. 18, 1912

2. Eleanor Katherine	Married:	Virgil Dimmer
Born: Dec. 20, 1911	Jun. 25, 1935	Born: Dec. 1, 1911
	Divorced	Died: Feb. 3, 1974

Children:
  (1) JoAnne Cecilia
  Born: Nov. 25, 1936
  Died: Dec. 26, 1936

(2) Ronald Joseph	Married:	JoAnne Ferch
Born: May 11, 1938	Apr. 8, 1960	Born: Oct. 1, 1940

Children:	Born:
[1] Vicky Jo	Apr. 25, 1966
[2] Gregory Scott	Feb. 23, 1971
[3] Brian Daniel	Jul. 10, 1975

(3) Donald Joseph
Born: May 11, 1938
Died: May 15, 1938

(4) Raymond Joseph	Married:	Katherine Stennett
Born: Sep. 13, 1940	Oct. 7, 1961	Born:
	Divorced	

Children: Born:
  [1] Debbie Ann   Single
  Born: May 22, 1962

  [2] Steven Joseph   Married: Susan Gallant
  Born: Jul. 21, 1964 Dec. 29, 1984

  Children: Born:
    (1) Jonathan Joseph Jun. 28, 1985

  [3] Dennis Joseph   Single
  Born: Jan. 12, 1967

(4) Raymond   Married: Betty O'Roucke
Born: Sep. 13, 1940 Apr. 22, 1969
                     Divorced

Children: Born:
  [1] Amy Marie   Mar. 9, 1970

(5) Marlin Joseph   Married: Joy McCafer
Born: Mar. 16,1942   Jun. 4, 1967   Born: Aug. 20, 1945

Children: Born:
  [1] Erick Joseph   Apr. 7, 1969
  [2] Eilene   Apr. 30, 1971
  [3] Sean   Oct. 17, 1974

(6) Mary Dianne
Born: Feb. 13, 1947
Died: Apr. 9, 1948

(7) Eleanor
Born: Oct. 11. 1949
Died: Oct. 11, 1949

(8) Duane Joseph   Married: Catherine Gross
Born: Dec. 9, 1951   Aug. 5, 1978   Born: Jun. 19, 1956

Eleanor Katherine   Married: Theodore Fraase

Born: Dec. 20, 1911   Aug. 3, 1959   Born: Aug. 3, 1897
                                                   Died: May 18, 1971

3. Alfred John   Married: Dorothy Aldous
Born: Jan. 10, 1913   May 30, 1953   Born: Dec. 28, 1909
Died: Mar. 17, 1986

  Children:
    (1) Lawrence Paul   Married: Adrianne London
     Born: Jul. 20, 1954   Nov. 7, 1974   Born: Feb. 14, 1956

      Children: Born:
       [1] Anna Marie   Jan. 14, 1981
       [2] Theresa Renee   Nov. 21, 1984

4. Cyrilous Theodore   Married: Tracy Fischer
Born: Aug. 13, 1914   Feb. 14, 1938   Born: Mar. 14, 1918
Died: Sep. 6, 1968

  Children:
    (1) JoAnn   Married: Fred Anderson
     Born: Mar.15, 1939   Jun. 19, 1976   Born:
                            (Divorced)

    (2) Nancy   Married: John Sanders
     Born: Mar. 26, 1942   Aug. 1959

    (3) Roger   Single
     Born: Jul. 25, 1943

    (4) Carol   Married: Bill Stansell
     Born: Dec. 31, 1947   Nov. 2, 1976

---

5. Evelyn Elizabeth   Married: Edmund Heitkamp
Born: May 13, 1917   Feb. 6, 1945   Born: May 13, 1911

  Children:
    (1) William Gerard   Married: Alice Solberg
     Born: Oct. 1, 1945   Jul. 12, 1966   Born: Jul. 30, 1946

```
Children:              Born:
    [1] Audrey Denise  Jan. 4, 1970
    [2] Wendy Allen    Aug. 30, 1971

(2) Marlts Ann         Single
Born: Sep. 8, 1947

(3) Cecile Marie       Married:         William Satrom
Born: Sep. 26, 1949    Jul. 23, 1970    Born: Apr. 6, 1941

Children:              Born:
    [1] Kenneth Bradley Nov. 22, 1971
    [2] Michael Garret  Oct. 13, 1972

(4) Jane Marie         Married:         Charles Nelson
Born: Oct. 6, 1951     Dec. 13, 1971
                       Divorced
Children:              Born:
    [1] Jason Charles  Feb. 24, 1972
    [2] Sonia Jane     Jul. 14, 1974    Died: Apr. 1979

(4) Jane Marie         Married:         Tom Zundel
Born: Oct. 6, 1951     1985             Born: Feb. 15, 1950

(5) Linda Ann          Married:         Dwaine Luke
Born: Dec. 4, 1953     1982             Born: Nov. 19, 1946

Children:              Born:
    [1] Ryan Anthony   Jun. 10, 1983
    [2] Joey William   Dec. 3, 1985

(6) Bonnie Marie       Married:         Ted Sheweyen
Born: Nov. 16, 1958    Nov. 19, 1976    Born: Nov. 23, 1943

Children:              Born:
    [1] Michelle       Oct. 3, 1978
    [2] Matthew        May 3, 1980
    [3] Ted Jr.        Jun. 2, 1982
```

6. Edmund Joseph	Married:	Raquel Laverne
Born: Aug. 23, 1919	Jun. 30, 1960	Born: May. 27, 1921

---

7. Rita Theresia	Married:	Douglas Kemmer
Born: May 15, 1921	Oct. 30, 1945	Born: Jul. 21, 1920

Children:

(1) Renee Cecilia	Married:	Richard Alley
Born: Sep. 26, 1946	Jul. 11, 1970	Born: Sep. 20, 1946

Children: Born:
  [1] Marla Marie   Mar. 6, 1974
  [2] Rachel Theresia Feb. 18, 1976
  [3] Shannon Nicolle Oct. 20, 1979
  [4] Douglas Bruce   Oct. 4, 1982
  [5] Brandon Richard Jul. 12, 1985

(2) Cheryl Marie	Married:	Randolph Cannon
Born: Nov. 10, 1948	Dec. 28, 1971	Born: Jun. 16, 1946

Children: Born:
  [1] Stacey Kathleen Mar. 22, 1975
  [2] Renee Kristine   May. 15, 1976

(3) Ward Douglas   Single
Born: Jun. 27, 1954

---

8. Leander Joseph	Married:	Ida Kearns
Born: Jul. 15, 1923	Jun. 30, 1952	Born: Jan 21, 1923

Children:

(1) Mary Ann	Married:	Daniel J. Dwyer
Born: Nov. 21, 1953	Feb. 25, 1977	Born: Nov. 11, 1953

Children: Born:
  [1] Joseph   Aug. 21, 1980
  [2] David   Mar. 25, 1982

```
(2) Rosemarie          Married:          Illig
Born: Nov. 9, 1954     Divorced

Children:              Born:
   [1] Angela Marie    Aug. 11, 1975
   [2] Charlotte Marie Apr. 15, 1978
   [3] Rebecca Ann     Feb. 2, 1985

(3) Jane Margaret      Married:          Gerald Miller
Born: Nov. 20, 1955    Sep. 5, 1975      Born: May 26, 1955

(4) David Emmett       Single
Born: Apr. 11, 1957

(5) Marla Jeanne       Married:          Steven Whitaker
Born: Sep. 14, 1959    Jul. 11, 1982     Born: Jul. 4, 1955

Children:              Born:
   [1] Jeanie Michele  Dec. 18, 1984

(6) Daniel Lee         Married:          Brigit Miller
Born: Nov. 17, 1960    Feb. 19, 1983     Born: Oct. 8, 1961

Children:              Born:
   [1] Markus Kyle     Feb. 13, 1986

(7) Carla Rose         Married:          Schumacher
Born: Apr. 27, 1962

Children:              Born:
   [1]. Brittany Rose  Jul. 17, 1984

(8) Dennis Lee         Single
Born: Dec. 31, 1963

(9) Douglas Mark       Single
Born: Jul. 22, 1965
```

9. Dorothy Susan   Married: Kenneth Edward Kapaun
Born: Feb. 12, 1925   Oct. 19, 1949   Born: May 6, 1924

Children:
   (1) Keith Joseph   Married;   Sandra Walton
   Born: Sep. 6, 1950   Feb. 13, 1971   Born: Nov. 15, 1950

      Children: Born:
       [1] Christine Denise Dec. 18, 1971
       [2] Kimberlee Ann   Aug. 17, 1975
       [3] Kelly Teresa   Feb. 25, 1977

   (2) Deborah Ann   Married: Leslie Wang
   Born: Mar. 12, 1952   Feb. 17, 1973   Born: Mar. 9, 1950

      Children: Born:
       [1] Rachel Jean   Oct. 23, 1975
       [2] Valerie Ann   Jul. 11, 1978   Died: Jul. 11, 1878
       [3] Daniel Lawrence Dec. 11, 1979

   (3) Darlene Marie   Married: Allah Wang
   Born: Oct. 1, 1953   Feb. 11, 1972   Born: Jan. 26, 1952

      Children: Born:
       [1] Lisa Marie   Jun. 6, 1972
       [2] Ryan Allan   Jan. 18. 1978

   (4) Denise Christine Married: James Hager
   Born: Dec. 31, 1954   Aug. 3, 1974   Born: Dec. 27, 1948

      Children: Born:
       [1] Paul Matthew   Sep. 12, 1976
       [2] Eric James   Sep. 10, 1978

---

10. Francis Adolphus   Married: Nancy Murphy
Born: Mar. 9, 1926   Jul. 3, 1949   Born: Jun.30, 1930

Children:
   (1) Theonita Marie   Married: Christopher Ketchum

Born: May 18, 1950   Dec. 15, 1973   Born: Dec. 6, 1950

(2) Edmund Leander   Married: Debra Westerdoff
Born: Jul. 15, 1951   Divorced

(3) Kim Frances   Married: Dale Zwingelberg
Born: Jul. 28, 1952   Jun. 19, 1976   Jun. 7, 1854

Children: Born:
  [1] Joshua Aaron   Sep. 1, 1983

(4) Craig Henry   Married: Renee Valerius
Born: Oct. 8, 1953   Nov. 20, 1982   Born: Feb. 6

Children: Born:
  [1] Chad Valerius   Jan. 28, 1973
  [2] Amy Valerius   1977

(5) Blaine Lloyd
Born: Nov. 4, 1954

(6) Elton Sylvester   Married: Shereen Geska
Born: Mar. 3, 1956   Aug. 18, 1978   Born: Jan. 23, 1956

Children: Born:
  [1] Chelsa Sophia   May 7, 1985

(7) Cynthia Louise   Married: Jens Nevland
Born: Apr. 30, 1957   May 20, 1983   Born: Dec. 29, 1956

Children: Born:
  [1] Jennifer Fay   May 17, 1986

(8) Aaron Kelly   Married: Jody Allen
Born: Sep. 10, 1961   Oct. 29, 1983   Born: Jun. 16, 1961

Children: Born:
  [1] Nicholas Kelly   Nov. 8, 1984

---

11. Marie Theresa   Married: Leo Baumler
Born: Jan. 26, 1928   May 24, 1952   Born: Aug. 21, 1926

Children:
    (1) Joan Theresa   Married: Bruce Presonil
    Born: May 3, 1953   Jun. 21, 1975   Born: Apr. 20, 1947

    Children: Born:
      [1] Thomas Joseph   Apr. 10, 1979
      [2] Joshua David   Nov. 30, 1981
      [3] Sarah Marie   Oct. 14, 1985

    (2) Martha Mary   Married: Gary Sehn
    Born: Dec. 10, 1954   Aug. 30, 1975   Born: May 2, 1953

    Children: Born:
      [1] Kevin George   Aug. 13, 1982
      [2] Kelly Jean   Apr. 16, 1984

    (3) Beverly Ann   Married: Peter Iwen
    Born: Mar. 20, 1956   Sep. 2, 1977   Born: Nov. 12, 1954

    Children: Born:
      [1] Rebecca Marie   Jul. 19, 1979
      [2] Benjamin Peter Mar. 29, 1982
      [3] Andrew Charles Jan. 3, 1985

    (4) David Gerard   Single
    Born: Jul. 3, 1957

    (5) Eugene Michael   Married: Brenda Richtsmeier
    Born: Aug. 1, 1960   Apr. 26, 1985

    Children: Born:
      [1] Jacob Lawrence Sep. 21, 1985

    (6) Diane Cecile   Married: Kurt Ward
    Born: Jun. 22, 1960   Sep. 14, 1985

    (7) Shirley Jean   Married: Shane Gunderson
    Born: Apr. 6, 1963   Sep. 14, 1985

Family Record of
Nick and Adeline Hathaway Fuhrmann

Nick Fuhrmann	Married:	Adeline Hathaway
Jan. 14, 1890	Apr. 10, 1929	Born: Jun. 11, 1894
Died: Aug. 1951		Died:
Buried: Portland, Oregon		Buried: Portland, Oregon

Children:

1. John Nick   Single
Born: Sep. 9, 1930
Plays the violin. Delivers mail in Portland Oregon

Family Record of
Theresa Fuhrmann and John Till

Theresa Fuhrmann and John Till
(Source: Marcella Thill Garman. 917
E. Oak St. Algona, IA 50511)

Theresa Fuhrmann Thill	Married:	John Thill
Jun. 13, 1891	Jun. 3, 1913	Born: Jun. 3, 1886
at St. Joseph, Iowa	at St. Joseph's	in Luxemborg, Germany
Died: Apr. 15, 1964		Died: Feb. 12, 1966
St. Benedict Iowa		St. Benedict, Iowa

Children:

1. Marcella	Married:	Gerald Garman
Born: Mar. 13, 1914	Sep. 7, 1954	

Children:

(1) Theresa	Married:	Dan Crum
Born: Jul. 31, 1949	Aug. 1, 1970	

Theresa Hobere, daughter of Zita (Thill) and Richard Hoberer, went to
live with Marcella and Gerald in the fall of 1955, and started school,
1st grade at St. Cecilia's Agona.

Children:	Born:	
[1] Libby	Dec. 7, 1973	
[2] Kathleen	Jun. 29, 1976	
(2) Paul	Married:	Sally Becker
Born: Sep. 3, 1953	Jan. 12, 1974	
		Divorced: 1977

Paul German went to live with them June 10, 1961, and they adopted him.

(2) Paul	Married:	Valerie Barnes
Born: Sep. 3, 1953	Aug. 1, 1981	

Children:	Born:
[1] Jennifer	
(Valerie's daughter)	Jan. 26, 1977
[2] Stephanie	Sep. 11, 1980
[3] Michael	May 10, 1983

---

2. Caroline	Married:	Irwin Eischen
Born: Fab. 22, 1916	Sep. 12, 1945	
Died: Jul. 8, 1978		

Children:

(1) Glenn	Single
Born: Dec. 30, 1946	

(2) Janice	Married:	Terry Demory
Born: Jan. 3, 1948	Sep. 1, 1972	

Children:	Born:
[1] Jeremey	Jan. 18, 1973
[2] Melisa	May 16, 1979

(3) Sue	Single
Born: Dec. 16, 1948	

(4) David	Married:	Linda Wilson
Born: Jun. 29, 1950	Apr. 1971	
	Divorced	

```
Children:              Born:
   [1] Angela          Jun. 13, 1971
   [2] Tanya           Nov. 27, 1972

   (4) David           Married:         Debbie Haase
   Born: Jun. 29, 1950 Jun. 18, 1983

   (5) Gail            Single
   Born: Mar. 19, 1952

   (6) Nickie          Married:         Julie Wagner
   Born: Feb. 18, 1955 Oct. 13, 1973    Killed: Nov. 4, 1973

   (6) Nickie          Married:         Susie Bolick
   Born: Feb. 18, 1955 Feb. 24, 1979

   (7) Donna           Single
   Born: Jan. 19, 1959
```

```
3. Zita                Married:         Richard Hoberer
Born: May 23, 1917     Nov. 26, 1945
Died: Jan. 10, 1951

   Children:
   (1) Therese Ann
   Born: Jul. 31, 1949
   (Theresa was reared by Marcella and Gerald German)
```

```
4. Roman               Married:         Mairie Kellner
Born: Aug. 7, 1920     Mar. 5, 1946
at Burt, IA

   Children:
   (1) Mairie Elaine   Married:         Ronald Pulpuff
   Born: May 11, 1947  May 12, 1973

      Children:        Born:
         [1] Monika    Mar. 18, 1974
         [2] Kelly     May 11, 1976
```

```
(2) Timothy            Married:          Donna Heinen
Born: Jan. 18, 1949    Jan. 31, 1970

   Children:           Born:
     [1] Chris         Apr. 10, 1972
     [2] Mark          Nov. 25, 1970
     [3] Wendy         Feb. 4, 1982

   (3) Ramona          Married:          Dick Yaeger
Born: Apr. 6, 1951     Jun. 17, 1972     Born:
                                         Died:

   Children:           Born:
     [1] Aaron         Oct. 17, 1974
     [2] Sarah         Oct. 23, 1979
     (3) Ramano        Married:          Doug Hall
                       May 3, 1980
5. Bernice             Married:          Robert Mayer
Born: Mar. 14, 1922    Nov. 16, 1954

   Children:
   (1) Barbara         Single
   Born: Aug. 10, 1955

   (2) William         Married:          Deanna Weydert
   Born: Aug. 10, 1955 Oct. 9, 1976

   Children:           Born:
     [1] Andrea Sue    Oct. 6, 1978
     [2] Joseph        Apr. 16, 1981

   (3) Nancy           Married:          Steve Conley
   Born: Oct. 9, 1956

   Children:           Born:
     [1] Casandra      Mar. 1, 1984

   (4) John            Married:          Kate Henley
   Born: Dec. 2, 1959  Jul. 21, 1984
```

Children:	Born:	
[1] Sarah	Oct. 15, 1985	
(5) Jim	Married:	Kim Leobig
Born: May 1, 1960	Sep. 4, 1982	
(6) Julia	Single	
Born: Apr. 27, 1965		

---

6. Harold	Married:	Marcia Downs
Born: Apr. 11, 1926	Apr. 7, 1952	

Children:

(1) Jeffery	Married:	Arlis Rettig
Born: Jan. 17, 1954	Divorced	

Children:	Born:	
[1] Josh	Nov. 9, 1977	

(1) Jeffery	Married:	Sue Willey
Born: Jan. 17, 1954	May, 1980	

Children: Born:
(Adopted children of Sue)

[1] Lisa	Jan. 7, 1973
[2] Brad	Apr. 15, 1974
[3] Brian	Apr. 15, 1974

(2) Joady	Married:	Karen Housten
Born: Nov. 8, 1955	Feb. 19, 1985	

(3) Tracy	Married:	Mark Judge
Born: Apr. 5, 1962	Oct. 30, 1982	

Children:	Born:	
[1] Levy Joseph	Apr. 23, 1984	

(4) Todd	Single	
Born: Apr. 25, 1960		

(5) Jason   Single
Born: Feb. 8, 1966

(6) Erin   Single
Born: Oct. 18, 1969

---

7. Orville   Married: Gladys Ziemet
Born: Sep. 11, 1927   Sep. 23, 1952

Children:
(1) Ronald   Married: Paula Mayne
Born: Aug. 6, 1953   Aug. 6, 1977

Children: Born:
[1] Amber Lin   Nov. 22, 1979
[2] Noland   Aug. 1983
[3] Natalie   Aug. 1983

(2) Richard   Married: Julia Hobbs
Born: Apr. 10, 1955   Feb. 3, 1970

Children:
[1] Heather Lea
Born: Nov. 12, 1985

[2] Alicia Ann
Born: Jun. 27, 1985

[3] Craig   Married: Jackie Redding
Born: Nov. 1959   Jul. 27, 1985

[4] Debra
Born: Aug. 29, 1961

[5] Diane
Born: Aug. 21, 1967

---

8. Elvira   Married: John Kajewski
Born: Jul. 12, 1929   Jun. 6, 1950
Died: Aug. 7, 1978

  Children:
    (1) Michael   Married: Teresa Ann Waters
    Born: Feb. 4, 1951   Jul. 29, 1972

      Children: Born:
        [1] Jessica   Dec. 15, 1972
        [2] Chris   Aug. 7, 1974
        [3] Mathew   Apr. 24, 1979

    (2) Steve   Married: Diane Engleborts
    Born: Jul. 28, 1952 Jan. 28, 1978

      Children: Born:
        [1] Nathan   Dec. 13, 1978
        [2] Amie   Mar. 29, 1980
        [3] Angela   Sep. 4, 1981
        [4] Abby   Jul. 26, 1983
    (3) Tom   Single
    Born: Feb. 27, 1956
    Tom lives in Dallas, Texas

    (4) Jan   Married: Dennis Lane
    Born: May 10, 1960   Aug. 18, 1979

      Children: Born:
        [1] Anthony   May 16, 1980

    (5) Lisa   Single
    Born: Dec. 12, 1966
    Lisa is in college

Family Record of
Valentine and Minnie Bennett Fuhrmann

(Source: Elsie Wanjoe. 21 Rosery Pl.
Calgary, Alta, CA T2k IL3)

Val Fuhrmann	Married:	Minnie Bennett
Born: Oct. 30, 1892	Oct. 20, 1919	Born: Aug. 17, 1894
Algona, Iowa		England
Died: Dec. 31, 1983		Died: Oct. 26, 1964

Children:

1. Harold Raymond	Married:	Mary (Anne) Agnes Wilson
Born: Aug. 16, 1920	Mar. 20, 1947	Born: Sep. 11, 1920
Kindersby, Sask. CA		England

Children:

(1) Lynda Rae	Married:	James Crittall
Born: Aug. 27, 1948	Aug. 9, 1969	Born: May 16, 1944

Children:	Born:
[1] Kyle	Sep. 2, 1975
[2] Russel	Sep. 25, 1978

(2) Donald John	Married:	Susan Strutt
Born: Nov. 17, 1951	Jun. 15, 1974	Born: May 20, 1952

Children:	Born:
[1] Deborah	Feb. 28, 1978
[2] Leto	Nov. 12, 1981

(3) Valerie	Married:	Raymond Washilew
Born: Apr. 12, 1953	Aug. 14, 1976	Born: Nov. 1, 1949

Children:	Born:
[1] Michael	Oct. 19, 1980
[2] Greg	Dec. 29, 1982

2. John Louis   Married: Yvonne Kelly
Born: Aug 10, 1923   Oct. 30, 1952   Born: Nov. 24, 1918
Died: Oct. 11, 1974

  Children:
   (1) Marcheto
   Born: Jul. 13, 1854
   Died: Sep. 2, 1954

   (2) Glenys   Married: Randy Gety
   Born: Apr. 10, 1965 Feb. 24, 1979   Born: Nov. 24, 1954

  Children: Born:
   [1] Leona
   [2] Dianne (Leona and Dianne are true sisters, adopted)

---

3. Dorothy   Married: Donald Jeoman
Born: Aug. 1, 1926   Sep. 30, 1945   Born: Jun. 11, 1921
Live at Marion, Ohio

  Children:
   (1) Donald   Married: Merriel Feaver
   Born: Nov. 18, 1947 Jul. 12, 1969   Born: May 13, 1948
   Children: Born:
    [1] Jodie   Sep.16, 1973
    [2] Jennifer   Nov. 22, 1975
    [3] David   Oct. 13, 1980
    [4] Mathew   Oct. 13, 1980

   (2) Connie   Married: Michael Rouse
   Born: Feb. 2, 1952 Jul. 28, 1973

                                         Divorced

   (3) Cindy   Single
   Born: Jan. 1, 1956

(4) Robert Scott   Married: Lynda ???
Born: Jul. 27, 1957   ???

Children: Born:
  [1] A boy   ???
  [2] A girl   ???

---

4. Alvin
Born: Apr., 1925
Died: Feb. 1936

---

5. Lorne   Married: Lorraine McNamara
Born: Jul. 1, 1928   May 29, 1954
                         Divorced

 Children:
  (1) Kim   Married: Jane Bach
  Born: De. 9, 1954   Dep. 16, 1983

  (2) Gail   Married: Greg Fawley
  Born: Apr. 24, 1957   May 20, 1978

  Children   Born:
   [1] One Son

  (3) Darcy   Single
  Born: Jan. 30, 1959

  (4) Jay   Married: Kathy ???
  Born: May 7, 1960   Jun. 28, 1985

  (5) Bruce   Single
  Born: Jun. 26, 1962

  (6) Murray   Single
  Born: Nov. 18, 1965

---

6. Elsie   Married: Harry Wanjoe
Born: Aug. 28, 1932   Aug. 18 1955   Born: Jul. 8, 1934

Children:
(1) Lori Ann   Married: Leslie Szelei
    Born: Jun.7, 1958   Feb. 25, 1978
                        Divorced

Children: Born:
   [1] Steven   Aug. 18, 1978
   [2] Luanna   Mar. 14, 1981

(2) Robert Val   Single
    Born: Jul. 8, 1961

(3) Kelly (Son)
    Born: Aug. 7, 1966
    Died: Apr. 23, 1972

Family Record of
Elizabeth Fuhrmann and Peter Erpelding

(Source: Adeline Erpelding Eagner.
1961 E. Lucas, Algona, IA 50511)

Elizabeth, Fuhrmann   Married: Peter Erpelding
Aug. 19, 1894   Jun. 8, 1915   Born: Oct. 25, 1880
Died: Jun. 5, 1921   Died: Jun. 24, 1982

Children:
1. Emilia   Married: Leo Frideres
Born: Feb. 29, 1916   Sep. 28, 1937   Born: Feb. 13, 1911
                                             Died: Jun. 24, 1982

Children:
(1) Kenneth   Married: Betty Lensing
    Born: Aug. 16, 1939 Sep. 16, 1961

Children: Born:
   [1] Kurt   Jul. 5, 1962
   [2] Bradley   Mar. 28, 1977

```
      (2) LaDonna              Married:           David McCleish
      Born: Mar. 19, 1942      Feb. 10, 1964


      Children:
         [1] Debra             Apr. 21, 1965
         [2] Lynn              Jun. 1, 1966
         [3] Douglas           Jan. 15, 1970



2. Adeline                     Married:           Nicholas Wagner
Born: Mar. 21, 1918            Jun. 1, 1938       Born: Jul. 17, 1904
                                                  Died: Jul. 26, 1953


   Children:
      (1) Donald               Married:           Melody Hanson
      Born: May 1, 1939        Jul. 5, 1969


      Children:               Born:
         [1] Nicholas          Jun. 21, 1971
         [2] Shannon           Jul. 20, 1972
         [3] Micah             Mar. 10, 1977
         [3] Stoney James      Apr. 11, 1986


      (2) Betty                Married:           Paul Bode
      Born: Oct. 11, 1941      Aug. 31, 1968


      Children:               Born:
         [1] Craig             Aug. 24, 1969
         [2] Chris             Aug. 11, 1972
         [3] Andrew            May 15, 1976


      (3) Virgil               Single
      Born: Aug. 27, 1944


      (4) Sandra               Married:           David Walker
      Born: Oct. 24, 1952      Apr. 23, 1977
```

```
3. Albin Henry                 Married:           Cleo Schneberger
Born: Sep. 6, 1918             Jan. 6, 1945       Born: Oct. 31, 1920
                               Pampa, Texas
Address: 5402 E. McKellips Rd. #230. Mesa, AZ 85205
```

Children:
  (1) Ava Elizabeth   Married: Michael Larsen
  Born: Jan 26, 1946   Sep. 20, 1969   Born: Jan. 26, 1947
                   In St. Joseph, MN

  Children: Born:
    [1] Nels Peter   Mar. 26, 1970
    [2] Kjell Andrew   Sep. 15, 1975

  (2) Nicholas Peter   Married: Pamela Ervin
  Born: May 3, 1947   Oct. 18, 1969   Born: May 14, 1948
                   In Lebanon, Ind.

  Children: Born:
    [1] Elizabeth (Libby) Apr. 13, 1970
    [2] Robert   Oct. 24, 1974

  (3) Susan Rebecca   Married: Lee Weseman
  Born: Jan. 10, 1950   Jan. 10, 1970   Born: Mar. 18, 1946
                   In St. Joseph MN

  Children: Born:
    [1] Theresa   May 28, 1971
    [2] Peter   Apr. 1, 1973
    [3] Joshua   Oct. 9, 1976

  (4) Candice Catherine Married: Steven Oliger
  Born: Feb. 24, 1951   Oct. 9, 1976   Born: Nov. 7, 1952
                   In Indianapolis, Ind.

  Children: Born:
    [1] Angelique   May 7, 1978
    [2] Zachary   Jul. 2, 1982

  (5) Margaret Mary   Single
  Born: Jun. 5, 1953

  (6) Joseph Charles   Married: Patricia Quillin
  Born: Apr. 5, 1955   Jun. 24, 1983   Born: Nov. 15, 1959

```
Children:                Born:
  [1] Adam               Jul. 19, 1984
  [2] Mary Alice         Mar. 14, 1986

(7) Celeste Ann          Married:              Kenneth Seanger
Born: Dec. 20, 1956      Aug. 20, 1977         Born: Oct. 13, 1956
                         In St. Joseph, MN

Children:                Born:
  [1] Nicholas           Sep. 21, 1980
  [2] Lisa               Mar. 20, 1982

(8) Valdon Henry         Married:              Gina Artese
Born: Dec. 6, 1959       Aug. 13, 1984         Born: Jul. 3, 1963
                         In Denver, Colo.

(9) Ann Therese          Single
Born: ???
```

```
4. Clarence              Married:              Catherine Swirczynski
Born: Jan. 29, 1920      Jun. 11, 1946         Born: Nov. 5, 1921
Address: 2403 Balboa St., Colorado Springs, Colo. 80907

Children:
  (1) Linda              Married:              David Allegre
  Born: Jan. 1, 1948     Dec. 20, 1968         Born: Dec. 19, 1946

  Children:              Born:
    [1] David            Jun. 25, 1969
    [2] Johnathn Douglas May 28, 1977

  (2) Curtis             Single
  Born: Nov. 29, 1950

  (3) Diana              Married               Edward Plank
  Born: Aug. 1, 1953     Oct. 13, 1979

  (4) Larry              Married:              Katie Mircle
  Born: Apr. 11, 1957    Jul. 19, 1980
```

Children: Born:
    [1] Jacob   Apr. 23, 1980

(5) Robert   Married: Donita Ann Smith
Born: Dec. 23, 1959   Nov. 3, 1984

Family Record of
Clara Fuhrmann And Charles Plathe

Clara   Married: Charles Plathe
Born: May 26, 1896   Jan. 30, 1918   Born: 1893
Died: Jun. 23, 1952   Died: Jul. 7, 1967

Children:
1. Arthur   Married: Helen Youngwirth
Born: Nov. 1, 1918   Jul. 14, 1943

Arthur worked for 25 years at Snap-on-Tools at Algona, Iowa. He retired
in April, 1984. Address: Rt.1 Boc, 38 Wesley IA 50483

Children:
    (1) JoAnn   Married: Gary Leety
    Born: Aug. 9, 1944   Oct. 1970

    (2) LaDonna Jean   Married: Dave Pickard
    Born: Nov. 18, 1946   Nov. 12, 1971

    (3) Betty Joyce   Married: Mike Gipple
    Born: Jan. 5, 1948   Apr. 18, 1870

    Children: Born:
        [1] Julie   1970
        [2] Jamie   1974

    (4) Jerry Edward   Married: Jeanne Vokulskos
    Born: Jan 22, 1952   Sep. 24, 1971

- 230 -

```
Children:            Born:
  [1] Jerry Jr.      1972
  [2] Danny          1974

(5) James Arthur     Single
Born: Jul.19, 1952

(6) John Charles     Married:            Sheryl Engelbarts
Born: Dec. 30, 1954  Aug. 21, 1976

Children:            Born:
  [1] Laura          1982
  [2] Lisa           1985
  [3] Michael        1985 (Lisa and Michael are twins)

(7) Larry Les        Single
Born: Nov. 19, 1960
```

```
2. Vernon            Married:            Dorothy Mergen
Born: Cot. 22, 1919  Jan. 29, 1946

Children:            Born:
  (1) Marilyn        1946               Lives in Florida
  (2) Sharon         1948               Lives in Cedar Falls, IA
  (3) Ronald         1950
  (4) Dale           1954
  (5) Dennis         1955
```

```
3. Delmar            Married:            Loretta Fisch
Born: Feb. 14, 1921  Jan. 20, 1942
Died: 1981 or 1982

Children:
  (1) Richard        Married:           Cecilia Schiltg
  Born: Jul. 7, 1945                    From Bancroft, IA

  Children:          Born:
    [1] Kelli Lynn   1972
```

[2] Donald Lee   1973
[3] Brent Allen   1974
[4] Charles Ryan   1976
[5} Jeffry Scott   1982

Family Record of
Louis and Susie Fuhrmann

Louis	Married:	Susan Thilgee
Born: May 2, 1900	Nov. 26 1931	Born: 1898
Died: Mar. 18, 1963	Died: Sep. 10, 1984	

Family Record of
Adolph and Amanda Kupper Fuhrmann

Adolph	Married:	Amanda Kupper
Born: Nov. 2, 1904	Sep. 6, 1933	Born: Sep. 9, 1912
Died: Feb 13, 1972		in Lindsay, Texas
Buried: Muenster, Texas		Lives in Muenster, TX

Children:

1. Robert	Married:	Jolene Zimmerer
Born: Jun. 29, 1935	Jun. 2, 1962	Born: Aug. 19, 1943

Children:	Born:	
(1) Kelly	Jul. 13, 1964	
(2) Scott	Aug. 20, 1965	
(3) Stacy	Jan. 26, 1967	Died: Feb. 14, 1967
(4) Toby	Jul. 4, 1968	
(5) Jessica	Feb. 12, 1974	
(6) Zachary	Sep. 18, 1979	

---

2. Marjorie	Married:	Jeff Bass
Born: Mar. 29, 1944	Jun. 1, 1974	Born: Aug. 12, 1947

Children:	Born:
(1) Thomas	Mar. 22, 1978
(2) Megan	Mar. 26, 1980

---

3. Michael	Married:	Kathy Nolte
Born: Feb. 12, 1946	May 7, 1976	Mar. 16, 1953

Children:	Born:
(1) Brian	Oct. 2, 1977
(2) Travis	Oct. 13, 1980
(3) Simon	Feb. 2, 1983
(4) Rene	Aug. 24, 1984
(5) Jacob	Mar. 5, 1986

---

4. Ronald	Married:	Pat Felderhoff
Born: Aug. 22, 1947	Mar. 4, 1973	Born: Mar. 30, 1953

Children:	Born:
(1) Holly	Dec. 12, 1977

John and Mary Fuhrmann celebrated their Golden Wedding, Nov. 27, 1933

Descendants of John and Mary

59 Grandchildren: 63 including 2 infants that died.
Over 200 Great-Grandchildren
Over 200 Great-Great-Grandchildren
One Great-Great-Great Grandchild: Jonathan Joseph Dimmer, son of Steven and Susan Dimmer. Born June 22, 1985. Great-Grandson of Eleanor Faber Dimmer Fraase of Cecilia and Henry Faber family.

Adeline Erpelding Wagner bought the original, 120 acre John Fuhrmann farm. Her son, Don Wagner, lives in a new home built there after the old house was torn down, and he still farms the land. Thus through Providence, there is a continuity of John Fuhrmann heritage through their children and their land.

Peter's trip to Germany 1912

Peter returned to Germany the first part of 1912 for a visit. In April he was ready to return to the United States and he tried to book passage on a new luxury liner that was leaving England on April 12th. To his disappointment there was no more room on the ship and he has to wait for another. The name of the luxury liner he missed was the "Titanic".

Peter was so grateful that he was spared, that he vowed to help complete the new main altar in the church in Kaifenheim which had never been completed.

Today there are large statues behind doors which are normally closed over the altar. These doors are opened for all to see only on special occasions. Even today, when descendants of Peter Fuhrmann visits Kaifenheim, the doors are opened while they are visiting.

Peter built a new home of native limestone rock on Kampstrasse in Kaifenheim in the year 1866. He sold the house in 1868, not fully completed when he migrated to the United States. The house still stood in 1978 when Alvin and Gracie visited Kaifenheim. It was on the crowded, narrow, winding cobble-stone street fully completed, and had that inscription, PF '66, on the main street side. Today the house still stands but the owner plastered the outside of the house covering up Peter's inscription.

St Joseph Centennial Book – St Joseph Iowa

Valentine and Barbara Engert

Valentine Engert was born in Bavaria, Germany, 1834. He came to this country in 1861, He and Barbara were married in Chicago where they were living at the time of the Chicago fire. They then moved to a farm twenty-five miles northwest of Chicago until 1881 when they come to St. Joe.

They purchased the old Hiram Howard farm in Riverdale Twp., Sec. 35. They became the parents of seven children: Regina, Elizabeth, Val, Barbara, Mary Ursula, Nick, and Mary. Regina married Jacob Fuhrmann; Elizabeth remained single; Val married Mary Lenertz; Barbara married a Mr.

Glad, and later, after his death, Jacob Fuhrmann; Mary Ursula became Mrs. John Fuhrmann; Mary was born in 1874 and died in 1896 at the age 22; Nick was a traveler and was shot and killed in a clubhouse out west.

After Valentine's death, Barbara and her daughter Elizabeth moved to a home between the Peyson house and the Knott home.

The Peter Fuhrmann Family as Recorded in the Centennial Addition Saint Joseph Parish 1876 - 1976

Peter Fuhrmann

Peter Fuhrmann, born Oct 18, 1823, and his wife, Anna Maria Wilhelmy, born May 24, 1821, and their children came from Germany to America and to Keokuk County in 1869. In 1872 they headed northwest by covered wagon drawn by oxen. Somewhere between Sigourney and Wilmar, Iowa, two of the Fuhrmann sons and another child became ill and died. They were buried in the corner of a field, and, as of 25 years ago, the graves had been preserved. (Sylvester Fuhrmann and his daughter Yvonne visited these graves.) The family continued on their journey and came to southern Kossuth where they lived in a sod hut and took whatever work they could find, herding cattle, etc., until they started to farm.

Their children were: John Joseph, Henry, Joseph John, and John.

John Joseph and his wife lived in Iowa City. They were instrumental in the organization of St. Mary's Parish there, and they had a family of eleven children, two of whom became nuns.

Henry and his family lived in Texas. There were thirteen children, one of whom, Paul, became Father Joseph Fuhrmann.

Joseph John married Anna Link. He was an assistant pharmacist at West Bend for a time and later chief pharmacist at Livermore and also a farmer. He purchased two farms near Livermore, one for each of his sons, John and Sylvester.

John married Mary Ursula Engert.

Peter passed away on December 4, 1883, and Anna on March 23, 1889.

The Marriage of Papa and Mama Fuhrmann

When John (Papa) and Ursula Mary (Mama) Engert Fuhrmann were planning to be married in November, 1883, Great-Grandpa Valentine Engert and Great-Grandpa Peter Fuhrmann drove to Livermore, Iowa, to get the beer for the wedding. They sat on a spring seat on a wagon and when they hit a big bump, Grandpa Fuhrmann fell backward off the wagon and broke his neck. He lived three days and died just before the wedding. Great-Grandma Fuhrmann then made her home with Papa and Mama Fuhrmann. (Recollection of Elsie Fuhrman of Muenster, Texas)

John Fuhrmann Family

John, the son of Peter and Anna Maria Wilhelmy Fuhrmann, was born November 4, 1857, in Germany, and came to America with his parents when eleven years old. The family came to the St. Joe area in 1872 and on Nov 27, 1883, he and Mary Ursula Engert were married in St. Joseph's Church. Mary was born Feb 14, 1868, a daughter of Valentine and Barbara Engert. Their children were: Anna, Mrs Matt Faber; Henry married Elsie Flusche of Lindsay Texas. They lived on the Fuhrmann farm in Sec. 28, Riverdale Township (Twp). (The present Ed Bormann farm) for several years before moving to Texas; Joseph married Elizabeth Ruf and also lived on the same farm before moving to Chicago, Illinois; Cecelia married Henry Faber, lived on the farm and later moved to Casselton, North Dakota; Nick married Adeline Hathaway and they made their home at Portland, Oregon; Theresa married John Thill; Elizabeth married Peter Erpelding; Theodore died in infancy; Val moved to Canada while single and married a girl from there and they have made their home at Saskatchewan and Calgary, Canada; Clara married Charles Plathe; Louis married Susan Thilges, daughter of John Peter and Anna Mary Erpelding Thilges; Edward died at the age of twelve; Adolph married Amanda Kupper, they lived on the farm in Sec. 27, Riverdale (presently Don Wagner) until they moved to Texas in 1946.

The John Fuhrmanns celebrated their golden wedding Nov. 27, 1933. John passed away Feb. 10, 1938 and Mary on July 30, 1942. Mary served as a midwife for a number of families in the area.

Mrs. Matt (Anna Fuhrmann) Faber

Matt Faber was born in the St. Joe Area in 1879 to George and Elizabeth Hauser Faber. His wife, Anna, a daughter of John and Mary Ursula Fuhrmann, was born in 1884. They were married in 1907 in a double wedding ceremony with John Frideres and Kate Faber.

Nov. 1, 1907: "John Fuhrmann and George Faber of St. Joe have purchased the old Joe Schreiber half-section farm, just west of St. Joe, Mr. Fuhrmann taking the quarter adjoining him, and Mr. Faber the balance." It was on this farm in Riverdale Twp., Sec. 33 (The George Faber quarter) that Matt and Anna Faber moved after their marriage and lived all of their lives.

Tragedy struck the Matt Faber family on Corpus Christi Sunday, June 21, 1919. Seven children had been born to them. Many of the members of the parish at the time tell how beautifully the children were dressed for the procession that morning. That evening the parents heard one of the children wanting a drink of water. When Anna reached the stairway, it was filled with smoke and was a fire.

Herb Roethler, the hired man, jumped out the upstairs window, and he and Matt hunted for a ladder. By the time they found one and had it up to the window, the interior of the house collapsed. The screams of the children stopped, one by one, until none could be heard. Those who perished in the fire were Raymond, Alvina, Lydia, Bernadine, Ernest and Leona. This was the first night that Leona had slept upstairs with the other children as they had coaxed their parents to allow her to sleep with them. Joseph, the baby, slept downstairs and was the only one of the children to survive the fire. Anna's agonizing cries could be heard throughout the neighborhood, and she had to be held back or she would have tried to enter the burning house, even though she knew the children had already died.

A new hoghouse was being built on the Faber farm and many times the children would climb to the roof top and sing. On this particular Sunday, Lydia climbed to the roof, and with a stick in hand, was directing the others in singing a song they had learned at school. Part of the song was: "I want to be an angel and with the angels sing, a crown on top my head, a sceptor in my hand." Her voice could be heard above that of the others, and her mother said that when hearing them sing she had silently hoped they would all be angels some day. Little did she realize that on that very night her thought would become a reality. Feeling there was more of their remains here than on the cemetery, Anna planted a flower garden where the house formerly stood, This flower bed is still being maintained.

A picture of the six children had been taken shortly before their deaths. Joseph wasn't along for the picture-taking as he a small baby and it was late in the afternoon; Anna felt she didn't have time to get him dressed for the occasion. The photographer was more than a little perturbed to think that they would bring six children in for picture-taking so late in the afternoon, so he took but one picture. Luckily, it turned out fine. It had not yet been developed at the time of the fire.

Mrs. Faber later had a dream or vision in which her children came from heaven to get her; that she might go back to heaven with them as she was so bereaved by their deaths. However, as she neared heaven, she looked back and saw her husband, Matt, and Joseph still on earth without her. Realizing she was more needed on earth than in heaven, she asked to be returned to her husband and son. From this time, she was able to accept the tragedy and had a great faith until her dying day. Probably no one read their Bible more than Anna.

Five additional children were born to Matt and Anna: Raphael; Herman; Mary, (Mrs. Reineld Salz), Florian, and Arlene, (Mrs. Clete Salz). Joseph and Herman are both single and reside on the family farm.

Matt and Anna celebrated their Golden Wedding in 1957. Matt died Jan. 13, 1959, and Anna passed away Oct. 9, 1974.

Henry Fuhrman

Henry Fuhrman, son of John and Mary Ursula Engert Fuhrmann, married Elsie Flushche, whose home was Lindsay, Texas.

Henry and Elsie lived on the parental John Fuhrmann farm in Sec. 28. Riverdale Twp. for a few years after their marriage. Elsie Mae was born in Iowa, and five additional children were born to them after they moved to Texas.

Henry passed away in April 1976 at age 90. Elsie, his wife lives in Muenster Texas.

Joseph Fuhrmann

Joseph Fuhrmann was born to John and Mary Engert Fuhrmann on May 24, 1887, on the family farm northwest of St. Joe. Elizabeth Ruf was born in Mertzalben, Germany to John and Kathern Heim Ruf in 1906. She came to the USA Feb. 3, 1923, with her sister Agatha, who was then married to Carl Emanuel. (They lived and worked in the St. Joe area before moving to Chicago.) Elizabeth worked for the John Fuhrmann family until she married Joseph, one of the sons, on Feb 26, 1924.

Joe and Elizabeth moved to the farm in Sec. 28, Riverdale Twp., now owned by Ed. Bormann. Here their four children, Ervin, Lillian, Dorothy, and Rita were born. Rita was only six months old when they lost their farm during the depression in 1932 and they moved to Chicago. Joe worked at various jobs until he joined the Janitors Union. They bought a six flat apartment building and Elizabeth took care of this.

Joe retired in 1958 as he was afflicted with arthritis of the spine. Joe passed away May 1, 1968, and is buried in St. Joseph Cemetery, Chicago. After Joe's death, Elizabeth sold the apartment building. She moved to Phoeniz, Arizona, in 1973, where she is now residing. She continues to raise flowers and garden vegetables and is active in church and neighborhood activity.

Ervin graduated from the University at Boulder, Colo., with a degree in engineering. In 1953 he married Mary Henry of Denver and they have five children. Ervin is employed by Phillips Oil Co., and and Mary and is now working on a project in the North Sea. Ervin and Mary and the younger children are living in Stravanger, Norway.

Previous to her marriage to Robert Schaub in 1947, Lillian worked for Borden Milk Co. in Chicago. She and Bob operated a school lunch business until 1974. Both are now employed at the Harris Trust and Savings Bank in Chicago.

Dorothy married Adam Berte. In 1956 Rita, married Edward Ellickson. They have two children, Gregg and Dona.

John Thill & Theresa Fuhrmann

John Thill was born Jun 3, 1886. On June 3, 1913, he married Theresa Fuhrmann who was born Jun 13, 1891, at St. Joe. They spent the first five years of their married life on a farm southeast of St. Joe in Delana Twp., Humboldt County, later moving to a farm in Sec. 4, Riverdale Twp., Kossuth Co. (presently occupied by Delano Grimm family), and still later to St. Benedict area.

John and Theresa were the parents of eight children.

Zita, born May 23, 1917, at St. Joe, married Richard Hoberer, Nov. 26, 1945, and died Jan 10, 1951. They had one child.

Marcella, born Mar 13, 1914, at St. Joe, married Gerald Garman, Sep 7, 1954. They have two children.

Caroline, born Feb. 22, 1916, at St. Joe, married Irvin Eischen, Sep 12, 1945. They are the parents of eight children.

Roman, born Aug 7, 1920, at Burt, Iowa, married Marie Kellner, Mar 5, 1946. They have three children.

Bernice, born Mar 14, 1922, at Whittemore, married Bob Mayer, Nov 16, 1954, and are parents of six children.

Harold, born Apr 11, 1926, at Whittemore, married Marcia Downs, Apr 7, 1953. They have six children.

Orville, born Sep 11, 1927, at Whittemore, married Gladys Zeimet, Sep 23, 1952. They are the parents of five children.

Elvera, born Jul 12, 1952, at Whittemore, married John Kajewski, Jun 6, 1950. They are the parents of five children.

Theresa was crippled by arthritis for many years before her death on April 15, 1964. John died Feb. 12, 1966

Charles Plathe and Clara Fuhrmann

Charles Plathe, son of Joseph and Catherine Lucas Plathe, and Clara Fuhrmann, daughter of John and Mary Engert Fuhrmann, were married in 1918. They moved to a farm northwest of St. Joe in Section 29, Riverdale Twp., that they purchased.

They became the parents of three sons; Arthur, Vernon and Delmar.

Arthur married Helen Youngwirth. After living at St. Joe for several years, they moved to a farm near Wesley. They have a family of seven children.

Vernon married Dorothy Mergen and they farm near LuVerne. They have a family of five.

Delmar married Loretta Fisch. They live on the home place and have one son. Charles Plathe, was elected County

Supervisor for District No. 1 in 1958 and served until his death.

Charles was born in 1893 near St. Joe and died Jul 7, 1967. Clara was born May 26, 1896 and died Jun 23, 1952.

Louis and Susie Fuhrmann

Louis, son of John and Mary Engert Fuhrmann, was born in May 2, 1900. On Nov. 26, 1931, he married Susan Thilges, daughter of John P and Anna Mary Thilges.

Louie and Susie spent the first few years of their married life on the John Fuhrmann home place (now Don Wagner) Sec. 27, Riverdale Twp. They then moved to the Fuhrmann farm in Sec. 28, 1963. Susie continues to reside in Algona.

Adolph Fuhrmann

Adolph Fuhrmann, son of John and Mary Ursula Engert Fuhrmann, married Amanda Kupper of Linsay, Texas, in 1933. They lived on the Fuhrmann farm in Sec. 27, Riverdale Twp. (now Don Wagner home) until 1945, when they moved to Texas.

Two of their children, Bob and Marjorie, were born while they lived in Iowa. After moving to Texas, two more children, Mike and Ronnie were born.

Adolph passed away in 1972. Amanda is employed in Gainesville, Texas.

PART IV

Synopsis of Flusche Brother's Enterprises;
Translations and Writings of Emil Flusche;
Translated Poems of the Flusche, Steinmetz Family

Flusche Brothers as German, Catholic
Colonizers in America:

Historical Data, Personal Journal
Translations and Perspectives

INTRODUCTION TO THE FLUSCHE BROTHER'S ACTIVITIES IN AMERICA

The seven Catholic German Colonies founded by the Flusche Brothers are:

> Westphalia, Iowa, in 1872
> Westphalia, Kansas, in 1880
> Olpe, Kansas, in 1884
> Muenster, Texas in 1889
> Lindsay, Texas in 1891
> Pilot Point, Texas, in 1891
> Mt. Carmel, Texas, in 1907

Biographical Synopsis of Flusche Brothers in America

Stephan Flusche, father of the six Flusche brothers, was a school teacher in Liesterscheid from about 1830 until his death in 1867. After his death, his family immigrated to America. Anton Flusche was the first to arrive in America in 1871. Emil, Joseph, and Carl came to America, May 15, 1872; August, March 16, 1873, and on May 20, 1873, Wilhelm, and the next day, the mother, Catherina Flucht Flusche, and an aunt, Clara Feldman.

In the 1800's, German immigration was heavy, and the plight of the German, Catholic farmers to find suitable locations induced the Flusche Brothers--those of a total livelihood--Anton, Emil and August, to take up the colonization activity; the rest of the brothers were involved in limited ways. Emil Flusche began the colonization of Westphalia, Iowa, (on September 14, 1872). On March 16, 1873, brother August arrived there; then, on May 20, 1873, Wilhelm (and the mother) came, and brought money to buy more land (560 acres). May 29, 1873, the first Mass was celebrated in the new colony. Anton had a drugstore in Conway, Arkansas. but had to give it up. Brother August went to Conway to bring him to Iowa. (That has Emil, Joseph, August, Wilhelm Carl, and Anton in Westphalia, Iowa.)

Brother Carl and Emil negotiated for the land for Westphalia, Kansas, 1880. On March 12, 1880, brother August and Carl and family moved to the new Westphalia, (Kansas). In 1883, August got married and went to Milwaukee and was on his own. Then it was Anton and Emil in Westphalia, Kansas. In the spring of 1884, Emil bought 80 acres of land. . . as a starting point for the new colony, Olpe, Kansas. Brother August moved to Olpe to conduct its colonization and had good results. (According to Emil's journal)

In March, 1889, August and Emil made their first trip to Gainesville, Texas. October 1, 1889, Carl and (Joseph Rueschenberg) and Emil made a contract to Flusche Brothers for 22,000 acres--future Muenster, Texas. Then things went badly in Olpe, Kansas; Emil stayed in Olpe, and Anton and August handled the business at Muenster. Wilhelm moved to Muenster in 1890. The Flusche Brothers' contract was canceled in Muenster and they decided to go elsewhere. August moved to Gainesville. Anton and Wilhelm moved to Lindsay, and August, Anton, (and Wilhelm) negotiated with J. M. Lindsay for a contract to colonize Lindsay. Anton became the land agent in Lindsay (1891).

Emil decided to move to Pilot Point, Texas, and started a German colony there in 1891. (He moved into his new home there in 1893.) Joseph went to Tioga (near Pilot Point).

On July 13, 1891, a contract was made between Clark and Plumb, etc, for 75,000 acres, which was declared suitable for the colony of Windthorst. August Flusche went to Windthorst in May, 1892, and took over the agency. The financial conditions in Windthorst became bad: Hard times, poor crops, and financial difficulties. A crisis was reached in 1895. Conditions improved, but much credit for this settlement (of debt) was due to a Dr. Bueohert who succeeded August Flusche as agent.

In October 1899, August lived in Chandler, Oklahoma, and Emil bought 169 acres of land there and stayed until 1902. In October 1906, Emil went to Electra and secured the colonizational rights for the colony of Mt. Carmel.

Anton died January 25, 1925, and is buried at Lindsay, Emil is buried at Mt. Carmel where he died January 24, 1930. August died February 28, 1928, at Crekola, Okalahoma, where, through his efforts a small settlement of Catholics was founded. (Dr.) Carl Flusche died in Westphalia, Iowa, from typhord fever on December 7, 1896. Joseph (the farmer) died in Pilot Point, October 22, 1895 and is buried in Muenster, Texas. Wilhelm, the oldest of the brothers, died in 1901, and is buried in Lindsay, Texas.

Writings of Emil Flusche - Electra, Texas

Translated by A.C. (Tony) Flusche

The writer of this, his life's history, Franz Emmerich, called Emil, was born in Wamge, near Attendorn, Westfalen, Germany on Feb. 10, 1849 and baptized in the parish church in Attendorn, on Feb. 12, 1849. My father was Stephen Flusche, born June 2, 1805 at Attendorn on der "Breitenstrasse" as son of Johann Adam Flusche, [born April 6, 1774, died Aug. 16, 1844] and Elizabeth formerly Gante. My mother was Eva Katherina formerly Flucht, born in Wamge Sept. 8, 1815, daughter of Johan Wilhelm Flucht and Elizabeth formerly Hitze of Hanemicke. Both parents of my mother died young. Her Uncle Johann Hitze of Hahnemicke took the two older orphan girls Eva Katherina and Margaret to his home; the two younger ones, Lisette and Maria Anna, went to relatives in Drolshagen. Their estate in the Wamge had in the meantime been rented, and as I have been told, had been sadly neglected.

My father was a schoolteacher in Liesterscheid, a village near Wamge, from about 1830 until his death on March 22, 1867. My parents were married Sept. 11, 1838 in Attendorn, and on the 24 of the same month moved from Attendorn to Wange. One of the first things I remember from my childhood is that the wife of our renter, Mrs. Peter Anton Kaufmann. was sent by my parents to Hahnemicke to ask my mother's cousin August Hitze to be sponsor at the baptism of my youngest brother, Frederich August, born July 23, 1863. This August Hitze is the father of the famous Msgr. Prof. Dr. Franz Hitze, active in social-politics and a member of the Reichstag. My next recollection centers on the sickness, death, and funeral of my only sister, who died at the age of 11 months on June 21, 1856. My other four brothers were: Wilhelm born August 9, 1839, Joseph born Dec. 21, 1840, Carl born Jan. 13, 1843, and Anton born Feb. 12, 1847.

My childhood was spent, without much excitement, in our little peaceful village, in our German and thoroughly Catholic home, with a few neighborhood children as playmates. Happy occasions were the annual visits we made with our mother or Aunt Anna Flucht to their sisters Mrs. Stamm and Kramer in Frankhausen bei Drolshagen, the visit to the Holy Grave in the parish church in Attendorn on Good Friday, and the Corpus Christi procession, which was a celebration in memory of the victory over the Swedes in the Thirty-year war.

From Easter 1855 until Easter 1863, I attended the school at Liesterscheid where my father taught. At that time there were not so many branches taught and not as many books used in school as now, but religion, Bible History, reading, writing and arithmetic were certainly thoroughly taught. My father was highly respected by both clergy and civil authorities as a very good and capable teacher. He also conducted a nursery, raising many fruit trees, also oak and Tannen [something like pine]. These Tannen were raised in large lots and sold to the government for reforestation.

I made my First Holy Communion on Low Sunday April 27, 1862. At that was still the custom that no child under 13 was admitted to Holy Communion. At Easter 1863 my schooldays at Wamge came to an end. Our Pastor Clemens Lohmann, a very close friend of our family, offered to give me instructions in Latin during vacation. I took him up on it and had good success. My knowledge of Latin enabled me to get into the second year Latin when I entered the gymnasium in Attendorn in Sept. 1863. My brothers Carl and Anton had already been attending this school and my brother August also did later on. From our house to this school was over an hours walk and we walked it every day in all kinds of weather, summer and winter. I enjoyed studying and was always top in each class.

The outbreak of the war against Austria in 1866 gave me the first idea of the seriousness of life. How clearly I remember the worry and sorrow of the wives and mothers of the men that had to go to war. Luckily none of my older brothers had to go. My father was at this time rather feeble and barely able to carry on his work as teacher. He did not think he would live to see the end of the war. However, the war soon ended with the battle of Olmuetz on July 3, 1866. On March 1, 1867, my father took pneumonia and died, well prepared, on March 22, 1867, [King's birthday]. His funeral on March 26 was very solemn and well attended, as he was one of the outstanding and highly respected citizens of the community. I felt his death very keenly. Since the last few years of his life,

I had been his companion and did much of his writing and other work. My brother Wilhelm succeeded him as teacher in the fall of 1867. While my brother Joseph, who on account of weak eyes, could not study, worked the farm.

I left school at Christmas in 1868. On account of having excellent reports and school records, I was fortunate in getting the a position with Gravenhorst Iron Works in Hoerstel, owned by Primavesi & Co. On July 3, 1870 my brother Anton, who now was druggist apprentice at Eylardi in Warendorf, and I were in Koeln, where they were celebrating the anniversary of the Prussian victory over Austria, July 3, 1866. From there we went home for a vacation with mother, aunt and brothers. A few more days brought the war against France.

When I started back to Gravenhorst, it was difficult to get passage on the railroads, as the army had taken them over. With feverish haste hundreds of thousand of soldiers, cannons, ammunition and other war material was rushed to the French border. At the outbreak of the war, all young men of military age were ordered to report and be ready for duty. The director of the iron works stated that I was indispensable and that my work was essential, so I got an extension for one year before I was due to report. At the end of that year, the war was over and peaceful conditions prevailed.

As the firm also had customers in Holland, I studied the Dutch language and soon took care of the Dutch correspondence and waited of on Dutch customers. In the fall 1869, I visited my brother, August, who was working for the firm, August Boehmer, in Telgte, which is also a famous pilgrimage place. After the war, on July 1, I left Gravenhorst and spent the summer at home. In the fall, through the recommendation of Rev. Pielstiker, I obtained a position as traveling salesman for the firm Gebr. Becker, in Fredeburg, dealers in tobacco, cigars and wine. I enjoyed this work very much, and now, at the age of 65, I still look back with pleasure at this very happy time during which I never missed a chance to attend Mass, even on week-days, and to visit my mother and Aunt Maria Anna [who was second mother to me]. Since I had no desire to be a soldier and since at that time there were rumors of war, I decided to accompany brothers, Joseph and Carl, to America. Brother Anton had already left for the US in 1871 and had a good position as druggist in St. Louis.

So on May 15, 1872 we sailed on the Norddeutscher Lloyd steamer, Herman, from Bremerhaven via South Hampton, England, where taken more freight and passengers were taken on board. After a very smooth crossing, without any mishap, we arrived in New York on June 1. Here we looked up Johann Meyer, brother-in-law of our old neighbor, Johann Zimmermann, were heartily welcomed. After having taken in some of the sights of the New York Central Park and others, we went by train via Chicago and St. Paul to Wilmar, Minn., a small new town and from there with some Norwegian farmers, by ox wagon 40 miles across open prairie to Hawk Creek in Rennville Co, where a certain Joseph Maier of Attendorn, a schoolmate of our father, had taken a homestead.

We found him living in a miserable hut in thinly settled neighborhood, inhabited mostly by Norwegians and quite a few Indians. We left Wilmar towards evening on June 5, the nicest weather, but as night came and we were on an uninhabited prairie far from any human habitation. A terrible thunderstorm arose and it seemed the world was coming to end. And so we traveled on through a cold driving rain accompanied by much thunder and lightning until sometime after midnight, we arrived at "Twenty-mile house," the first sign of human habitation.

Early in July, we went back to Wilmar and from there to Milwaukee, Wisc. where we were kindly received by our country-folks, Theo. Stamm and the widow Lohagen. Since we could not find any suitable work in Milwaukee, Carl went to Grand Rapids, Mich., where a cousin of our mother, Caspar Henze, a well-to-do farmer, lived. I soon followed him. Carl established himself as Doctor in Grand Rapids. After two weeks I went to our former neighbor, Franz Schnettgen, in Wesphalia, Clinton Co., Mich. This man had changed his name to Snitgen, to conform with English pronunciation, otherwise he still remained a staunch German. He owned an implement store, was running a wagon factory, was County Treasurer, and had 14 living sons. He was a highly respected man and I spent several enjoyable weeks with him.

Westphalia, Mich. is one of the oldest and best German Catholic country parishes. It was founded in 1845 by a small group from Helden, Germany, a village near Wamge. Here, life seemed so carefree, peaceful, Catholic, and attractive - just like home and it fascinated me. Here I conceived the desire and determination to establish such a colony or colonies here in the US. An advertisement by A. H. Ketteler of Harlan, Iowa, in the "Milwaukee Seeboten" attracted my attention. In August, I left via Chicago, Davenport, and Avoca for Harlan, Iowa. On this lonesome trip, it came to me as a vision that I would be instrumental in finding homes for many of our countrymen. I arrived in Avoca about midnight. How elated was I when at daybreak I saw this beautiful countryside. From here we went by horse-drawn coach to Harlan where I was welcomed by Mr. Ketteler. The date of my arrival at Harlan was August 31, 1872.

The next day, a Sunday, a neighbor of Mr. Ketteler drove us around over the colony land. This land was a township belonging to the Chicago Rock Island & Pacific RR. The SE corner of it was the about 2 miles north of Harlan. [A township is a piece of land 6 miles square, or 36 square miles.] In this whole township there was no road of any kind, no human trace, except the stakes to make the sections and half sections. These stakes were set on little mounds of dirt, so they could be found in the high prairie grass, but even at that, they were hard to find. Ketteler drank heavily and could not write German. He had an agreement to sell this land to German Catholics only. According to this agreement with the RR Co., he was to add $1.00 an acre to the price of the land, 50 cents of this was his commission and the other 50 cents went into a building fund for a church. He asked me to carry on his German Catholic settlers. On Sept. 6, 1872, he agreed per contract to deed me 80 acres S 1/2 SW 1/4 Sec. 23 and $400.00 a year. I went to work with enthusiasm and met with unexpected success. Several days were spent looking up and properly locating the section corners. We marked them with long willow poles.

Then in one day, we bored a wall 6 inches in diameter 20 feet deep without hitting a rock or other obstruction and had plenty of good water. Then we dug a cellar. We walked back and forth to Harlan, a distance of 5 miles. My brother Joseph came from Minnesota on Sept. 14. On Sept 19, Mr. Griffith of Harlan started building our house, the first house in the new colony, now named Westphalia. On Oct. 31, brother Carl came. In November, Herman Schwarte built the second house, a quarter mile southwest of ours. Joseph had married on Oct. 5 in Dunlap Iowa. From now until Feb. 1873, we four and Herman Schwarte were the only settlers. The winter was cold with much snow. One morning a whole herd of deer was encamped right near our house.

For 12 cents a bushel, we had corn brought to our house and sometimes used some of it for fuel.

On Dec. 14, 1872 I received news from home that our entire family was coming in the spring. Also, they sent money and wanted us to buy more land. So, we bought 560 acres of land, and in Feb. 1873, we got two teams of horses and farm implements from two Englishmen in the neighborhood who decided to move back to Holyoke, Mass.

On March 16, 1873, came brother August and our neighbor's son, Johann Rueschenberg and Emil Zimmermann from Germany. On May 20 came brother Wilhelm. The next day we went with three wagons to get our mother, Aunt Clara Feldmann, the family, Johann Zimmermann and August Schnuettgen, from Avoca, where they had been resting from their trip across. They had left Bremen on April 31 and landed in New York on May 16, 1873. On May 28, for the first time a Catholic priest, Father John Kempfer, asst. at Council Bluffs, came to our colony and read the first Mass in the parish on May 29 and 30. On this occasion, Carl Flusche and Clara Feldmann were married.

Johann Zimmermann built the third house in the colony. One hot summer evening as he and his oldest daughter had gone a way east of their home to get some willows for roofing and had not returned by night, his wife became very worried. She sent the children to our house to tell us. So, all of us including Franz Hesse and Richard Schneider, who had just arrived from Germany, joined in the hunt. Suddenly a thunderstorm came up and the heavy rain put out our lanterns and we had trouble finding our way back. We discovered tracks in the grass showing that they had gone north. Since it was too dark and raining, we went home. The next morning after having ridden about 7 miles north in this uninhabited prairie, we saw a wagon in the distance. It was a Mr. Pratt who lived about 10 miles northwest of us. Mr. Zimmermann and daughter had arrived at his place after midnight, lost and very tired and he was now taking them home.

In Oct. 1873, the land commissioner of the Rock Island RR, John L. Drew, came to me at Westphalia and transferred to me the sole agency for the colony land. Mr. Ketteler had not done very satisfactory and had not kept his contract with me. The record of the progress and conditions of Westphalia can be found in the archives at the rectory.

In 1874 came many new settlers from other states, mainly from Wisconsin. From our old home in Germany came the families Hendricks, Sasse, August Mester, Joseph and Heinrich Hesse, Peter Book, and M.E. von Tersch, and in 1875 many more, among which we mention from the old country: Louis Anastasi, Neinrich Mertens, John Bock, Albert Assmann, Peter Schnuettgen, Peter Hesse, Joseph Berghans, Joseph Rueschenbert, Casper Schneider, Joseph Kramer, and H. Sondermann. In May 1876 two Jesuits, Fathers Haag and Wochner held an 8 day Mission in Westphalia. The parish now numbered over German Catholic families. After the close of the Mission the Missionaries spent a day at our house and Father Haag said to me that there was no more meritorious and greater missionary work then to gather German Catholics in such parishes and give them the opportunity to practice and keep up their faith. This encouraging remark impressed me very much and gave me encouragement in later ventures in other colonies.

In the fall of 1879, a typhoid epidemic hit Westphalia. I was also hit and spent two months in bed. At that time, there were in our house our mother, brother Carl and wife and baby daughter, Tonchen, brother August and I. Aunt Maria Anna had died Feb. 13, 1877.

Brother Wilhelm was postmaster at Westphalia. Joseph lived on a farm east of us. Anton had a drugstore in Conway, Ark., but on account of being afflicted with malaria, he had to give it up. Brother August went to Conway to bring him to us. On account of his continued sickness, the venture was a financial failure.

These were hard times for me. Making financial settlement with Wilhelm, the big household, taking care of the homeseekers and new settlers. The low prices of farm products - corn 15 to 20 centers per bushel, hogs 2 to 3 cents - made it impossible to advance. I had been dividing my income from the land sales with my brothers for their upkeep of the household and of improvements of the farm. So it came to pass that we sold our farm to H. Wagemann of Illinois for $10,000., which by values of that time was considered a good price.

Later on, when the CM & St. P.R.R. came through near there, land prices went up quite a bit. From 1874 on, I was a Notary Public and also Justice of the Peace. I was also a member of the committee for the appraisal of land values for the right-of-way for the new railroad that was being built from Avoca to Harlan.

Animated by the desire to find a place in Kansas for a new colony, Brother Carl and I, in Feb. 1880, made a tour through eastern Kansas. On Feb. 15, we met with Mr.

M. L. White in Garnett, in the western part of Anderson Co. where a new town, Cornell, was laid out. A railroad through this town was under construction. There was much cheap land available in this open prairie and since the location and opportunity seemed desirable, we bought a few blocks of the townsite and 320 acres of the prairie. On March 12, 1880, brother August and Carl and family moved to the new Westphalia. On March 15, I bought from S. P. Cornell his 160 acre farm with a large two-story house about half finished. After the house was completed, brother Carl and his wife conducted a hotel in it.

On April 13, 1880, V. R. P. Anastasius Peters OCC read the first Mass in the new colony. Our mother came to Westphalia, Kansas in Oct. 1880. I came to Westphalia, Kansas, on March 16, 1881. In the meantime, I went back to Iowa to close out our business there and scouted for settlers for our new colony and had good success. Our mother died on May 21, 1881 and was the first to be buried in the new cemetery. In July, at the request of brother Wilhelm, I went back to Westphalia, Iowa, and found him and his wife, Christine very sick and I myself was stricken with malaria. Christine died rather unexpectedly. Wilhelm suffered terribly with his eyes and lost the sight of one of them. Since he was postmaster and, of course, could not get around, I had to care of the mail, although on account of my malaria, I could barely stay on my feet. This was a hard time.

In September, after I had recovered, I had to take Wilhelm's children, Willie and Clara, to an orphanage in Dubuque, Iowa. The oldest daughter of M. Wilwerding went with us to enter the convent there. Brother Joseph moved into the house with Wilhelm. On Nov. 23, 1881, I and Anna Heese were married in the Catholic Church, corner 9th and McGee St. Kansas City, Mo. by Rev. Zechenter. Anna had come from Germany to Westphalia, Iowa, where we met and learned to love each other. She was very religious, cheerful, had a good education and was a model housewife and cook. Ours was indeed a happy marriage. Our children were; Emil born Dec. 19, 1882, Hugo born May 3, 1884, Anton Heinrich, called Albert born Aug. 6, 1885, Paul Vincent Jan. 9, 1887, and Bertha Margaretha July 12, 1889. These children were all born in our house in Westphalia, Kansas. Our youngest daughter, Anna Maria was born in Pilot Point, Texas.

In Westphalia, Kansas, we, my brothers Anton and August and I, conducted, besides the farm, a general merchandise business, loan office, insurance, and land office, under the name "Flusche Bros." August got married in 1883, and went to Milwaukee and was on his own. Then it was Anton and I.

In the spring of 1884, at the suggestion of Rev. Dominic Maier O.F.M., I bought 80 acres of land on the Sante Fe at Bittlertown, 10 miles south of Emporia, from John Thye, as a starting point for the new colony, Olpe, Kansas. Brother August moved to Olpe to conduct the colonization and had good results. On August 6, 1885 the first church in Olpe was blessed.

In the winter of 1888-89, it was announced that the western part of the Indian Territory would be open to white settlers, under the name of Oklahoma. At the invitation of the German Frater, Placidus O.S.B. of Sacred Heart Mission I.T., I went there in Feb. 1889, to discuss with him if it would be possible to make arrangements to gather Catholic settlers in one place and establish Catholic parishes.

From Purcell we went by wagon across the swift running Canadian River through the desolate Pottowattomie region. The Superior of the Mission, Rev. Thomas Buperon O.S.B., received me very cordially. He, a Frenchman, told me that the priest in Purcell, told him to advise me against any colonization activity for German Catholics, because they wanted to reserve this part of Oklahoma for French settlers.

In March, 1889, August and I made our first trip to Gainesville and Nocona. On April 23, 1889, the western part of Oklahoma was opened to white settlers. At the request of Dr. Preuss, editor of the "Amerika". I made this landrush as correspondent for the "Amerika". In August 1889, John Koll of Westphalia, Iowa, and I went to Gainesville again to take a look at Gunter's pasture at Myra and Lazarus but could not come to an understanding with the young John Summerfield. He insisted that the entire 22,000 acres should be sold in one year. So, we went home without having accomplished anything, since I considered this as unreasonable.

Shortly after we received a letter from Jot Gunter, stating that he was ready to make some concessions and invited us back soon to talk it over. Oct. 1, 1889 brother Carl and Joseph Rueschenberg of Westphalia, Iowa, and I went to Gainesville arriving in the evening, and late the same night drove to the home of our countryman, August Pulte. We spent the night there and the next day viewed the land for the new colony. On our return to Gainesville, we were surprised to find out that Jot Gunter had arrived from Dallas by special train and was waiting for us in the Lindsay Hotel. In the night of Oct. 4-5, the contract between me and Jot Gunter was orally concluded, with John Hird and Captain Schopmeier of Gainesville and Carl Flusche and Joseph Rueschenberg of Westphalia, Iowa, as witnesses.

The next day the contract was written and signed in Dallas. This contract which had several cunning and deceitful clauses, provided that Gunter & Wellesly turned over to Flusche Bros. their 22,000 acres to be sold in two years, the east half for $12.00 acre, the west half for $10.00 per acre, that a new town to be laid out between Myra and Lazarus, 25 acres to be donated for church, school, and park. Our commission to be 10%, 5,000 acres must be sold in 6 months, 12,000 in one year, no commission for selling town lots until the amount of money received from these lots would be enough to equal $25.00 per acre for the whole township. Then the balance should be divided equally.

The surveying of the land and plotting the town took nearly two months, causing many homeseekers to leave without buying. The first building in the new town was our office on a slight elevation north of the R.R., a small two room affair. About the middle of Oct., Mr. Cross, receiver for the M.K. & T.R.R., came through Muenster by extra train, visited us, and promised to make arrangements for a car of lumber to be unloaded at Muenster. There was as yet no side-track at the future Muenster. He made his promise good. A German carpenter, Bundschuh of Gainesville, built the first buildings in Muenster.

From Kansas, we sent Gerhard Stephens with a team of horses, two wagons, a large tent, several barrels of apples, etc. John Koll came with his family from Westphalia, Iowa and conducted a boarding house in this large tent. The homeseekers were mostly acquaintances from Iowa and Kansas and came in large numbers. On Dec. 8, 1889, our good friend, Father Brickley of Gainesville, read the first Mass in the new colony in our land office. On Jan. 1, 1890, a meeting was held in our office regarding the building of a church. Present at this meeting were among others: Franz Hesse, three Wiesmann brothers, John Koll and myself.

It was decided to put up at once a building to be used for church and later on, for school. Jot Gunter had promised to give $500.00 for this.

In the meantime, as a result of several crop failures in Kansas, panic conditions existed, most banks went broke, land was practically valueless. Unfortunately, we had bought a lot of land cheap [we thought] and had loaned more money on some land than it was now worth. With outstanding debts from the store and other conditions, we saved hardly anything out of this "shipwreck." So, in order to save what could be saved out of this crash, I stayed in Kansas and Anton and August handled the business at Muenster. I made several trips during this time to be of assistance. In December 1890, through the envy of some of the settlers and the baseness of the men with whom we made the contract, our contract was canceled. Anton and Wilhelm then moved to Lindsay.

At the request of the banker Gee and J.M. Sullivan of Pilot Point, who were surprised at the marvelous growth of Muenster even such in such an unfavorable year, so much could be done, in the spring and summer of 1891. I decided to move to Pilot Point and start a colony there. On Sept. 3, 1891 we left Westphalia, Kansas, after a short visit with the family Springob at Wichita, Kansas, we arrived at Gainesville on Sept. 8, at my brother August's. On Sept. 10, we moved to Pilot Point into a house belonging to a Mr. McFarland, cashier of the bank.

Some of the wealthier citizens of Pilot Point showed a lively and active interest in the colonization project by donating a good sized tract of land for church and school and a donation of about $1,500.00 for construction. So I could go ahead at once and make arrangements for the construction of a building 28 x 70; 24 feet high [two story] for church, school and sisterhouse. On Dec. 8, 1891, the digging of the foundation was begun and, on March 7, 1892, St. Thomas day, the first Bishop of Dallas, Most Rev. Dr. Thomas F. Brennan, blessed the new church. He arrived the night before; he brought along a newly ordained priest, the Rev. Hugo Bardenhewer, who was the first priest ordained by the new Bishop in the new Diocese, and who was supposed to stay in Pilot Point as our pastor. However, this did not entirely materialize. Also Rev. Dr. John Coffey, who since October had been visiting us every few weeks and reading Mass, was present for the occasion, and five other priests were also there and at our house for dinner. A large crowd came to attend the blessing of the church. Many non-Catholics, who knew nothing about Catholics, except having heard the word "Catholic" were there to see how the Catholics adored their wooden God.

Herman Boerner and his son-in-law, Louis Tschoeppe from New Braunfels, were the first colonists, soon came, Heitzman, Zipperer, Geis, Phillips, Zimmerer, Tischler, the Bauer Bros.

Since there was as yet no rectory, Father Bardenhewer made his home with us. In the summer, he fixed up a little room in the second story of the church, as his residence. In the fall, a small rectory was built. Two sisters of Divine Providence from San Antonio arrived in September, 1892, and opened the parochial school. In May, came Franz Blumberg Anton Steiger, Anton Brekel and Joseph Fritcher from Heron Lake, Minn. who through me bought 1750 acres of nice prairie land from Col. Elijah Emberson for $15.00 per acre and divided this land among themselves and several other families, who arrived in December, 1892.

On election day we moved into our new house near the church. Our youngest daughter, Anna, was 3 weeks old. On April 1, 1894, we had solemn First Holy Communion for children, for the first time in the parish, under Father Bardenhewer. Our oldest sons, Emil and Hugo, were in the class. Fabian Heitzmann died suddenly and, there was no cemetery as yet, he was buried on the church property, west of the church. Mr. A. H. Gee, who had donated the land for the church, protested this. Then the pastor and the church committee bought 3 acres northwest of the church and the body of Heitzmann was transferred there.

On May 6, 1895, my wife became suddenly very ill, and on May 11th gave birth to a little girl. Brother Anton's wife took the baby to her home in Lindsay and tried to raise it, but it died July 21. My wife died on May 15th, well prepared and resigned to God's will. Of all the misfortunes that had befallen me, this was the hardest one. However, my religion and my responsibility for my children kept me going. Brother Carl of Westphalia, Iowa took little Anna in June, and in October also our son Albert. Brother Wilhelm's daughter, Clara kept house for us for a while, and then Joseph's daughter Lizzie. Both are now Sisters of Divine Providence of San Antonio. After that Emil went to my brother Joseph, Hugo to Wilhelm, Paul and Margaretha to brother Anton in Lindsay.

During the summer of 1897, I, in partnership with J.M. Sullivan, was engaged in some land business in the new harbor city Port Arthur. I returned to Pilot Point in time to miss the flood at Port Arthur on Sept. 8, in which many lives were lost. In October 1899, I went to Chandler, Okla. where my brother August now lived, and bought 169 acres and built a house on it. Before Christmas my three sons, Emil, Hugo and Albert came and we set up housekeeping. In the spring, Paul came and a year later Margaretha. At the end of 1902 we sold the farm to Rev. Anton Pieke of Mascoutah, Ill. He in turn donated this and two adjoining farms to Bishop Jansen of Bellville, Ill. for orphan children.

On Jan. 27, 1903, we moved to Tulsa, hoping to be able to buy some cheap land near church and town, when Indian land became available. Tulsa was at that time one of the few places in the Indian Territory where there was a church and a resident priest, Rev. Theophil van Hulse. We lived in the southeast corner of the Osage Nation on land owned by a family named Harlow. In Nov. 1903, Emil went to St. Francis College in Quincy, Ill. to take a business course. In September 1904, Hugo and I went to the World's Fair in St. Louis, also attended the Catholic Convention there, and made a tour through southern Missouri and went via Knoble, Ark. In 1905, Hugo took a course in the A & M College in Stillwater, Okla.

In October 1906, I came to Electra and secured from R.S. Allen the colonization rights for a part of the Waggoner ranch, for the colony, Mt. Carmel. In February 1907, we moved into our new home in the center of the colony.

(The above was originally written in German by Emil Flusche about 1914 and some years later translated by his nephew A.C. Flusche.)

Guthrie, Okla. April 22, 1889

The Oklahoma Land Rush by Emil
Flusche of Electra, Texas

The 22nd of April, 1889, will always be remembered as the most eventful days in the history of the southwest. The opening of Oklahoma to settlers on this date, a veritable migration of people is being set in motion, the result of which can, at present, hardly be estimated.

Oklahoma, said to mean in the Indian language, "The beautiful land," comprises 1,800,000 acres, over or something 71 full for townships. Since from every township two sections are reserved for school purposes, one can figure that only about 10,000 farms of 160 acres each are available. Take from this the worthless land and that occupied by cities, it would leave actually only about 7,000 good farms available. Compare herewith the surprising and inconceivably large mass of people from all parts: states and cities of the US and even parts of Europe that are already on the spot, and many others are arriving by train, wagon and horseback and even on foot--like a living river, and you find your automatically asking "What is going to become of this?" For instance from Arkansas city, Kansas, the nearest town north of Oklahoma, since about 9 o'clock this morning, at least 4 trains, with an average of 600 passengers, left every hour. Probably the same amount arrived over the other three lines, and yet by comparison to those that came overland, and are mostly intent on staking claims for homesteads, this human mass was the smallest. In general one may assume that the R.R. passengers are mostly interested in the new cities.

As our train crossed the Oklahoma border, shortly after noon, one man had already put up his tent on the first quarter section of the RR and greeted the passing trains with triumphantly waving his hat. He was greeted by the passengers with resounding "Hurrahs" for his bravery. Every half-way usable claim, from here on, had already been staked or inhabited. All kinds of odd identifications had been employed: tents made by laying articles of clothes across sticks, stakes with whisps of hay, and poles with tags. One man even put up a pole with a straw man very similar to a human being. About 6 miles north of Guthrie we saw a troop of cavalry with five tents and provision wagons, surrounded by a large crowd of people, horses and wagons. From the train as far as one could see, in all directions, endless rows of covered wagons were visible. At every creek and convenient stopping place, there were groups--some small, some large--of campers stopping for rest and meals. Some were helping to get a wagon that was stuck in the mud, going. At several creeks in the Cherokee outlet, that were impassable on account of high water, the Santa Fee RR had laid planks across the N.M. bridges to enable the claim seekers to cross with their wagons. This favor was greatly appreciated. All this was no comparison with what greeted us when we arrived at Guthrie.

As our train neared Guthrie, we could see, on the east side of the RR track on a gradual sloping, long stretched hill, an unnumberable mass of humanity in many hundred if not thousands tents. After having untangled ourselves from the ball of humanity that had accumulated at the depot, as a result of three passenger trains having arrived at about the same time, and having managed to cross the tracks and made our way into the city, we encountered a fantastic spectacle. Every foot of land for at least a mile east and half a mile north, had been layed out in building sites about 25 by 140, and had been "improved" some way or other. Either the owner put up some kind of "residence" or decorated it with his name. The main building in the new town was, of course, the land office, a one-story simple frame building 14 x 24 with store front. The Post Office, like all already reported business, was located in a small white tent, as are also the hotels, restaurants, etc. The lots seems to have been laid out in a haphazard pattern, without any space between, and every minute more are filled.

That the streets are momentary narrow and crooked is not surprising. But the whole city of Guthrie, when today at noon, did not have any inhabitants, and tonight, as is estimated and generally believed, harbors about 6-8,000 men [one sees very few women and childred] is as alive as an anthill and one can not the town on account of the people. Tonight many thousand, wrapped in blankets, will spend their first night on their newly captured homestead.

That this was really a contest and race is evident from the fact that today at 12 o'clock noon April 22, 1889, the soldiers, who had been guarding the northern border of Oklahoma, were almost crushed to death and could hardly get out of the way of the avalanche of humanity, that had been gathering here for several days, and was now, at a given signal, released. Now the race started, now to find a good piece of land and take possession of staked it. They tell of one cowboy who, 19 minutes after 12, claim 6 miles from the northern border. That such a wild contest too was not without bloodshed, is only natural. At Guthrie one all zezlous contender for a piece of ground, was killed by an equally determined one.

The land office is open only from 9 A.M. to 4 P.M. The claimants lined up in long rows outside and only one was admitted in the office at one time. The actual taking possession and occupation of the land is considered legal and important, the recording at the land office can be done any time within three months, if one stays on the land during that time.

According to reports a "Town Company" had demanded four and one-half sections of land [2800 acres] for the townsite of Guthrie, but were, of course, turned down, since only 320 acres were reserved for each town. The result will probably be that this will be circumvented in various ways by keeping up different names for occupying the sections, until title of ownership can be established. A piece of land that has been claimed for homestead, can be transferred to any one else and be included in a townsite, and vise versa.

Each person is allowed only one building site in one town and must live on it himself. A maximum of twenty men is required before they can apply for a town site.

The towns that sprang up today will have elected officers in a few days, and then will probably have some law and order. It is rumored that several prominent men from some of the northern states have their eyes on the position of mayor of Guthrie.

By Emil Flusche of Electra, Texas.

This article appeared in the German paper "Amerika" of Louis in German. Was copied from the files at St. Louis by Father David Flusche O.S.B. and translated by his father A.C. Flusche/ [Tony Flusche]

Biographical Notes of Wilhelm Flusche

Until April 1, 1873, I was teacher at Listerscheid by Attendorn, Westfalen. Our father, Stephen Flusche, preceded me as teacher there. My father was born in 1805, in Attendorn, Westfalen. He was a teacher in Listerscheied from 1829 untill his death in 1867. Rest in peace! We lived in Wanger, ten minutes from Listerscheid. That was my mother's home. We lived in my mother's home. Our good mother was born in 1815 in Wamge. 1873, on 20 May, I came to Westphalia, Iowa, accompanied by my mother, and Tanta Maria Anna. My brothers were there already. Uncle Anton was in St. Louis. In 1874, I went back to Germany, 2, November, on 29 May 1875, I and Christina arrived here and married. She was born 1852 in Nierst, Crefeld. Christina's father was Johann Peter Flucht. They originally came from

Wamge, the family home of my mother. From 1858 until 1860, I was a teacher at Leher, a seminar in Buren. From there onto the death of my father, I was a teacher in Bekinghausen on the Lippe.

1885. On 5 September, Willie and Clara came back from the convent.

1885. On 29 October, Augusta Steinmetz and I married by Rev. J. A. Weber in Westphalia, Iowa.

1887. On 26 May, Grandfather and Grandmother Steinmetz and Anna came from Germany. They lived with us until we moved to Texas.

In 1890, November 8, I and my family and brother, Joseph, went to Muenster, Cooke County, Texas. which I in connection with my brothers had founded the year before. I had bought a farm in Muenster the year before. (Muenster originated in 1889.) The church, school, and railroad were there. Seventy-five families were in Muenster already. I moved there with the intention of bulding a nice home for me and my family on my 100 acres of land, south of the depot. (Where Arthur Bayer lives now.)

In the meantime, John Koll and Richter were trying to get the real estate business away from the Flusches. The real estate business was not lucrative enough to support two real estate agents. Koll and Richter splashed mud on the reputation of the Flusches; they were in cahoots with the town loafers, and turned the people against us. Franz Hesse who was my best man at my wedding to Augusta was also against us. We Flusches got together and studied the situation thoroughly and we agreed it would be best for us to leave Muenster. We discussed our plans with Father Hugo, a Franciscan from St. Louis, Missouri. We decided that we would start other German Catholic colonies. Anton and I went to Lindsay in 1891. On March 20, we met with J. M. Lindsay in Gainesville. We made out a contract, but we didn't come to an agreement at the first meeting. There was nice, good farm land all around Lindsay. August was in Gainesville, working on the deal with J. M. Lindsay, but he did not get anywhere. During the winter of 1891 and 1892, he decided he could get a better deal in colonizing Windhorst, Texas.

(Uncle Emil went to Pilot Point in Denton County. His family was still in Kansas. His wife was very sick and Emil moved to Pilot Point in 1891. He moved into his new home there in 1893.)

In 1892, March 25, the first Mass was read by Rev. Bardenhewer in our house in the south room. Fr. Bardenhewer served Lindsay and Pilot Point. During the year after making the contract with J. M. Lindsay, we had to go to church either in Muenster or in Gainesville. Anton build the first house in Lindsay and he moved in May, 1891. I build the second house, and I moved my family in the new house on October 7, 1891. My wife had been in ill health while we lived in Muenster (the water made her sick) She had gone back to Iowa to my brother, Dr. Carl Flusche, to have the baby. She came back with six-week-old Otto. Fritz was with her while she was in Iowa. Robert, Willie, Clara and I lived with Uncle Anton. Little child, Gusta, was with Tanta Anna in Muenster. (Joseph's wife).

The first church built was intended to be used as a school later on. In April, 1892, it was finished. The first Mass read in this church (school) was by Father Bardenhewer; he read Mass in Lindsay every other Sunday.

The first business in Lindsay was a saloon opened by Joseph Becker (Augusta's cousin) on April 9, 1892. From February, 1892, to February, 1894, he lived with us; then he got married. He had a good home with my wife and me for two years and he thanked us with "God reward you for it." (Meaning, they didn't get paid for his lodging). (Joseph Becker had been a baker. He had had a bakery in Waco. He had debts all over Waco. He married a Galasky and they had twins that died. Joseph weighed 300 pounds, but had been good-looking before he got fat).

In April, we built a fence around the church property and cemetery. J. M. Lindsay donated eight acres of land for the church. He also donated $300. for the material for the fence. Other business men gave $300. I gave $50. We only had a $100. debt for the church.

At the end of February, 1892, the first funeral was held in Lindsay. The young girl of J. Ruppaner drowned and she was the first to be buried in the new cemetery. She was five years old. In July, 1892, 14 year old Theresia Gieb died of burns from a coal oil accident. Her's was the second funeral in Lindsay, (Mama always called her Appolonia Gieb).

On July 1, 1891, the first postoffice was established in Lindsay with Anton Flusche as postmaster.

1892. In November, the first road was laid west from Lindsay to Muenster.

1893. In May a road was laid north of Lindsay.

1892. December and January, 1893, a sister's house was built. Father Bardenhewer who was living in Muenster, was urging us to build a priest house. He wanted to have his residence in Lindsay. Judge Lindsay loaned Lindsay $800. to build the first priest house in Lindsay. We took up a collection and the parish volunteered to give $25. per month.

1893. January 11, was a beautiful day for Lindsay. Thirty busy "arms" were working on the priest house. The floor was laid; the walls were plastered. (Slats were placed two inches apart; then plastered on it). The chimney was built. A glass of beer helped a little bit; it made the workers hammer and saw faster. As we worked, the new church bells in the tower rang for the first time. Seyler from Muenster was digging a water well; once in a while, the noise from the dynamite he used could be heard. During the construction of the priest house, Jos. Ortner came with the new organ. We put it in the church the same evening; but later, he took it along back with him when he returned to Iowa. Then, Wm. Topf came with the first (permanent) organ in 1893.

1893. In April, Bishop Fitzgerald of Little Rock (Lindsay's diocese) advised us that he had asked the Benedictine order to send priest to the German Colonies (Muenster and Lindsay). A few days later, German priest, Rev. Bonaventura of Diocese of Little Rock, served Lindsay and Muenster. Under his pastorage, the first parish council election was held in the church. Members were: Christopher Hundt, Wilhelm Flusche, Jos Ortner, Andrew Zimmerer, and Fr. Bonaventura. Father Bonaventura demanded $250. from Lindsay $450. from Muenster because he made his headquarters there.

1893. July 31, a tornado destroyed the first church in Muenster for the second time.

1893. October 15, the first sisters came to Lindsay and opened the school with thirty-two pupils. In December, there were fifty students.

1893. December 14, Father Weber came to Lindsay from New Jersey.

1893. December 25, Lindsay celebrated its first Christmas and no other place could have had a more elaborate celebration. We had three holy Masses and we had Benediction with the monstrance for the first time; I had asked Father Weber to bring the monstrance when he came.

1894. March 1, The new bishop arrived from Dallas. Right Rev. Dunne from Chicago installed Rev. Father Weber as the new pastor of Lindsay. Father Weber built a one-story priest house and left the first two-story priest house for the sisters.

1894. March 26, 27. It was very cold. There was over an inch of ice. The priest house was finished in May.

1894. Seyler from Muenster drilled a new water well @ 80 cents per foot. It was 115 feet deep.

1896. March 29. Father Weber quietly left during the night and went to Muenster. He had to leave Lindsay because he had a drinking problem. "I feel much sorrow for you," Father Weber," Mighty at one time, you were capable, brilliant with your work and with your word, Your star glimmered brightly in the heavenly sky. Go home and may God be with you."

Wm. Flusche

1896. In March, we got a new priest, Father Mielinger. In September, Frank Seyler dug the city well (downtown) in five days. It was 160 feet deep.

1895. October. Grandfather, and Grandmother Steinmetz and Paul and Anna Wiese came from Iowa and Paul Wiese rented Lindenau and lived there.

1895. December 4, Leo Wiese was born on St. Nicholas Day. Grandfather and Grandmother lived with us in Lindsay.

Grandmother died January 2, 1896, from edema (dopsy). Grandpa Steinmetz brought $1,000. from Iowa and bought ten acres of land and built a nice house on it. (Where Hoelkers live, back to the Blocks). He moved in it with Paul and Anna Wiese in 1896

1896. In September 10, Uncle Paul Wiese opened the second saloon in Lindsay in his father-in-law's house. It is called Jayerlust (Jolly hunter).

1897. May 16, Father Mielinger said good-bye and moved to Pilot Point. A priest, Father Heuchener, came from Gainesville to say Mass; he only stayed sixteen days. The parishioners are getting discouraged because we have no resident priest. It has caused much strife in the parish.

1897. June 8, we got a new priest, Father Baumgartner; he left us real soon--quietly--which was good.

1898. A good, energetic priest has come to Lindsay, Father Johannes Baptist. (Dec.?) (The rest of this journal appears to have been written by Grandma Flusche Theisen) In 1900, all the church debts were paid and we even have a $200. surplus. Under Father Johannes guidance and managing, within two years after he came, we started to build the brick church.

1899. January 24, Father Johannes O.S.B. had the first Mass as our paster in Lindsay and he gave a sharply worded sermon. Father Johannes had gotten the impression from Muenster parishioners Lindsay was not a stable, agreeable parish. After the High Mass, the church committee congratulated Father Johannes. In the name of the parish, they pledged that they would go through "thick or thin" with him. The parishioners paid their dues to the church building fund. On June 28, 1903, to the pleasure of the parish, the new church was dedicated. (In the words of Grandma Theisen) To our dear but very ill pastor, the church is dedicated as an everlasting monument. The kind Father John donated the high altar and the statues of St. Peter and Paul to the Church. (Father John died in 1904)

(Grandma Flusche Theisen wrote a poem commemorating the dedication of the new church in Lindsay, 1903.)

ENGLISH TRANSLATIONS

OF

GERMAN POEMS

COMPOSED BY VARIOUS MEMBERS OF
THE FLUSCHE-STEINMETZ FAMILIES

```
*  *  *  *  *  *  *  *  *  *  *
   *  *  *  *  *  *  *  *  *  *
      *  *  *  *  *  *  *  *
         *  *  *  *  *  *
            *  *  *  *
               *  *
                *
```

TRANSLATION OF POEMS

(This poem about my home town Lindsay was composed by my mother, the late Mrs. William Flusche-Theisen)

I know not what it presages
That all is so jubilant to behold
For a long, long time
Was Lindsay never so wonderous fair.
The banners proudly wave their glory
Each expressing its distinguished fame.
Numerous marks of joy sparkle and enhance the festive glow.

And, no wonder! Our famous town of Lindsay is celebrating a double feast today.
Our beloved and Right Reverend Bishop Dunne of Dallas, Texas is coming to bless
Our new St. Peter's Church, and our zealous and dearly beloved Pastor Father John Baptist
is celebrating his 40th anniversary as a priest.

Speak Lindsay! Say who made thee so great and glorious?
Who brought the peace and joy?
Say who built this church which portrays such dignity and love?
Its impressive tower pointing upwards, leading us Christians heavenward
Who directs and guides our children toward God and Church?

Speak Lindsay! Talk loud and clear. Who loved that thee so sincerely that he would
Give his lifeblood to point the way to heaven?
Our wise and prudent Father John did, and does all this in order to save our souls,
This priest of God, so pure and noble, was born in Germany. His love for us,

As well as all his fatherly actions will always be a
living example throughout
Our earthly lives.

Father John, we pledge thee anew our hearts of German
trust. With thee we give glory
And thanks to God that He steered you to Lindsay. Full
of joy we look to
The future that God may keep you with us for many years
to come.
May our Lord send His Divine Blessing upon you, just as
you bless all of us, big and little.

May the Blessed Mother intercede for you at the Throne of
God in order to give
You courage to continue His work in our parish.
And when your life span is ended, may the Divine Saviour
reward you for all
When you reach the heavenly shore.

This we say to you anew: "Happy Jubilee for you!"
May God bless you always 'til eternity we all share!

* * * * * * * * * * * * * * * * * * * *

The Man and the Housework

Yes indeed, the nicest life is the married life
of an American housewife.
Hardly is she engaged, she begins to impress her man
That her "yes" and "no" are it.

When they are married, it takes not many hours,
Before the poor man obeys a look.
Too late now sees the man how wonderful his life had been
When yet he had been free.

Hardly has the morning dawned, must the man already care
That the breakfast may be there.
Water, wood, and coal must be fetch without delay
And what else may missing be.

Then the table decked, and the wife aroused from sleep
Yet beware, not before ten it be.

Or else, God spare the husband
For the wife likes to get up late.

Also must he early in the morning shiny dollars provide
That she may play the lady fine.
She sits in a rocking chair, rocking back and forth,
All the while reading Uncle Tom's Cabin.

To make her yellow cheeks a rosy hue,
She does apply with haste some rouge.
Likewise does she use hoops--fishbone--ironstripes
And maketh herself thin beyond reason.

Velvet and silk portraying, gazing in all places
She then up and down the street proceedeth
Whether the baby cries--whether it snows or freezes,
Nothing is holding her back from her promanade.
Comes her husband home at last, does the lady rest?
Has not paid a thought to supper?
Ah, then he must rush up and down
Til the lady has prepared the tea.

And when after a short year the pair
With an heir is happily surprised,
The sufferings of the man can not be painted.
The shoe then nearly crusheth him.

Then it will be: "Carry the baby, chase the mosquitoes"
Serve you lady here and there. Yes, the nicest life
Is the married life of an American housewife.

                                    Wilhelm Flusche, 1883

        *

                The Man and the Housework

Child of the wide world, that poet I should turn,
I should ne'er have believed in all my life!
Yet your mocking poem forces me to judge.
It has robbed me of peace and rest.

Therefore you mocker hear: we are no gods.
Humans we are full of mistakes, all alike

Whether it be a slipper or a boot--it hurts
Everywhere--even in far off Chinaland.

From the married state--there in the Thinkerland,
God preserve in mercy me!
Fourteen, sixteen children--and if out once goes the man
Takes he six or eight always with him.

I saw in German lands--yes, it is a shame to say.
In the market place with the gracious lady,
Many a lieutenant's servant--yet a beast of burden
Inspite of his dark blue uniform seemed he to be.

Has the soldier a sweetheart, then he says: "Dear,
When I am free, then we shall wed."
She feeds him bacon??????????
Well then he sails for America.

Germans in foreign lands gripe without end;
Nobody thinks a thing about it.
Men, let me tell you, you have enough to bear,
Whether German or English your lady be.

                                        H. Wheeler.

(Composed in response to the previous poem.) A German
newspaper Milwaukee. 1883

Sentiments before the Examination

The examinations approach, poor me, poor me.
I am trembling from head to foot.
Already I see in spirit the worst image.
The Prior looks so stern--so mild.

The teachers ask so many questions hard,
And torture the pupils in gruesome art.
These Fraters look so very smart,
As though they were the only servants.

And yet most of them have not
Wisdom with spoons been fed.
They mock, and they grin, and they laugh at us
When we our answer delay.

How then does the poor student feel?
Hardly he knows what he says or does.
His wretched little bit of courage is gone.
All the answers are gone from his mind.

The poor students tremble and are cold from fear.
Now the spectacle breaks loose in a terrible way.
The Fraters' mockery rains down.

Thunders the Prior a threatening, "Sit down."
Constantly this image before my eyes is kept
Even into the dreams of the night it is webbed.

What is the name of the wretch who exams did invent?
Would that I had him in my hands.
He would be rewarded the measureless pain
He has prepared for pupils always.

(Poem by my brother Fritz Flusche while a student at
Conception Mo. College where He studied for the Priesthood
in 1902-190 _)

COME BACK AGAIN
for Elsie

I must tell you a little story
About this birdie sweet.
Each time I see other birds,
I only of this one can think.
It hopped so happily from place to place
Enjoyed so much living in May.
Lo, I threw a stick,
And its spring was over.

Poor field lark! Is it really you?
And I went and picked it up.
Ah, how quickly came to an end
Thy so grief sojourn.

Your tiny eyes so pleadingly
For a longer span of life were asking.
Twice, it raised its little head;
Through its dying body a tremor went.

And I held it lifeless, wilted,
Like a rose which has faded;
Like a carnation torn by storm,
Because the breath of life was gone.

I gave it all I could.
In all stillness I dug a grave.
I laid there as gently as I could,
The small frame of my dead bird.

There, in front of the smoke house it lies.
When in the field potatoes bloom,
Its sweet lays it sings,
Free from life's care and trouble.

Already a year has gone by,
Bird song in lilac bush and mulberry tree.
Yet amidst all lovely tunes
I miss the field lark's sweet warbles.

All the birds are here already,
Sing to me of bliss in love.
Can you never come back
Never---don't say it.

(This poem was written by my brother Fritz for me.)
14-II-1906

* * * * * * * * * * * * * * * * * * * *

WHO?

Clara, what are you crotcheting again?
You are crotcheting a round thing.
Clara sat down
As Fritz began to speak.

On the east side of the home
Built in 1890 in Texas
Sat the two together,
So full of love and trust.

Spring from the neighboring heights
Descended greeting and blooming into the vale.

Feathered singers laughing
Echoed from the woody hall.

Clara crotcheted faster,
Barely she noticed the words
'Til stitch after stitch she placed,
Finishing the last round.

"It's a round table cover
Made for the center table.
When later on it will be used,
Perhaps they'll think of me."

And the hand which did the crotcheting
Rested in Fritz's with bliss
Then she stroke back with silken fingers
The whitish strands.

Shall this hand crotchet again
Down in sunny San Antonio!
Who shall then ask again
In little Fritz's naive tone?

(This poem was composed by my brother Fritz for my sister
Clara who entered Our Lady of the Lake Convent in San
Antonio in 1897)

* * * * * * * * * * * * * * * * * * * *

FORWARD!
January 1, 1910

Quietly, bathed in pale moonlight,
Stands the lonely fawn;
Bathed by the evening dew,
By its dead mother.

Soon the faithful watcher's windows;
Merciless the forest closes.
Shall yet I be alive--
Until the sun greeteth again?

Thus asks herself the poor orphan,
And looks anxiously into the night,

Where the wolf may slowly prowl,
And the fox bloodthirsty watch.

Art not 'thou' that orphan now,
"Katholische Rundschau?" Courage!
From your wide circle of friends,
You'll an editor good and true yet receive.

                              Fritz Flusche

(Kath. Rundschau, June 1, 1910; due to the lack of a
manager this German newspaper folded up.)

TO HERMAN
July 30, 1911

Brother, I greet you so far away.
Brother, I greet you; I think of you.
No matter what they may say,
You were always good to me;
That's why I love you so.

Brother, I long for you,
                              Far in the world.
Brother I long for you,
                              Cold is the world.
I love you still as I did there.
Where in the same place,
Strangers we were.
Brother, I greet you, be so kind.
Write and tell me, where there is need.
You are far from home.
Should with the cold North you meet,
Be careful!

                    (Fritz Flusche to his brother Herman.)

      * * * * * * * * * * * * * * * * * * *

FOR ELSIE

"A happy Feastday! A Happy Feastday!"
Already in the early morning hours

Calls the mother--calls Augusta.
"Prosit" is heard from every mouth.
Soon also the feastday cake
Is placed on the breakfast table,
And the largest of all pieces
Is, of course, for Elsie dear.

And so sweet tastes the cake
So beautiful look the gifts
Yet my Elschen sits so sad,
I dare not even think of it.

Has he then quite forgotten me?
Does distance separate his heart?
Only a word, dear brother!
Your good wishes to convey.

Be comforted, my dear Elschen!
My love knows no distance,
Just as if I would see you now,
I love you just the same.

Let others present you with gifts;
I have only a heart full of love
Which wishes only this one thing:
To remain forever with you.

May angels guide you;
Jesus be you leader.
May you some day in heaven's realms
Enjoy perpetual Christmas.

Fritz Flusche, 13/12/05

* *

HAIL, THOU MORNINGSTAR
(For the feast of the Assumption)

Over forests and dales
Evening shadows creep.
To the chapel there on the hill
I see pious pilgrims go.

And the waves of the river roar.
Happy the crowd of pilgrims sings
Through the leafy bows of birches;
The last rays of the sun gleam.

I had to think of Mary,
of the Mother of our Lord.
Hark! how the pilgrims sing;
Hail Thou morning star.

Gate, Thou, of Heaven's realms;
Holiest of all women
Who bore for us the Lord;
Hail Thou morning star.

Hail Thou Star of ocean,
Long in my ear resounded.
And the beam of the brilliant star
Deeper pierced into my heart.

William Flusche

(One should think of the beautiful pilgrims chapel of
Waldenburg near Attendorn in Westfalia, Iowa.)

* * * * * * * * * * * * * * * * * * * *

TO MY AUGUSTA
(October 1885)

Poem by my father to my mother on the eve of their
marriage in Westfalia, Iowa.

Maiden from the fatherland
Take my heart and take my hand.
I will gladly share with thee
Your joys and your sorrows.
My whole heart beats for you
True as only Westfaliens's do.

Give thou to me also hand and heart.
Share with me joys and sorrows.
Let united in love us be
That above the angels may rejoice.

Such love is God's breath;
Such love makes happy too.

Wilhelm Flusche

Westfalia, Shelby County, Iowa.

* * * * * * * * * * * * * * * * * * *

The Departure
at
Antwerpen, September 19, 1885

[This poem was composed by my mother's father when he
escorted her to the ship in Antwerpen, Holland, when she
went to America to marry my father.]

You went away--you have now gone
Into a distant land.
You left your fatherland--
The German fatherland.

You did not delay--you did not complain
As many a coward does--
You went as though it were your duty.
You went with a man's courage.

In many a jest--a whole heart
You bore in your breast.
You did not forget your parent's grief
It was too clear to you.

Heavy though my heart, it was glad
When you wished to go.
When on the ocean shore I stood
Seeing you part on the waves.

You nodded to me--you waved to me;
I saw it all too well.
Then through my veins ran
The warm father's blood.

One more look--I went back to the ????Hotel.
I wish you the best on the waves.
Hasten then fast to you fatherland.

        I think of you--think of me
As often as you read this.
This is the best monument
Which never shall be effaced.

        Your father, Wilheim Steinmeiz.
              Lindsay
    on the Occasion of November 7, 1905

(The poem was composed by my grandfather Steinmertz when
my mother married John Theisen, her second husband.)

    Greetings! Congratulation!
    Your heavenly patron bless you
    For gifts which adorn man.
    We beg God in his kingdom;
    May through the thorny world
    The path which only leads to heaven,
    Lead you God's fatherland
    As a father leads his children.

    May fate's hard blows
    Always pass you by.
    May you in misfortune, to your honor,
    Faithful to your virtue's banner stand.
    Not for riches, not for honor
    Do we beg our Creator today.
    Only virtue, only Christ's teaching
    Becometh wife and husband.
    Love and faithfulness-don't forget—
    Adorn a happily married couple.
    Zeal is called limitless
    When in words it is expressed.

    Farewell in your cosy Texas home;
    Near the Red River shore.
    Always remember your dear ones at home
    In the near and far land.

    Your Father Wilhelm Steinmetz Aged 85 years.

    *

GREETINGS TO MY FATHERLAND by
My father.

(Melody: O STRASSBRUG)

O Germany--O Germany
You fatherland so dear and true.
How lovely to my ears
Sounds the tone of your language.

Your language, your language—
So lovely and so mild.
Of the good German people
Despised image.

Of the people --of the people
Which holdeth love and truth.
Which fears God alone
And outside him nothing on earth.

God bless --God bless
The new Germany.
And make it to the old

     *

GERMAN COMFORT
By my father

We sons of Germany likely
Wander into foreign lands
Yet to us it does not go like unto others
We are most of the time despised.

A clear eye we have
Red bloom our cheeks
Besides God's gifts:
Intelligence and deep feeling.

Because they envy
What a good God has given us
We can well understand
The foreigner's hatred and mockery.

We are arguing with none
We stand our test.
Exactly, the hatred of the mean
Is the best ones praise.

Wilhelm Flusche 1888

* * * * * * * * * * * * * * * * * * *

O, do not be ashamed of the German tongue;
It is so clear --so noble and so true.
Forget not, that your mother's first word to you
Was a word in the German tongue.

O, be not ashamed of the German tongue
Even though other sounds are better known to you,
As pure and warm as the German word
Sounds no other tongue's most beautiful sound.

Do you notice approaching lies and deceit
And do you fall without fault into danger
Speak German, my child, --the German word
Is an enemy of deceit, the German word is true.

O, be not ashamed of the German tongue
It is so clear --so noble and so pure
And lo! Your mother's last word
Shall be a word in the German tongue.

Wilhelm Flusche 1888

You are a child and must forever remain,
The true wife remains forever a child.
A white sheet, upon which the gods are writing
How precious meekness and simplicity are.

I would love to carry you on soft hands
As only true love can.
And fate I would love to beg
O, do not touch this child.

Full of devotion I would lovingly guard you
And restlessly care for you early and late
That not life's storm from your blossoms
Innocence's sweet-scented dust blow adrift.

And when in death my eyes break
Then I shall in my last prayer mild
With tired lips dying speak to you:
Remember me and stay a child.

Wilhelm Flusche

* * * * * * * * * * * * * * * * * *

FAREWELL FROM LINDSAY
August 18, 1906--my brother Fred
To my mother.

TO MY DEAR MAMA

HOME

You, who still live in the circle of your loved
ones.
You, whom no serious moment
From the fatherhouse has driven
Oh, call blessed your fate.

Not to all is it given to stay
In the sweet dwellings of home.
Childhood's beautiful hours hurry
Spring has hardly come.

Here comes fate with earnest miene
And shows us another path.
With haltering step--with deepest pang
I shall soon board my ship.

And must I wander, must I sail
Into the wild world a stranger
Then I call unspeakable toughed:
Fare thee well, you quiet home.

You dear home--where every spot
Once a heaven in it bore.
Where a sparkling well
The well of golden days once flowed.

You little spots of happy games
Farewell, farewell you quiet place
Me beckons to another goal
Demanding fate away.

And grieved I send in parting
The last look upon the dear home.
This home of the beautiful joys of youth
Sadly I go out of thee.

So clear shines no evening again.
So friendly does not green nature.
So lovely does not bloom May again
As does the field of my father's house.

Deeper yet than on father's hearth
Grip sorrow and pain outside.
And 'no' heart on this wide earth
Beats more tender than a mother's heart.

Love's burning feeling
Which raised us with a thousand pains,
We cannot find it twice,
It cannot glow elsewhere as bright.

Therefore from afar off
Longing sends greeting and wishes,
Even if there shone the brightest stars
And if I found the greatest luck.

For deep childlike feelings
No heart shuts up cold and rough.
You awake even in the world's flurry
remembrances sweet and gay.

O, give thou me forever again
Innocent childhood days.
Don't you live in memories again,
O blessed, thrice blessed past?

You unforgettable precious place,
And even though thou be a home so small,
And if I had all the world's goods
In touching contemplation I think of thee.

You holy home so loved by all
I think of you in sorrow and in joy.
And should I wander a thousand miles,
Yet I think back of thee.

                                        Fritz Flusche.

        * * * * * * * * * * * * * * * * * *

LINDSAY--LINDSAY, you disappear
And fade from my gaze.
Where can I find you again?
When shall I return to you?

Long already did I hear "You must part."
Sadly it sounds in my ears.
Even though I tried not to hear the word
It pursues me in all my paths.

Dear Mama! On account of lack of time I was unable to
finish the above poem which was to be for you. But it
matters not! You know that in spite of it, I am always
your loyal, devoted and loving son, and that I shall
remain it-- just as I know that you will not forget me.

                        Your most loving son Fritz.
                    Lindsay, Texas, August 13, 1906

        * * * * * * * * * * * * * * * * * *

        THE PILGRIM'S CHAPEL AT WALDENBURG BEI
              ATTENDORN IN WESTFALEN

There, where the runes of the Waldenburg greet
From the sunny turret this blooming land.
There stands in the forest, at
the foot of the cliff
A cozy little chapel, known to so many.
There thrones on a beautiful altar, the image of
THE MOTHER OF SORROWS.

So peaceful it beckons in the green woods
From hallowed shadows, it buries your sorrows.
Here does not touch a disturbing sound

The outpouring sufferer in the silent hill.
There opens the heart with childlike confidence
TO THE MOTHER OF SORROWS.

Here walks the mother the bedewed paths
Her babe is sick, and all hope is gone.
Now she flies quietly to the Mother of Grace
Raises in sorrow her trembling hands.
O, give me, for Thy son's sake, my darling again.
Mother of Sorrows!

And all are coming, sisters, brothers
And all are coming, sisters, brothers
To reveal human misery and anguish;
Here resound prayers and holy songs
Through murmering treetops--at the golden sunset.
And the little birds of the
woods, sing in between
TO THE MOTHER OF SORROWS!

O, be thou blessed, you holy peace
Which hovers 'round the chapel
and soothes the pain
Till, at last, silences the tongue in song.
O, lock me also in your merciful heart
Assists us all at last in death's hour.
O MOTHER OF SORROWS.

Wm Flusche (Sr)

* *

GREETINGS TO THE QUEEN OF MAY
Fritz Flusche, 1905

Ring out you May song
Resound your anthem
Full of love and bliss.
The mistress of the world
To her the first greeting from a happy heart!

Thee Mother of our Lord
Heaven's most beautiful star
To you we sing.
You, our pride and renown.

Protect Christendom.
You, our protection and quard--Hail! o queen!
virgin to you is this song
Full of love and trust
Full of grace!
In your crown of glory
You glow in highest bliss
Brilliant example for us-- in word and deed.

Faithfully may your hand
Protect the dear fatherland.
Thus we pray!
And from ardent breast
We cry with happy hearts
Resounding for evermore
HAIL THOU QUEEN!

"In February, 1906"

Fierce winter! Long enough thy snowy hand
Stripped nature's farirest shrines throughout the land;
Thy ebb has come and inward flows a tide,
Though distant still, it rises far and wide.

Bold robber! Now thy ways are scrutinized.
Doesn't notice how old sol of thee apprised,
Ashamed of southern flight at thy untimed attack,
E'en nearer draws his circles' fiery track?

Fair nature now will in rebellion rise;
Her accents fill the earth, the sea, the skies;
The night, foul emblem of thy darksome ways;
Thy sole conifer, her cold mantle lays.

O'er azure lakes reflecting heaven's cheers
And leaves them deadly pale when dawn appears:
Her reign is shortened; whether willing or no,
The parting day's warm echoes she must blow.

Then winter flee to north pole's furthest pole
And there thy hasty adieu in senseless thunders roll;
Prometheus bound for chilling fair sol's fire,
There fight his fierce, fiery fangs in uselss ire.

Fred C. Flusche IV. Class

"Hope"

Though sable clouds conceal the heavenly dome,
By darkning frowns unseen appears some smiling star;
Though desert sands the weary foot annoy,
Blue mountains beckon kindly from afar.

No more the blue bells silvery peal awakes
The valley's echoes dreaming of better times;
Nor answers feathered bard to tethered choir,
Nor wooded bell the brooklet's laughter chimes.

But no landscape so bleak but silhouettes
A lively evergreen's 'gainst the rising moon;
No tempest sounds so dissonant,
But on its wing some soothing tone is born.

Though northern blasts play nature's funeral marches,
Still some sweet voice must have preserved its lay,
For nature's oracle and interpreter,
Dearious melodies that bear the charm of May.

Some say, that ever 'gainst that season comes
Wherein our Saviour's birth is celebrated,
This bird of dawning singeth all night long:
And then, they say, no spirit dares stir abroad.

The nights are wholesome; then no planets strike,
No fairy takes, no witch hath power to charm,
So hallowed and so gracious is the time!
(Fourth line missing).

E'ven as the Almighty strikes hope's fondest keynote;
Makes baling spring dawn on a winter's cold:
Thus He will shed on our spirit's darkness,
His glorious sunbeams, endless fold and fold.

Fred C. Flusche, BI Class.

"A Prayer"

Lightly, lighly,
Prayer, blithely:
Heavenward wing thy humble way,
Tell my mother of my sorrow
That before the distant morrow,
Mary, Virgin, hear my lay.

Flowers, flowers,
In their bowers,
Are as yet well stowed away.
And their perfume cannot soften
Many harsh tones returning often
When I sing to Her my lay.

Kindly, kindly,
Somewhat blindly,
Look to me but for today.
Noting not my love so dreary,
Only that I'm weak and weary
While to Thee I sing and pray.
Lowly, lowly,
Toilsome, slowly,
Give me grace my cross to bear;
Only grant to me the light
That will let me see Thy height:
Easy is my burden's share.

Spending, spending,
But unending.
Could this moment of prolong,
That the echoes ringing, ringing,
Mary's blessings downward bringing,
I could listen again and long.

Fred C. Flusche. VI Class

A PROFILE: WILHELM FLUSCHE

Much can be learned about Wilhelm Flusche, by reading his poems and his journal. His relationship with the Flusche Brother's colonizational efforts is more clear. Since he was a school teacher and a poet, and since his brothers needed a suitable livelihood, three of them became land agents as immigrants poured into unsettled areas of the U. S. during the late 1800's. But as the eldest of the Flusche brothers, Wilhelm was directly involved in their colonizational work. He was a part of the collective discussions of their work. He gave them financial aid, his advice, and the use of his personal facilities for colonizational purposes. His sharing of their colonizational zeal appears to have been one with them in common cause: The retention of their German, Catholic heritage in their adopted land.

Wilhelm's earlier poems about Germany reflect a deep nostalgia for his "Fatherland." He expresses this openly in the poems, "O Strassburg," "The Pilgrim's Chapel at Waldenburg: Attendorn, "and "Hail, Thou Morning Star." Like most German immigrants that grouped together when they fled Germany in the 1800's, he had hoped to see German communities like those of Germany in the United States. He suggests this in the poem, "O Strassburg": "The new Germany./ And make it to the old." The poem "German Comfort," written in 1888, indicates that he feels "the foreigner in a foreign land": "We sons of Germany likely/ Wander into foreign lands;/ Yet, to us it does not go like unto others/ We are most the time despised."

He also feels the pressure to be assimulated into the America culture. In the poem, "O, do not be ashamed of the German tongue," he exhorts his fellowmen to remain true to their German communal isolation: "Do you notice approaching lies and deceit,/And do fall without you fault into danger?" In his last poem, "Texas," however, he realizes that unprecedented changes were taking place;

that events were occurring that would sweep away the old world of his youth.

Wilhelm's acquiescence to progress in his poem, "Texas," is applicable to other German immigrants of the German communities that took roots and grew in Texas. Thus, the poem becomes an appropriate tribute of these communities to the sesquicentennial celegration in 1986.

TEXAS
Last poem by my father – 1890

Do you know the land so wondrous fair--
With its plains, its mountains--
Where the sun brightly shines--
Cool breezes from the gulf blow-
Where large rivers flow-
Towns and factories bloom-
Where trains rush on rails-

Transport goods without delay-
Where proud steamers land-
Which sailed across, the ocean-
Where stand the golden harvests-
Flocks in the meadows feed-
Where flowers bloom more beautifully?

On the trees the fruit hangeth.
Where everything drives and forward goes
And nothing and nobody stands still
Here is a land, a beautiful land.
It is Texas--well known Texas.
That's why with prudent mind
Germany's children move there,
Acquire renown and good luck
And never more return.

Wilhelm Flusche

* *

DAS IST ALLES

SOURCES

Part I

Wilhelm Flusche's letter to his brother, August.

Part II

Record of The Wilhelm Flusche Family by A. C, (Tony) Flusche, son of Anton Flusche.

Part III

Taped interviews of Henry J. Fuhrman by Jerry and Alvin Fuhrman.

Letter of Joseph Fuhrmann to Anton Flusche, taken from Anton's research of the Peter Fuhrmann family.

The Fuhrman Family Bible.

Information supplied by descendants of John and Mary Fuhrmann

Saint Joseph Parish Centennial Edition: 1876-1976, st. Joseph, Iowa.

Part IV

Writings of Emil Flusche. Assembled by A. C. (Tony) Flusche; and later, translated by him.

History of the development of the colonies founded by the Flusche Brothers in Texas; Muenster, Lindsay, Pilot Point, Windthorst, and Mt. Carmel. By A. C. (Tony) Flusche.

Excerpts from the personal journal of Wilhelm Flusche. After the illness of Wilhelm Flusche (1898), the journal appears to have been continued by Augusta Flusche Theisen. The translator is not identified.

A collection of poems written by the Steinmetz, Flusche family. All the poems were written in German except for three English poems by Fritz Flusche. The translator of the poems is not identified, but evidence indicates it was done by Sister Christina, Wilhelm Flusche's daughter.

www.ingramcontent.com/pod-product-compliance
Lightning Source LLC
Chambersburg PA
CBHW051134120626
46547CB00012B/804